CARMEL IN THE WORLD PAPERBACKS

2

Essays on Titus Brandsma

D1593909

Titus Brandsma
Carmelite

Essays on

TITUS BRANDSMA

CARMELITE, EDUCATOR, JOURNALIST, MARTYR

Edited by
Redemptus Maria Valabek, O. Carm.

CARMEL IN THE WORLD PAPERBACKS
Rome 1985

Cover design by Riccardo Palazzi, O. Carm.

BX
4705
.B 815
E88
1985

ISBN 88-7288-000-9

Institutum Carmelitanum
Via Sforza Pallavicini, 10
00193 Roma

PREFACE

With the imminent beatification of Fr. Titus Brandsma, requests for more material about the martyred Dutch friar have multiplied. The following collection aims to gather under one cover items which have been published in various magazines of Carmelite vintage; a few items are newly translated, e.g. from the process of beatification. Inevitably, there will be repetitions in such a collection; a systematic elimination of such would have mutilated the contributions sometimes beyond recognition. The items were chosen with an eye for various approaches to the appreciation of Fr. Titus and his message.

Section I is biographical. It means to situate Fr. Titus in history and in the life of the Church. His life and work are highlighted, as the prelude and life experience necessary for his final ordeal at the hands of the Nazis. Though studied from various angles, Fr. Titus' life shows a marvelous consistency which makes his stance vis-à-vis Nazism as inevitable as was his extermination in Dachau.

Most requests for more information about Fr. Titus insist on the need to know more about his spirituality. Although he was not prone to write about his spiritual growth, still there are many external indications of the sturdy Carmelite spirituality of this thoroughly religious friar. Section II has gathered articles of a more general scope: they give a broader overview of Fr. Titus' spiritual stance. Section III is made up of more monographic studies, which concentrate on various aspects of his multifaceted personality. The specific virtues which were particularly incarnated in Titus' spiritual vision are studied, mainly from the beatification process documentation.

The final Section (IV) provides an anthology — all too brief when compared with the volume of Fr. Titus' actual writing — of this professor and preacher's extensive and varied literary output. The letters from prison are given in their full form, to show the real Titus — never content to remain in the realm of abstract pricinples, but rather immediately involved with the people who embody and live and sometimes must die for those principles.

The Editor

4

CONTENTS

INTRODUCING
FATHER TITUS BRANDSMA
CARMELITE

Adapted from a talk by
Falco Thuis, O. Carm.,
Former Prior General of the Carmelite Order

WHEREVER Carmelites are found—and that is on every continent of the globe—the name of Titus Brandsma is known. Far beyond the areas where the priests, brothers and sisters of the Order live and work, the fame of this capable and efficient yet humble friar has aroused profound admiration. Even France—where the Order of Carmel has not existed since the French Revolution—has produced a marvelous little work *Ce petit moine dangereux*, now translated into several languages.

Thus the news that our Father Titus may be beatified in the not-too-distant future has caused joy throughout the world, and preparations for appropriate celebrations are under way.

In my travels throughout the world I have met many Carmelites who knew Father Titus personally, either in Rome where they lived and studied with him, or in Canada, Ireland or the United States where, a few years before World War II, the Dutch Carmelite gave a series of lectures on the spirituality and the mystical doctrine of Carmel. Many still recall their confrere, this expert on the history of spirituality, especially that of the Carmelite Order; they treasure vivid memories of a small, friendly man who was vitally interested in everyone he met, a man whose spirituality and genuine piety were but external manifestations of his intimate walk with the Lord. So too is he remembered by his professional colleagues within and beyond The Netherlands.

Following his violent death in the Nazi extermination camp at Dachau, Titus Brandsma quickly became known throughout the Order as a martyr, as a witness to the faith, a servant of the truth: a man loyal to the Church and constant to the end. If during his lifetime his fellow Carmelites had thought of their confrere as a man of deep faith, now they knew it for certain.

Almost spontaneously, first in The Netherlands and then in ever broadening circles, people from all walks of life, even non-Christians, became interested in the life of Father Titus. They began to see his final steps on the path to martyrdom within the overall context of his Christian and religious life: of his love for everyone he met and his zeal to foster each individual's personal growth as men and women called to union with God.

As biographies of this saintly Carmelite began to appear in various languages—his conferences on Carmelite spirituality had already been published in English—his own human qualities began to be understood in greater depth and color.

In the well-known address on the concept of God, which he delivered in 1932 on the anniversary of the foundation of the Catholic University of Nijmegen, the martyred Carmelite continues to speak to his fellow Christians: it is his own vision that he puts into words, but they are words that are relevant for everyone who has been touched by the Mystery of God.

Father Titus' simple but moving poem—composed in his cell in the "Hotel Orange" as the prison at Scheveningen was known—has been reproduced worldwide: "O Jesus, when I look at you . . ." These few lines embody the nucleus of Carmelite spirituality: the experience of God's presence and of the soul's invitation to union with him. To this Titus remained serenely faithful, as he had promised years previous in his religious profession, *usque ad mortem*, until death.

Father Titus Brandsma, Carmelite, is honored throughout the world. Schools and auditoriums, religious houses, a library, even streets are dedicated to his memory; and artists attempt to capture his spirit in sculpture, in painting, and in stained glass.

More than any merely visual image, however, we Carmelites—whether of the first, the second or the third Order—will discover that it is Titus Brandsma's practical understanding of what it means to live in the presence of God after the example of Mary and Elijah, which he demonstrated by his life and work, that embodies the charism of the Order. It is his example that makes our mission clear: to serve our fellow men by drawing them to a personal experience of the divine presence in their lives.

Father Titus continues to inspire: by his life of communion with God and by his authentic faith, so completely in harmony with his enormous apostolic activities in myriad areas; by his love and concern for the "poor little ones" who always had free access to him; by his appreciation of local cultures and of all that promotes the human, and therefore the spiritual, development of man; and by his consuming love for the Church, for which he willingly gave his life.

Because of his love for the Church, even before the notion of ecumenical relationships had become popular, Titus was in the vanguard of those working for the reunification of the churches. For him the Church is a body that must continually grow during its pilgrimage through time, if it is to become ever more fully the Kingdom wherein God's holy people find their home. And due to this same love for the Church, no matter what other duties might be pressing him, he always found time to join his Carmelite community for the celebration of the Liturgical Hours and of the Eucharist.

The Order of Carmel is proud of its confrere, Titus Brandsma. May he continue from heaven his ministry of teaching, today and in each generation to come.

I
LIFE AND WORK

Young Titus
with his
lifelong friend
and mentor
Hubert Driessen,
O. Carm.

A light
moment
en route
to America

I

THE LIFE AND WITNESS OF FR. TITUS

Aquinas Houle,
edited by Mark Ciganovich, O. Carm.

WHEN we hear of relics, we think of saints. And when we hear of saints, we think of relics. Dachau helps us off this mental merry-go-round. For in this notorious concentration camp thousands of religious men were destroyed—their living bodies tortured and their lifeless corpses reduced to ashes. There are no relics. And this did not happen in the days of Nero or Diocletian, or in the thirteenth or sixteenth century, but in the twentieth century.

These holy men who died at Dachau were no haloed figures from the musty pages of ancient history. These were men who wore the clerical garb of today, who grappled with the twentieth-century problems of their people, and who died with their people—bravely, but in the anonymous fashion of modern warfare. Father Titus Brandsma was one of these men.

Father Brandsma's journey to Dachau began on the evening of January 19, 1942, when he was arrested by the Nazi security police at his home monastery in Nijmegen. Shorn of his Carmelite habit, without time to put his papers in order or to pack any belongings, Father Titus was hustled off by his captors to Arnhem prison. The next morning he was transferred to the state prison at Scheveningen. Here, and in The Hague nearby, Dutch Nazi authorities subjected him to several interrogations. After seven weeks, he was assigned to the concentration camp at Amersfoort.

Here, Father Brandsma was deprived not only of his precious breviary and rosary but also of the solitude he had found so congenial at Scheveningen. However, he soon made the transition from solitary to apostle, forming a group to whom he gave lectures and sermons, hearing confessions, giving encouragement to the sick by word and deed until his poor health landed him in the infirmary. These activities, particularly his preaching, displeased the camp authorities, and on April 28 the aging priest was returned to Scheveningen.

After two weeks of further interrogations, the authorities consigned Father Brandsma to the concentration camp at Dachau. On May 16, he and several other prisoners were herded into a train for the cross-country trip to the transit camp at Kleve. Father Titus spent several days there.

Finally, after another torturous train ride in which the passengers were treated more like animals than men, he arrived at the small town of Dachau just north of Munich on June 12. Mercifully, Father Brandsma's waning physical strength could not long endure the hard labor and the beatings which were everyday fare at Dachau. Within six weeks of his arrival, he died in the early morning of July 26, 1942. His body was cremated three days later.

This is the mere geography of Father Brandsma's last days. But what of the man who travelled this path, and how did he come to end this way?

Early Years

Father Titus Brandsma was born at Oegekloster near Bolsward on February 23, 1881. He was the fifth child of staunch Catholic parents who lived on a farm in the almost completely Protestant province of Friesland in the Netherlands.

Born Anno Sjoerd Brandsma, Father Titus gave early signs of his vocation. At the age of eleven, he entered the Franciscan Fathers' school at Megen and began his studies on the junior seminary level. His studies were continually interrupted by reason of ill health, and it was with regret that the Franciscans sent such a promising student home.

At Oegekloster his vocation grew and was strengthened by the decidedly Catholic atmosphere of his home life. Of the six Brandsma children, five were destined to enter religion. His brother Henry was ordained a Franciscan priest, while three of his sisters entered religious life.

During his convalescence Anno gave serious thought to his choice of a religious order. The Cistercians and Carthusians had great appeal for him— an early indication of his contemplative spirit. Realizing that the physical demands of these Orders were far beyond his endurance, he decided in favor of the Carmelites.

At the age of seventeen, Anno left home once more, this time to travel some distance to the south. At the centuries-old monastery of Boxmeer, he entered the novitiate on September 17, 1898. As is the custom for novices, he assumed a new Christian name and became known from then on as Titus Brandsma. He professed his vows the following year and began his studies in philosophy.

As a Student of Philosophy and Theology

Father Titus gave positive indication of the keen intellect and depth of soul which would so pervade his priesthood in later years. His bent for journalism came to the fore during these early years when he began what was to become his life-long practice of contributing to both the devotional and scientific periodicals of his day.

Also as a seminarian Father Titus published his first book, an anthology of selected writings of St. Teresa of Avila. These were the years in which Father Titus developed his great love for the spiritual heritage of the Carmelite Order. By delving into the works of the great Carmelites of the past, he arrived at convictions which were further developed in his later writings and preaching.

Priesthood

His student days passed rapidly and he was ordained on June 17, 1905, in St. John's Cathedral, Hertogenbosch. Following the ceremony, Father Titus consecrated himself and his life's work to Our Blessed Lady.

After his ordination Father Titus was sent to Rome for graduate studies in philosophy. At the Gregorian and Leonine Universities Father Titus gave himself not only to a deeper and more concentrated study of philosophy, but also to a study of the history of mysticism. While working for his doctorate the young priest continued his practice of contributing articles to Dutch periodicals. Despite all his work Father Titus was a sick man. His stomach ailments were growing worse and gave his superiors cause for concern. At their request, he would occasionally allow himself a brief rest.

Finally sickness overcame him and he was confined to bed with the order to remain there until fit to carry on his work. Yet he prevailed upon his superiors for permission to take his oral examinations for the doctorate. With their permission, he arose from his sickbed and set out for the Gregorian. It was May 17, 1909. He took the examinations while running a fever. The inevitable: failure. The response: return in October. The disappointed friar returned to the Netherlands and strove once more to master the material. With the help of an old friend, Father Hubert Driessen, O. Carm., he utilized the summer of 1909 for a complete review of scholastic philosophy. The following October found him back in Rome. On the twenty-fifth of that month he walked out of the Gregorian a second time, this time with his doctorate.

Teacher and Scholar

Father Titus returned to the Netherlands and began his work as professor of theology and philosophy at the Carmel in Oss. His students recognized his intellectual vigor, his pure insight into matters of dogma, and real love of his work.

While teaching at Oss, Father Titus began his systematic study of the masters of Carmelite spirituality. Whereas previously his study had been guided by love and a desire to learn, he was now able to couple these advantageous qualities to the mind of a research scholar. He was later on to concretize his thought on Carmelite spirituality, at least in an historical sense, in his *Carmelite Mysticism—Historical Sketches* and in his article on the Carmelites in the *Dictionnaire de Spiritualité*. Certain of his conclusions were so fixed in his mind that he even worded them in the same fashion over and over again.

Not long after his return to the Netherlands, Father Titus helped to re-establish a systematic course of studies for the students of his province. In spite of this and the various other duties that were given him, he continued to find time for his love of journalism. He wrote numerous articles for periodicals and newspapers. Between the years 1904 and 1921 he published eleven works ranging in subject matter from a literary study of the works of Baptist of Mantua to *Lessons in the Frisian Language*.

Whether Father Titus was busy teaching some distinction in philosophy, mapping out a year's schedule for a dogma course, or proofreading one of his articles, each and every duty he performed was done so as to coincide with the dual spirit of the Order. This twofold spirit of prayer and action permeated his whole life.

Apostle

This man who could explain so clearly Carmelite contemplation was never found to neglect Carmelite activity. Father Titus used whatever means were at hand to bring God to man and man to God. The sound of his voice was familiar to the thousands who heard him on the radio; his style of writing, his brevity and concise phraseology, were well known to the countless Dutch people who read his articles in many periodicals.

Yet the contemplative side of this man was always apparent. Mental prayer was not confined to that period set aside for it in the monastery schedule. Rather, mental prayer was his day. "To live is to pray," he often said; and it can be truly said that his life was a prayer—and this prayer encompassed his fellow man.

In his relations with others Father Titus was always the smiling little professor; he was the humble little Carmelite who appeared in the parlor with a box of cigars under his arm, saying: "Wherever we are, there should be a feast." He greeted the poor of the neighborhood with as much cordiality as he did the doctors of the university.

Father Titus was involved in so many different activities that it is a wonder he was able to keep up with his duties as a religious and a priest. We can single out three distinct activities which claimed much of his attention and time: the Catholic University of Nijmegen, the Apostleship for the Reunion of Eastern Churches, and the Catholic Journalists' Association.

For years Father Titus had been sympathetic to the idea of establishing a Catholic university somewhere in the Netherlands. Catholic educators of the time sought his help. Together with them and the Dutch hierarchy he did much to help found the Catholic University of Nijmegen in 1923. With the university a reality Father Titus' efforts brought about the foundation of a new Carmelite monastery which was constructed in Nijmegen under his direction and first occupied in 1929.

Although the Nijmegen Carmel was to be his

home until shortly before his death in 1942, he was equally at home in his classroom at the nearby university where he taught for nineteen years. Here, the modern apostle of mysticism enkindled in the hearts of his students the desire for their own spiritual betterment and for a better understanding of the great spiritual heritage of the Dutch people. Along these lines, Father Titus—in conjunction with the Flemish Jesuits Stracke and Reupens and the Dutch Benedictine Dom Huijben—became one of the founders and driving forces behind *Ons Geestelijk Erf* ("Our Spiritual Heritage"), a periodical which considered the study of the spiritual life of the Low Countries from the earliest times to the eighteenth century.

His study of the spirituality of his own country must have done much to give him the understanding heart that he had for the eastern churches separated from Rome. He expressed his desire for the return of these churches not only in his classroom work and prayers but mainly in activities in the Apostleship for the Reunion of Eastern Churches, an organization in which he was a most enthusiastic and interested worker.

Some of his statements concerning this movement have been called prophetic. On one occasion Father Van Keulen, a co-worker in this apostleship, forecast in the presence of many, "Father Brandsma will bring our work to overwhelming success."

Devotion to Mary

"Father Titus lived by love;" his love was of a Marian nature. By profession Father Titus was a man of prayer, by commission a man of action, and by dedication a man of Mary. Mary was a driving force in his spiritual life. He constantly stated that all men, and especially Carmelites, should be other *theotokoi*—God-bearers like Mary. God's activity on the soul and his grace in the soul are the starting point of the spiritual life. Mary is the mother of that life.

19

Father Titus was eager to bring this Marian devotion to the attention of people whenever the opportunity presented itself. For example, when delivering an address on the occasion of the ninth anniversary of the Catholic University of Nijmegen, he concluded with these words:

> Once there was a virgin who became the mother of the Incarnate God and who gave us God as our Emmanuel. He died on the cross, that we might live in union with Him and that we might have grace abundantly. So He was born in us also, through grace. God did this that our union with Him in the natural order should be fully restored and be made even more intimate and fruitful. In this way the Mother of God gave us that close union with God and became herself the most perfect example of that union.
> May this example always be before our eyes! There is more than an example here. It is the Blessed Virgin's task to direct our eyes toward God. Just as we, in the light of divine revelation, recognize God in the child in her arms, so may our Lady likewise guide our understanding, that we may recognize God in all that He has created; so that He may live in us, as He once lived in her, that He may be born again in us and come into the world through our godly deed.

Father Titus achieved the end of his Marian devotion by bringing Christ to the world as well as, and as often as he could. He saw Christ in his fellow men; he gave Christ to those around him. It has been said that people always departed from the little Carmelite with the idea that they knew a little more of the charity and love of Christ than they did before they met Father Titus. On his travels, he brought Christ to the traveller; in his teaching, to his students; and in his counselling, to professional people and to the poor alike. By his suffering he was soon to bring Christ to the world of Nazi prisons.

Zeal

During his priestly life Father Titus had been assigned several responsible positions: provincial counsellor, teacher, prior. But, of the many assignments, perhaps most exalted was his position as *Rector Magnificus* of the Catholic University of Nijmegen for the scholastic year 1932-1933.

Before his term as rector he had frequently represented the university by presiding at various functions. But as rector he was called upon to represent the university as the major official of Dutch Catholic scholarship. He presented a report of the university's progress to the Holy Father; he attended the anniversary ceremonies of the great University of the Sacred Heart in Milan.

His activities stemmed from the Catholic University but extended to the general life of the Church in the Netherlands. In the 1930's the name of Titus Brandsma became synonymous with Dutch Catholic endeavor. During those days and earlier, Father Titus was connected in some way, either as a leader or an ardent defender and promoter, with almost every external function and organization sponsored by the Dutch hierarchy.

His name was known abroad; and in 1935 at the invitation of the American Carmelites he crossed the Atlantic to visit that country. During his stay in the United States he visited many houses of the two American provinces and the Carmelite nuns in Allentown, Pennsylvania.

While visiting the Carmelites in Niagara Falls, Ontario, Father Titus gave a series of lectures on the spirituality of the Order. These lectures, given at Mount Carmel College, resulted in the book *Carmelite Mysticism—Historical Sketches*, which Father Leo J. Walter, O. Carm., helped to prepare.

Besides his book on Carmelite spirituality, another memorial of Father Titus' visit to Niagara Falls has come down to us. During his stay there Father Titus prepared some notes for further talks on mystical theology to the students of the Order. Meditating before the mighty cataract, he concludes these notes with the statement:

> I personally meditate rather about what lies beyond this beautiful phenomenon; not only eye and ear are fascinated, but much more my intellect, which ponders over all God has hidden in the water. I see not only the beauty of nature, the immeasurable potentialities of water, but I see God at work in His creation, in His revelation of love. Nevertheless, my eyes and ears are also captivated and time after time I return, to see and hear.

His was a discerning and whole-souled response to the beauty and goodness of God in His creation.

His zeal prompted him to volunteer for foreign missions; but the wisdom of his superiors refused his offer. Accordingly, he did the next best thing: he sacrificed himself for the missions by working at home. One night after being out late raising funds to support the Carmelite missions, he collapsed upon his return to the monastery. The Prior picked the little man up and helped him to his bed.

The Prior was worried about Father Titus' health. For one thing, he wanted Father Titus to give up his wooden bed and straw mattress. But Father Titus remonstrated that he had a much sounder sleep in his "wooden box."

Father Titus sought to be poor in all things and acted accordingly. Occasionally the Prior had to send him to the Brother tailor for a new habit. On the other hand, he was not the sort of person who mortified other people with his poverty.

Poverty meant sacrifice for him, and he felt its sting. Because of financial difficulties, the Prior had to cut drastically Father Titus' long list of subscriptions to scientific journals. The little priest readily submitted, and from then on when he wished to quote or make reference to some article, he went to the University to find the place of a period or comma.

Both in the material and spiritual orders he showed the genius of an architect. He was a constant builder of the material as well as the spiritual. Today granite and marble stand to testify to his enthusiasm for the material progress of his province. It was due to his labor that the building program of the Dutch province in the 1920's and 1930's produced some of its most beautiful monasteries, churches, and schools. But more than these edifices in stone, there remain the edifices of minds and souls who inwardly and outwardly proclaim the greater enthusiasm exerted by Father Titus in building concepts of God and Mary in the hearts of men.

Nazis and Catholic Schools

But the problems concerning spiritual life were not the only ones which confronted the little friar. Shortly after his return from the United States in the autumn of 1935, the world witnessed Adolph Hitler's rise to power. The Hitler philosophy of the superiority of the Aryan race was being propagated more and more throughout Germany and its border nations.

Father Titus saw the unreasonableness of the Nazi theories; he condemned Nazism in his classes and wrote condemnatory articles in which he upbraided the general tenets of Nazism and in particular its treatment of the Jews. In 1938 Germany invaded Austria and the free countries of the world watched with anxious eyes for the next move of the "little dictator."

The Netherlands, along with Belgium, declared neutrality and took some precautions against a possible invasion. But on the whole the Dutch people did not give the impression that they were worried over Germany's desire for land. In January of 1940 William Shirer in his *Berlin Diary* wrote:

> The Dutch people still lead the good life. The food they consume both in quantity and quality (oysters, fowls, meats, vegetables, oranges, bananas, coffee—the things the warring people never see) is fantastic. They dine and dance and go to Church and skate on canals and tend their business. And they are blind—oh so blind—to the dangers that confront them.

But not all the Dutch were blind to the dangers. Certainly the hierarchy and zealous priests must have had some concrete plans in case of an invasion, otherwise they would never have been able to carry out such a successful program against their oppressors.

Dutch serenity was jolted on May 10, 1940, when German tanks and infantry finally invaded the Netherlands. State authorities realized that defense was out of the question—defense, that is, with guns and ammunition. Dutch defenses resided in the mind and heart, and in the love of God. This was true for non-Catholics as well as for Catholics. Although Catholics comprised only one-third of the population (about three and a half million) the Church was destined to bear the brunt of the attack.

Dutch Catholicism meant unity, and not merely in matters of faith. The Catholics had their own radio station, and a superb system of Catholic schools from the primary grades to the university level. A phenomenal Catholic press flourished in the Netherlands. The Church was influential in the political and economic welfare of the nation. Is it any wonder that a man of Father Titus' ability and love for his homeland would attack an anti-Christian organization which would destroy what blood, tears, and love had built over the centuries?

Once the invasion was complete and the occupational forces secure in their new offices, the Nazi propaganda machine went to work. The wheels of de-Christianization began to turn. On February 24, 1941, the Department of Education decreed that "from the first of May, 1941, no priest or religious is allowed to be principal or director of any school or similar institution." Archbishop De Jong of Utrecht summoned Father Titus and asked him to represent the hierarchy in its fight against the Nazi overthrow of Catholic education.

Father Titus first consulted with the leaders of Catholic education throughout the nation. He pointed out the course which had to be followed in order to insure the Church's jurisdiction over her schools. His next move was to represent the hierarchy at the Nazi-controlled The Hague.

Finally, after many months of procrastination on the part of the Nazis, Father Titus was allowed to have his say. He spoke to deaf ears; he pleaded in vain to hardened hearts. His endeavor and subsequent failure to secure ecclesiastical control of the schools involved him all the more in the dangerous controversy between the Church and her oppressors.

The Church entered open warfare with the Nazis on August 24, 1941, when the pastoral letter of Archbishop De Jong was read in every church throughout the Netherlands. In the letter the Archbishop in union with the rest of the Dutch hierarchy condemned Nazism; the faithful were told of the Nazi plan for disbanding Catholic organizations and of the decision to overthrow Catholic schools. The clergy were told to refuse the sacraments to any member of a Nazi-controlled organization.

The Catholic Press

The hierarchy realized only too well that the Catholic press had to be kept free and in the hands of the Church. If the Church lost her press, then—for all practical purposes—she would lose one of her most efficacious contacts with the faithful. The Archbishop had cause for concern as he again sought the help of the little Carmelite of Nijmegen.

Father Titus set out on this, his last venture of resistance, with characteristic enthusiasm. He travelled the length and breadth of the Netherlands holding conferences and explaining to editors and newspapermen the stand the Church would have to take if the occupational forces infringed upon her right to a free press. Father Titus was already a marked man!

Father Titus' resistance measures were answered by the Department of "Information," which issued a communique on December 18, 1941:

The Catholic Press is no longer allowed to refuse on the ground of principles, acceptance of any advertisement of the National Socialist Party or any of its Branch Organizations, so long as those texts do not contain anything contrary to public order. This decision has been taken because nothing must be neglected which promotes the unity of the Dutch people.

The Nazis had played a trump card. The Archbishop, working through Father Titus, had either to submit or play a higher trump. On the last day of 1941, Father Titus wrote his stirring *De grens is bereikt* ("The limit has been reached"). In the name of the Dutch hierarchy Father Titus's letter to the editors and journalists presented the *God or mammon* proclamation to Dutch Catholic journalists. As spiritual director of the Catholic Journalist Society, Father Titus fearlessly told the Catholic press to choose sides:

If you still want your paper to be called a Catholic paper, then this sort of article has to be refused, no matter what the consequences may be for the paper or even for yourself. We cannot do otherwise. The limit has been reached. I trust that you will all, without hesitation, maintain this our Catholic standpoint. The more unitedly we all follow the same line, the stronger our stand will be... We are not sure yet if those responsible will resort to violence. But in case they do, remember, God speaks the last word and He rewards His faithful servant.

New Year's Day, 1942, saw Father Titus begin a second tour of the country; but this time he visited the bishops of all the dioceses to obtain their personal views in regard to the press. With first hand information of the hierarchy's plan for resistance, the indefatigable friar retraced his steps to consult a second time with the editors and directors of Catholic papers.

He reported his progress to the Archbishop on the tenth of the month. Five days later the Nazi propaganda machine sent articles to all the Catholic papers with orders that they be printed in the morning edition. The Archbishop answered this move with another letter to the press referring to Father Titus' earlier letter and obliging the editors to abide by the instructions therein.

But the Archbishop was not merely content to communicate with the journalists by mail. Again he called Father Titus and sent the weary Carmelite for a third time to contact the newspaper people. This time Father Titus secured written pledges that the papers would remain loyal to the Church.

Arrest and Imprisonment

By the nineteenth Father Titus had completed his last assignment; the signed pledges rested on the Archbishop's desk and the Carmelite returned once more to his monastery in Nijmegen. That night two young men knocked on the door of the Nijmegen Carmel; they asked to see Professor Brandsma. Father Titus appeared in the parlor: exhausted, yet willing to sit and talk to anyone who chanced to call on him.

One of the two men stood to greet the aging priest. He told Father Titus his name was Stephen and in the same breath that Father Titus was under arrest. Father Titus could do nothing but submit.

But before the two young officials led Father Titus from the monastery they thoroughly searched and ransacked his room. Taking what papers they wanted, the police then told him to remove his habit and to follow them without any ecclesiastical garb whatsoever. When the three men arrived at the front door, the Nijmegen community was on hand to bid farewell to their illustrious confrere. Father Titus gave them his blessing and knelt to receive the blessing of his prior. He said that he would try to be home early.

Accompanied by his captors, Father Titus was taken to Arnhem, where he spent his first night in a prison cell. The following morning he left Arnhem for the state prison at Scheveningen, a seaside resort town. Here he spent seven weeks undergoing several sessions of interrogation at near by The Hague.

During these "inquiries" Father Titus defended the Church's teaching, saying that he had no other alternative than to be obedient to the superiors God had placed over him. He was ordered to answer in writing: "Why the Dutch people, especially the Catholics, are opposed to the Dutch National Socialists." On January 22, Father Titus wrote the answer to this query in eight pages, a summary of what he had lectured on at the university years before: the evils of Nazism.

Seven weeks at Scheveningen prison—solitary confinement for a lover of solitude. Here Father Titus wrote one of the most beautiful passages that ever flowed from his pen: *Mijn Cel* ("My Cell") which gives us a better understanding of the interior life of this great man.

His cell, about ten feet by six, consisted of a small cot, a three-legged stool, a table fastened to the wall, a dust pan and a hand brush, a small window, and four bare walls. Father Titus arranged a little altar on the table; he opened his breviary to a picture of Our Lady of Mount Carmel and propped it on a shelf so that the face of Our Lady greeted him each morning upon arising.

He mentions that, lacking both knife and scissors, he used a cigar box nail to cut some slits in paper in order to mount some holy cards that were in his breviary. One of these pictures was Fra Angelico's Crucifixion; another was St. Teresa of Avila and her motto: "To die or to suffer." The third card he mounted was a picture of St. John of the Cross with his motto: "To suffer and be contemned." Father Titus would bear witness to these mottoes during the next six months. He also tacked on the wall what he refers to as his favorite motto: *Prenez vous les jours comme ils arrivent* ("Take each day as it comes").

Each morning he would rise from bed and say a spiritual Mass, repeating as many prayers as he knew by heart. He made a spiritual communion, and after his "Mass," his thanksgiving. After saying a portion of his Office he took his breakfast which had been brought to him much earlier. He broke his black bread into several pieces and poured his coffee over it. He did not find this much of a sacrifice as he states that he had often had such a breakfast in Bavarian convents. Breakfast finished, he took a walk and smoked a cigar; the walk consisted of pacing back and forth the length of the cell. He enjoyed his cigars while they lasted and happily offered another sacrifice to God when they were gone.

To help pass the time of day he began writing a biography of St. Teresa of Avila. He had used all of his writing paper for his *Mijn Cel*; so he began his last contribution to the spiritual literature of the Church by writing this biography between the lines of his Breviary, which he had fortunately been allowed to keep.

By the time he was transferred from Scheveningen, Father Titus had not yet completed the life of the woman who had such a great influence on his life. Fortunately, this work and *Mijn Cel* were secured by the Dutch Carmelites from the police official who had been favorable to Father Titus.

During the internment at Scheveningen Father Titus had been allowed to communicate with his confreres at Nijmegen by mail and on one occasion he was permitted a phone call. In these contacts with his loved ones his optimistic spirit prevailed. His optimism was not a cloak by which he hid his sufferings and sorrows; rather, it was a deep-rooted sense of interior peace. He writes:

> Blessed solitude. I am quite at home in this small cell. I never get bored here—just the contrary. I am certainly alone but never was our Lord so near to me. I could shout for joy because now, when I cannot go to the people nor the people come to me, He reveals Himself to me so often. Now He is my only refuge, and I feel so secure and happy. If He ordered it I would stay here forever. Seldom have I been so happy and content.

In these lines we get a glimpse at the serenity of this man's soul, of his nearness to God, and of his

deep life of prayer. A few weeks after Father Titus
wrote these lines his poetic nature found expression
in his last poem: "Before a Picture of Jesus in My
Cell."

> A new awareness of Thy love
> > Encompasses my heart:
> Sweet Jesus, I in Thee and Thou
> > In me shall never part.
>
> No grief shall fall my way but I
> > Shall see Thy grief-filled eyes;
> The lonely way that Thou once walked
> > Has made me sorrow-wise.
>
> All trouble is a white-lit joy
> > That lights my darkest day;
> Thy love has turned to brightest light
> > This night-like way.
>
> If I have Thee alone,
> > The hours will bless
> With still, cold hands of love
> > My utter loneliness.
>
> Stay with me, Jesus, only stay;
> > I shall not fear
> If, reaching out my hand,
> > I feel Thee near.

Amersfoort

The Carmelite's "retreat" was at an end when,
after seven weeks at Scheveningen, he was transferred to the concentration camp at Amersfoort, a
town about midway between the coast and the German border. Solitude was not Father Titus' lot here;
rather he was quartered in a large barracks with a
great many prisoners. There was no longer time to
write out the experiences of one's soul; Father Titus
spent the greater part of each day doing manual
labor which taxed his strength tremendously.

Within the confines of the dreaded Amersfoort
Prison Father Titus welcomed the company of many
other priests, doctors, lawyers, and Protestant ministers. A group of Catholic intellectuals banded to-

gether and took the name "Tilburg Circle," after the Catholic city of the same name.

Father Titus became quite influential in this group; he led the rosary and meditations, gave instructions, and carried out various functions within the little clique. He earned for himself the familiar nickname "Uncle Titus," an indication of his amiability and friendliness toward all with whom he worked.

At Scheveningen, Mass had been out of the question, but Father Titus had at least been allowed to keep his breviary. At Amersfoort, on the other hand, even his breviary was gone, and so too his rosary. There was not a rosary in the whole group of prisoners, and accordingly the Tilburg Circle got busy and did all they could to make one for Father Titus. At last the rosary was made and the treasure was secretly presented to him. It was on these make-shift beads that the priest led the rosary each day.

Shortly after the Tilburg Circle had made its beads, an *Imitation of Christ* and a missal were smuggled in to the prisoners. These two books did much to aid the Carmelite in preparing the conferences that he delighted in giving. Father Titus' followers now included more than the Tilburg Circle; Protestant ministers and people of all faiths and walks of life came to hear the holy priest preach when the opportunity presented itself.

His first letter home, like those from Scheveningen, was very optimistic. He spoke of comparatively good health and of getting along well in his new environment. But if his health was poor in Scheveningen, it was worse in Amersfoort. During Lent he was sent to the infirmary and confined to bed. He was not there long before he again was active in apostolic work; he preached each day, giving some anecdote from the life of the day's saint.

One day he left his sick bed in the infirmary in search of some rocks. Returning with his find, he

31

heated them at the fire; next he wrapped the hot rocks in towels and placed them near the stomachs of those who could scarcely bear their pain. All the while his own stomach ailments were getting worse. No doubt his charity for his neighbors won him many graces, but it also won him the wrath of the authorities.

On Monday of Holy Week, the doctors decided that Father Titus could return to his barracks and be free to move about as he pleased—a convalescent measure. This was all he needed. He heard confessions, preached, led the rosary, and performed all the priestly ministrations that he could.

On Good Friday he gave conferences to the Tilburg Circle and the countless others who came to hear him. He preached on the spiritual heritage of the Dutch people; the author of the *Imitation* was presented to these abandoned souls as an example of abandonment to God. Father Titus enlivened Gerhard Groote's ideas on the passion for the hundreds who heard him.

On Easter Sunday, tired and exhausted, Father Titus delivered a sermon drawn from the ideas of the great medieval Dutch preacher, Father Brugman, O.F.M. The camp authorities had had their fill. Father Titus had been warned about his public preaching; the commandant wanted to send him to quarters reserved for prisoners who received a more severe treatment. The camp doctor forbade this on the grounds of the priest's poor health. The next-best thing for the commandant was to be rid of Father Titus altogether.

Father Titus received word on April 27 that he was to be transferred back to Scheveningen where he had enjoyed the peace of his solitary confinement. But this time his stay was destined to be short-lived. Less than two weeks after his return to Scheveningen, he was summoned for interrogation. The Nazi authorities wanted him to sign papers testifying that he would no longer preach or carry on his movement of resistance toward the occupational forces in the Netherlands. He was told that if he signed there would be a good chance that he would be released, and that if he refused he would, in all probability, be sent to Dachau.

He wrote a paper saying why he could not sign the document offered by the Nazis. Again he gave the reasons why the Church is opposed to Nazism. He told the Nazis that if they gave him his freedom he would not abuse it by keeping quiet about the principles and ideals of Catholicism. The authorities told him that he was sentencing himself to Dachau.

However, from information gathered after his death, it was found that the Nazis had a dossier in their files concerning the endeavors of Titus Brandsma. Items branding Father Titus were his work for the Catholic schools, the question of Jews and his defense of them, and his operations at the Catholic University. Father Titus was considered one of the men most dangerous to the system established by the occupational forces.

With the permission of the authorities Father Titus phoned his prior in Nijmegen and told him of his departure for Dachau in the near future. The Nijmegen Carmelites were told not to worry about him, that everything would be all right. On May 16, 1942, Father Titus began his weary way to Dachau. He boarded a train for Kleve, Germany—a train in which the passengers were treated no better than animals. The train travelled cross-country to the southeast, and shortly after crossing the German border terminated its run in Kleve.

Kleve and Dachau

At Kleve Father Titus was able to attend Mass and receive Holy Communion. A German priest from the town acted as chaplain to the prisoners of the transit camp. The chaplain advised Father Titus to do all in his power to keep from going to Dachau, for once there it was practically the end.

He saw the wisdom in this advice and accordingly wrote to The Hague asking the authorities to spare
him from going to Dachau on the grounds of his poor
health. His feet were swollen; he could not sleep; he
suffered from dysentery and kidney infection. He
stated that if he played checkers, he saw checker-
boards all day, that he heard bells ringing: in short
he was suffering from hallucinations. He knew that
he could not survive Dachau and thought to save
what he could.

He agreed to spend the remainder of the war
with a limited freedom confined in a German monastery to insure the occupational forces in the Netherlands of his willingness to desist from any further
resistance measures. We see Father Titus reasoning
to the lesser of two evils: either go to Dachau and
certainly not be able to continue his priestly work, or
leave the resistance movement for the time being and
take a chance of getting back into it later.

He also wrote to friends of his in the Netherlands, requesting that they try to do something to
help his plight. His friends had interceded on his
behalf even before he wrote, but they had been refused. The Nazi reply to his appeal stated that he
knew of his poor health before he began his resistance to the German occupation and should have tak-
en that into consideration then.

After the short delay at Kleve Father Titus was
sent to Dachau. The journey lasted three days and
four nights. On Friday morning, June 12, 1942, Father Titus was stripped of his clothes, his head was
shaved, and he received a prison uniform. As number 30492 he took his place with the newly arrived at
Dachau. He spent two weeks in the initiation blocks
where he and those who had arrived with him were
to acquaint themselves with their new camp
life. His stay at Dachau was to last but forty-seven
days.

The priest who had once undergone the care of
specialists in Amsterdam for his stomach ailments
was now undergoing the care of specialists in brutali-

ty. Besides his internal sickness he now had to endure beatings and insults from without. Any manifestation of religion was forbidden. He could no longer preach; he could no longer administer to the sick and comfort the afflicted. Day by day his strength was leaving him.

But there was strength at Dachau in the Blessed Sacrament. Occasionally a village priest would smuggle Christ in to the men who worked in the fields. These priests ran the risk of being caught and severely punished. Likewise, the priest-prisoners took their lives in their hands by daring to administer the Blessed Sacrament to the faithful.

One day when Father Titus had charge of the hosts, he was apprehended by a guard, thrown to the ground, kicked and bruised. Brother Tijhuis, O. Carm. (of the Nijmegen Carmel, also at Dachau), ran to comfort the suffering priest. Father Titus smiled and told the Brother not to worry, for he had Comfort Itself with him. From under his arm he produced an old eyeglass case which held the Blessed Sacrament. He had guarded it there during the beating.

Father Titus feared going to the infirmary where he could no longer continue his subversive apostolate. But the inevitable happened! After withstanding another severe beating he dragged himself to the camp hospital. He remained there for six days, unconscious for the last two. He died at 2:00 A.M., July 26, 1942; he was sixty-one years old.

Three days later his body was cremated. The Dachau authorities notified Father Titus' brother-in-law of his death. The death certificate states that he died of *Darmkatarrh* [pneumonia]. Today at Dachau there stands a memorial to Father Titus and the thousands who died with him: a modest stone bearing the inscription: Grave of Thousands Unknown.

The Dutch people mourned Father Titus' death. Queen Wilhelmina of the Netherlands sent her personal sympathies to his family. Archbishop De Jong wrote to the prior of Nijmegen:

> He was a holy religious and a holy priest, a man of great merit, possessed of great qualities, a founder of many works. He was always ready to assist me and I am greatly indebted to him. He gave his life for the Catholic Church.

The men and women of the Dutch Catholic Press remembered him; one of them, H.W.F. Aukes, published a biography of Father Titus only five years after his death. The Dutch province of the Order will never forget him. Dr. Brocard Meijer, O. Carm., published a definitive biography in 1951, and the Italian biography of Titus Brandsma appeared in 1960. In 1961, the Aukes biography was revised in the light of information gathered throughout Holland for the process of his beatification.

Intercession

Since his death Father Titus has won more renown in the Netherlands than during his life. His name has spread to every part of the globe. The Carmelite Order may have lost a great man in Titus Brandsma, but it has gained a powerful intercessor before the throne of God.

The influence of Father Titus is still felt in his native country. In a small village of Holland in April, 1948, a man by the name of L. Gommans was ordered by his doctor to take a rest cure for what was diagnosed as a gastric ulcer. In a few months the pains returned and Mr. Gommans was taken to the hospital for X-ray photos which showed that part of the stomach was affected. After a long rest he returned home.

His condition did not improve and by January, 1951, the situation was so acute that he was rushed to the hospital where the ulcer was removed by surgery. New X-ray photos showed still more ulcers but no further surgery was possible due to Mr. Gommans' extreme weakness. He remained in the hospital and began to suffer even more pain. Finally, the doctors' verdict was that nothing more could be achieved by surgery; only a rigorous diet could alleviate the pain. Still, the suffering became greater.

Mr. Gommans then heard about Titus Brandsma. He started a novena to him and his prayers, joined with those of his family, had an immediate effect. Suddenly, all pain vanished and his condition returned to normal. The patient was soon allowed to return home and has had no complications since that time. The various doctors involved in the case could find no explanation for the cure.

There is also the incident concerning little Frans Bordens of Amsterdam. He was struck by an automobile while playing in the street and rushed to the hospital where it was found that he had a serious concussion of the brain, interior bleeding, and a fractured skull. Doctors worked feverishly on him but he was given only a short time to live. He received Extreme Unction while unconscious and paralyzed on one side.

The mother of Frans Bordens informed a community of sisters in Nijmegen of the condition of her son and they immediately began a novena to Titus Brandsma. The doctors held little hope for the boy's life but in a few days he regained consciousness momentarily and his temperature was almost normal. Soon, his condition took a turn for the worse and the doctors could see no chance for recovery. On the eighth day of the novena Frans suddenly regained consciousness again and was even able to receive Holy Communion. From that time his condition rapidly improved and the boy was allowed to return home.

Encouraged by such events, the Carmelites of Holland, in 1952, began to take the necessary steps in the process which they hope will lead to the canonization of Father Titus Brandsma. The aim is to show that Father Titus died a martyr's death for the Faith, since his resistance to National Socialism through his guidance of the Catholic daily press caused him to suffer and die in defense of Catholic principles.

In January, 1955, the diocese of Den Bosch set up a commission to study the issues of sanctity and martyrdom and to investigate Father Titus' writings. On December 8, 1957, the diocesan process was ended in Nijmegen. Eighty sessions had been held in which fifty witnesses were heard, among them three bishops and four non-Catholics. The writings were gathered into 136 volumes and submitted to Rome.

Hundreds of priests who knew the forceful Carmelite during his stay at Dachau have expressed their wholehearted support of the work now being done. Both Dutch and German bishops have voiced their praise of such a heroic life. These and many more who knew and loved Father Titus Brandsma are offering their prayers that soon this Servant of God may become an official Saint of the Church.

2

CHALLENGES IN LIFE

Redemptus Maria Valabek, O. Carm.

THE hero of today is the little man who meets and beats challanges that loom over him. This is at least partly the reason for the present attraction of Fr. Titus Brandsma, the Dutch Carmelite who died in Dachau in 1942. Fr. Titus' life seems to be a series of challenges, some apparently insurmontable, which shaped the personality and holiness of this 20th century Carmelite. The remarkable feature is that far from beating him down or souring him on life, these challenges seemed to strengthen his basic optimism and charity, whether he was successful in coping with them or not. Even the challenges in which he came out second best or in which he failed, he accepted as part of God's plan for him. He accepted them as God's will for him, even when a superior twenty years his junior would refuse him permission for some new project. He would reply: "The superiors know better than Titus Brandsma where Titus Brandsma can be useful."

From the very first, he had to grow accustomed to the unexpected. Born into a Frisian farming family as the first male after four girls, mother and father Brandsma were delighted that they would have help in their arduous farm tasks. But it soon became evident that Titus, or Anno, as he was called at baptism, was of too weak a constitution to withstand the rigors of a farmer's life. Plowing, sowing, harvesting might be beyond him; but books and writing, study and research were not. These were to become his avocation.

First signs of a vocation

His staunch Catholic parents were justifiably proud when their young son asked to enter the minor seminary of the Franciscan Fathers. Not only did Titus excel in studies; he was also noted for his deep piety and devotion to God and to the Church. Yet, the third requisite of a vocation seemed to be lacking: his health was, at best, precarious. The Franciscans decided most reluctantly that they could not take a chance with him; Mr. Brandsma agreed and took his son home. But far from discouraged, Titus began looking for other possibilities. His openness to God and love for the things of God made him spontaneously think of the Carthusians or of the Trappists. But he was aware of his own limitations; these orders led too rigorous a life for his weak constitution. He looked for an atmosphere where deep prayer was the rule, however mitigated by a certain amount of activity. His cousin, a Carmelite priest, suggested his own Order. Listening to a description of their way of life, Anno thought he had found what he had been searching for. At seventeen, he entered the Carmelite novitiate at Boxmeer on September 17, 1898.

Early life in Carmel

Although he had been warned by his cousin of the difficulties he would experience during the first few weeks in Carmel, Titus (as he was called upon entering the novitiate, taking his father's name) from the very first felt perfectly at ease. His student days were already a foreshadowing of his future life of expansive charity, research and teaching. He was an exceptional student in every subject but preaching. In this subject, his voice was too monotonous, his gestures too many, his delivery too bookish. But accepting this as a new challenge, Titus worked on his preaching and in the end was probably the only one of his six classmates whose voice would be known throughout Holland due to innumerable conferences, radio broadcasts, and lectures. Though he never became an exceptional orator, his sincerity and the conviction with which he spoke swayed his listeners. They listened because they could tell that this preacher was not expounding beautiful, but practical material. Fr. Titus spoke as one who lived the love of God and the service of neighbor of which he was speaking.

Also during his student days, Titus developed a passionate interest and love for the spirit, the prayer life, the mysticism of his Carmelite Order. As a student he had already translated an anthology of the works of St. Teresa into Dutch. This was to remain his major interest for the rest of his life. If he became an expert in anything, it was history of mysticism with special stress on the Carmelite school and the mysticism of the Lowlands. As for his Order, he could not stand any chauvinism and it was later noted by other orders that he worked as hard for them as for his own—but he constantly grew in devotion and faithfulness to the middle, conciliatory road that Carmel took between a more intellectual or a more affective form of spirituality. Because Titus' nature made him strive to embrace good wherever he found it, this spirituality seemed to fit him.

His student days also forged another characteristic of this enthusiastic Carmelite—his penchant for writing. The pen, and later his Underwood typewriter, would be his constant companions for the rest of his life. Both scientific and popular journals and newspapers featured articles by Fr. Titus, who was in this way able to express his manifold interests—from the missions undertaken in Brazil and Indonesia by his Dutch Carmelites to the preservation of Frisian folklore and dialect. Not only did he contribute to existing publications; he was the first to endorse and help plan several magazines himself. As a student he was the moving force behind a magazine called *Dutch Carmel*. That he was the inspiration of the undertaking is clear since the publication failed once he left the seminary. But far from discouraging him, this failure spurred him on to new and better plans, so that as a priest he was instrumental in founding a more professional publication by the Carmelites, *Carmelrozen*.

Once he finished his ordinary theological studies and was ordained a priest in 1905, many expected this bright student to be sent to Rome for higher studies. Instead, two classmates were chosen above him to teach philosophy, and Titus was sent to a parish as sacristan. It seems that one of his professors, Fr. Eugene Driessen, feared that the young Frisian priest was too independent-minded and not orthodox enough in his views to warrant further study in the sacred sciences. He prevailed on the provincial superior not to send the promising student to Rome. Disappointment this must have been, but it never turned to cynicism or useless self-pity. A year later the Procurator General from Rome, Fr. Hubert Driessen, arrived in Holland and arranged for his young friend Titus to go to the Eternal City to further his studies. The basic humility and loyalty of Titus squelched his natural desire to continue his studies as he reminded Fr. Hubert, "Are you aware of my independent spirit?" The answer he received was direct: "Perfectly. That is why you must go to Rome."

In Rome, Fr. Titus' already precarious health broke down. He was in bed more than not; on weekends he was sent out for the fresh air of the Alban hills. Despite constant bouts with sickness, which were actually to plague him for the rest of his life, the first two years of philosophical studies at the Jesuit Gregorian University were both successful. The third and decisive year proved more difficult. Because he kept pushing himself, as also with other projects, the candidate for the doctorate had a protracted and serious relapse demanding a three month period of complete rest. When this was over, Titus decided that he would try for the doctorate nonetheless. He drove himself to learn the required material, but was unsuccessful—he failed his doctorate exam. But his tenacity made him more determined than ever to succeed. He went back to Holland, studied the material again during the summer months, presented himself for a retake of the exam in

October. This time be passed and became Doctor Titus Brandsma, Ph. D.

Apostolic Life

If his superiors and companions thought that Fr. Titus had overdone it during his student days, they would be hard put to describe the intense life of diverse activity into which he threw himself once he had been appointed professor at his Order's school of philosophy. And this extraordinary activity did not slacken with the years; rather, as Fr. Titus became known in his native land and elsewhere, there were more and more calls on his talents and advice. Far from being a dreamer, he was esteemed precisely as a first-class organizer and planner. Whether it was the centennial of a national patron saint like St. Peter Canisius, or a mission exhibit aimed at rousing interest in the Church's missions, or the organization of new schools, Fr. Titus seemed to have a flair for thinking up a suitable program. His articles on diverse subjects continued, and he considered himself fortunate to be able to use the stipends he received for these writings in favor of so many of the poor who came to him asking help. He travelled throughout his native land giving conferences on the subjects close to his heart—mysticism, the missions, the glories of the Netherlands and especially of his own province of Frisia.

He was particularly in demand after being named professor of philosophy and of the history of mysticism at the newly formed Catholic University at Nijmegen. The daylight hours did not provide him with enough time for all he had to do, particularly in regard to the preparation of classes, as well as the constant contacts he had with his students, so that he had to work late into the night. Since his health was always a worry to his superiors, they used to remind him each evening at recreation to get to bed early. So many times it was a penitent Titus who reported to his prior the next morning that he had gone on until quite late in the night to finish some urgent research. Yet he seemed to thrive on this work. At one point, after a long and delicate cure, two specialists decided that the best cure for Fr. Titus was to let him immerse himself once more in his work.

However setbacks and further challenges were not wanting. There were those among the professors and students who complained that with all his activities, despite his wealth of good intentions, Fr. Titus could not possibly do justice to the scientific level of teaching and research that was required by his university position. The Carmelite tended to agree with them, but he could do little about it since by nature he could not say no to any worthwhile venture that was presented to him. As a priest, he had made it his policy to reach as many people as possible. This was the fundamental reason for the fact that he did overextend himself.

No one, on the other hand, could deny the deep-seated kindness and charity of Fr. Titus. At faculty meetings, he sought to find a way to resolve contrasting opinions. His cheerful attitude was a byword, so that whenever he came to some Carmelite house, word spread rapidly that Fr. Titus had arrived. Although he was not a comedian or a mimic, his interest and his ability to listen to others, like his ability to offer so many useful suggestions, made him always a most welcome guest.

Despite his organizational abilities, Titus was not a success as a superior. He was appointed prior of his community for only one three-year term. Though excellent as an assistant and counsellor (positions which he held all his life), he was not decisive enough to be put in command. Financially, he would have brought the Dutch Carmel to bankruptcy had he been in charge. He would have given away everything to the poor, who found him a constant friend. The true mettle of Fr. Titus shines out in an episode recorded by all his biographers: a family, finding itself in financial straits, appealed to Fr. Titus for help. Though unable to do anything personally, he went to seek his superior's aid. The superior, twenty years younger than Fr. Titus, answered, "If everyone were as generous as you, all the poor would be rich, and all the rich poor. You are poor. Let things alone, there are limits." Fr. Titus put up no argument. He was sorry he could not help the pressed family, but he returned to his cell to continue his work.

Spiritual Life

His own spiritual life was in no way neglected with all his work. He made every effort to be with his community for prayers in common, both mental and vocal prayer, to such an extent that a colleague once complained that Titus was excusing himself from meetings to get home for the noon-day prayers: "Why don't you do one thing at a time? Dedicate yourself to it and do it well rather than being occupied with so many things." Still, his life of union with God, the wellspring of all his success, was the primary concern of Titus for the rest of his life. For him, even philosophy should in the end lead to God and show the marvels of God's love for us in a new dimension. Perhaps this radical theocentric outlook was what made him prefer the study of mysticism to all other studies.

Plans for research into the doctrine of the mystics of the Lowlands were given priority on his list of commitments. He collected manuscript after manuscript, obtained photocopy after photocopy of the classics of Lowland spirituality. One of the projects which he had elaborately worked out, but which never reached fruition, was the publication of a series of scientific monographs on these various subjects.

Fr. Titus was not sought after because he bent over backwards to change his views to every new tendency that appeared. Actually he was known to be quite entrenched in his opinions. And he could speak quite frankly on occasion, precisely because his listeners knew his great charity and simplicity. Once he addressed his Carmelite confreres:

Without poverty the religious is pharisaical; he is a gentleman in the monastery dressed like a poor man. Here in Holland, more than anywhere else, we are too attached to all kinds of things, and used to comfort. We want everything put in order under the pretext of Dutch solidity, cleanliness and neatness. We seek the rich and give more honor to them even in our heart. The poor are ours, but we do not want to be theirs. We make ourselves ridiculous before God who heard our vows.

The uncomplicated way be had of uniting himself to God and of teaching this union to others reminds one forcibly of the doctrine of Carmel which St. Therese of Lisieux enunciated so well. On one occasion, Fr. Titus gave a hint as to the secret of his spiritual life:

Do as perfectly as you can the tasks of your everyday life, even the most trivial. It is quite simple. Follow Our Lord like a little child. I skip after him as best I can. I put my trust in him and abandon all care.

He was speaking to one of his four sisters, three of whom became nuns. His only brother joined the Franciscans.

His untiring efforts on behalf of the Catholic University won him acclaim, highlighted by his appointment as Rector of the University in 1932. In his official capacity he became an even more familiar figure on the Dutch scene. Among other duties, he travelled to Rome to present Pope Pius XI with a dossier on the standing of the Dutch Catholic University. Fr. Titus, a man who never stood still, was not content to isolate himself in the Netherlands. He made numerous study trips abroad: to Spain, Germany, Ireland, and in 1935, the United States, at the invitation of his American confreres, to give a series of lectures on Carmelite spirituality. These resulted in a book, *The Beauty of Carmel*.

Observation and Arrest

The final challenge he was required to meet was the Nazi occupation. In character with his nature,

Titus Brandsma would not keep silence about the situation. From the pulpit and in the classroom he openly showed the evils of Nazism and the reasons why the Church must oppose it. This attitude, judged imprudent even by many of his confreres, put him on the Gestapo's list. He admitted that he noted unfamiliar students taking copious notes at his lectures, and so he was not unaware of his dangerous position. The occupying powers deemed him a "dangerous little friar."

But the proximate cause of his arrest by the Nazis was his work with the Catholic journalists. Among his many other duties, he had been asked by the Archbishop of Utrecht, Cardinal DeJong, to act as chaplain to the Catholic journalists in Holland. The Catholic press was a powerful instrument through which the bishops could make their views known. The powers in authority knew this and were determined to utilize this perfect means of getting their ideas across to Catholics. The Nazi government, then, imposed the publication of several Nazi-slanted articles on the Catholic papers. The Cardinal saw the end of all free expression in this act, so he asked Fr. Titus to convince the Catholic newspapermen to stand firm and refuse to publish the articles. Fr. Titus was not content to write directives to his friends the journalists. He visited them all personally and managed to preserve a united front. All refused to collaborate.

This type of resistance the Nazi regime could not cope with except with imprisonment. On January 19, 1942, two Gestapo agents came to Carmel and after ransacking Fr. Titus' room, led him away under arrest. He was told to leave behind his frayed brown habit and to put on an ordinary suit. The Carmelite experienced dire conditions in several prisons during his arrest, ending in Dachau. During his captivity, Fr. Titus remained true to form, as charitable and direct as ever. He gave away the last of his prized tobacco. But when his captors promised him freedom, were he to promise not to speak out against Nazism, the short Carmelite said that he would again do as he had done if he were so asked by his superiors. When reminded that he need not be so critical openly, he answered the judge: "I cannot keep the truth to myself. I am not the Archbishop of the Netherlands nor a director of instruction, but it would be a sad state of affairs if Msgr. DeJong and Dr. Verhoeven were alone to proclaim the truth!"

Term of Imprisonment

The solitude of his first prison in Scheveningen was a joy to him who had so often hankered after time to give himself up to his Lord during his busy days. Undaunted and grateful, he wrote home, "Seldom have I felt so happy and content... If God ordered it, I would stay here forever." These exclamations were further clarified in a short work about this period in Fr. Titus' life entitled *My Cell*. It was here too that the Carmelite returned to his first love. He began a biography of St. Teresa of Avila, later completed by Fr. Brocard Meijer and published in 1946.

But this respite was brief. Titus was sent off to Germany, where prison camps were much cruder and solitude of the cell had to give way to living in barracks. Accepting, yet this other challenge, Fr. Brandsma thanked God that he could do something good by talking to, encouraging and comforting his fellow prisoners of every nationality and religion. The example of courage and good spirits, dispite his chronic stomach ailments, impressed one and all.

Just before he was deported to Dachau, the terror of all concentration camps, his captors tried to break him for the last time. They promised freedom for silence. Fr. Titus gave the same answer as before. But he too, was a man. Influenced, no doubt, by the German chaplain who had befriended him, he decided on the eve of his departure for Dachau to ask for freedom in some German monastery, where he would remain for the duration of the war. We, weak and unfaithful as we are, perhaps never feel closer to Fr. Titus than in this circumstance when he wrote not only to the judge of his case, but also to influential friends of his to do all they could to prevent him from being buried in Dachau. Among the reasons he adduced for his request was his failing health. The judge's reply: "He should have thought of his health before getting into this brawl."

In Dachau, a hell on earth for the inmates, Father Titus continued to be himself. Even at the limits of his strength, when he dragged himself to the fatal infirmary, where shameful experiments were conducted on him, he knew how to forget himself. The nurse who administered the fatal injection to him and who later returned to the faith due to Father Titus' intercession, noted:

> Generally there was a group of sick people around his bed; this took place every day. He always had the knack of reanimating them. Once I was present when a man, standing close to his bed, was telling him about his life in tears. And I heard the Servant of God tell him, 'But my good man, what you are saying is not all that serious. Everything is passing.' For the most part, sick persons are concerned about themselves and think only of themselves, but the Servant of God was always in good humor and was a support to all, and myself in particular.

This invaluable witness mentions that other deaths made no impression on her. Father Titus' death was indelibly etched on her spirit, because he was "always so kind and cordial... That injection made such an impression on me, while in other cases no impression was left on me." She was amazed that Father Titus was so genteel towards her and even towards the doctor, while both were hated by the other prisoners.

> He had great compassion for me. He asked me how I had ended up there. I told him how things had gone. He did not show the slightest bit of hatred for me. Once he took me by the hand and said, 'You're a good girl, I will pray for you very much...' He gave me his rosary for me to pray. I told him that I was not capable of praying, and so it was of no use to me. He told me that even if I could not pray, I could at least recite the second part of the rosary, 'Pray for us sin-

ners.' I laughed at that. He told me that if I prayed much, I would not be lost. For other patients I often felt aversion. Hundreds of priests made no impression on me; only Father Titus I immediately found attractive and I liked him, since he was a good patient.

The indomitable spirit of Father Titus conquered the horrors of human degradation. Till the end he was intent on living out the Carmelite spirituality about which he had written so widely and so effectively. He refused to add to the hatred, cruelty and prejudice which he saw around him. This is why the emaciated friar shared his meagre daily portion of bread with those he felt needed it more. This is why he kept consoling, uplifting, counselling, forgiving. He even loved and forgave his tormentors, felt compassion for his eventual slayers. Once when he had the privilege of having the Eucharist with him, hidden in his eye-glass case overnight, he considered it one of the greatest of graces that he woke up at 2 a.m. and could spend the rest of the night in the company of the Lord. "My brother, I knew Whom I had with me," he commented to Brother Raphael. The Jesus he found in the midst of human degradation and inhumanity to man has become his eternal Treasure. When he was exterminated and cremated like thousands of others, his fellow prisoners in their misery commented, "If anyone is in heaven, he is."

3

"THE LIMIT HAS BEEN REACHED"

Thomas Winship and Titus Hoekstra

PERHAPS nothing shows better why Fr. Titus Brandsma died than his own letter of December 31, 1941, to the editors of the Dutch Catholic newspapers and the record of his trial at Scheveningen in January, 1942. Following the German invasion of Holland in the spring of 1940, a systematic attempt was made by the occupying authorities and the Dutch Nazi government to indoctrinate the people with the Nazi ideology. Even before the war, Fr Titus had condemned outright the unchristian materialism of Nazism. Undaunted by the presence of the German army and the Nazi political machine, he continued to do so, courageously defending the liberties of the people and the Catholic Church, the chief source of resistance to the regime. In the spring of 1941, difficulties increased for the Catholic schools and the press of which he was spiritual adviser. Fr Titus became the champion of the Catholic cause. Even though suffering from a severe illness, he hurried from one end of the country to the other to exhort the Catholics to stand firm and to remonstrate with the occupying powers. He warned the press of the enemy censorship, "a sewer of falsehood and imposture," from which the newspapers had to draw their information. To the journalists whose counsellor he was he once said, "The day will come when The Hague will expect us to become the propagandists of Nazism. No, my friends, we must give way no further; there are limits and we have reached them." That day came soon afterwards on the eighteenth of December when the following order was telegraphed to all editorial staffs:

The Ministry of Instruction and Culture hereby informs the Dutch Press that it is not permitted to refuse publication of the advertisements of the N.S.B. (*Nationaal Socialistische Beweging,* i.e., The Dutch Nazi Party) or its co-organizations on doctrinal grounds, if the content of the advertisement in no way unlawfully attacks the honor or well-being of persons or societies, harms their good name, or runs contrary to public order and common sense. This measure is taken that nothing calculated to further the unity of the Dutch people may be omitted.

Then followed a period of some uncertainty. It was clear that liberty of conscience would no longer be respected. On Tuesday, the thirtieth, Father Titus conferred with Archbishop de Jong and on the next day sent to the editorial staffs of all the Catholic newspapers the following letter, by which he took his stand for the liberty of the Church:

December 31, 1941

Dear Sir:

In view of my appointment by His Grace Archbishop de Jong as ecclesiastical adviser to the Catholic Journalists' Association, I feel obligated to draw your attention to the following remarks:

The statute for the editors and the explanation given with it explicitly acknowledge not only the existence of, but even the desirability of confessional newspapers in the Netherlands. The Catholic newspapers have been maintained by the "reorganization" of the press, that is to say, those newspapers are allowed which are inspired by Catholic principles.

The Dutch law recognizes the Catholic Church as one of the greatest societies in the country and allows her to follow her own principles in her internal organization. In that internal organization the Bishop's right to make decisions for the Diocese binding in conscience with regard to faith and morals and the upkeep of church discipline comes first. The Bishop has the right to decide what course must be followed by the faithful of his Diocese in faith and morals. According to her own principles as well as according to the principles of international law, the Church of the Netherlands is expected to recognize the laws of the occupying power. But the episcopacy has been forced to take measures according to its own principles against a movement which attacks those principles and preaches others contrary to them. At the present time much is presented to the newspapers in the Netherlands with express orders for its publication. Where it was not flagrantly contrary to Catholic principles the order has been obeyed in such a way that the Catholic people have not been scandalized since it is known that the directors and editors have been acting under constraint. Whether they have already submitted too much cannot be judged by the common reader, who does not know of all that has been offered for publication. The episcopacy, much to its regret, has been obligated to assert in its first circular letter that the former glorious Catholic newspapers can now hardly be called "Catholic." It, however, willingly recognizes that the directors and editors who are sincerely attached to Catholic principles and do their utmost to maintain the Catholic character of their newspapers as far as possible, face a very difficult task and it also understands that it is very difficult in practice to draw the line between what can and cannot be done. The episcopacy affirms that, as long as the directors and editors sincerely strive to maintain their own Catholic standing, their efforts earn them honor and recognition.

How difficult it is to know how much one can submit under constraint! This, however, is cleared up now, because a few days ago the authorities of the press issued an order, obedience to which would place the editors and directors of the Catholic newspapers in conflict with their principles. In this order, which obliges the printing of advertisements of the N.S.B., it is explicitly stated that one cannot resist it on fundamental principles. Through this order the principle itself is made a point of contradiction. There the Catholic newspapers cannot compromise any longer if they do not want to disregard the command of their Bishop who forbids them to give their support to those ideas and this movement. This instruction has not yet been issued as an official decree but as news through the teletype. Perhaps it will not become an official regulation. So much the better! But if the order is given or if the publication of advertisements of the N.S.B. in accordance with this piece of news is insisted upon, even under the threat of grave penalties such as suspension or suppression, the directors and—in agreement with them—the editors must categorically refuse those articles if they appreciate the Catholic character of their newspapers. It is not possible to act otherwise. We have reached the limit. I trust that the

Catholic newspapers will maintain the Catholic point of view without hesitation. The more we are united in refusing, the stronger we shall be. I hope you understand that I write this declaration only after mature reflection and discussion with various people in authority and with His Grace, the Archbishop. The directors of the newspapers are to take note of this point of view. If they do not acknowledge it, they make the Catholic paper an impossibility and it ceases to exist, if not materially, then certainly formally; with the consequence that if it continues materially, it can no longer rely upon the assured support of Catholic subscribers and thus will be ruined dishonorably. It will certainly be very hard for many of you who till now have had an honorable and remunerative position. Only those who, against all promises, try to force the conscience of the directors and editors will bear the consequences. I do not yet dare to think that the responsible authorities will go as far as that, but if they do, God will have the last word and will reward the faithful servant.

With every good wish for the New Year,
Father Titus Brandsma, O. Carm.

For ten days from the first of January, 1942, Father Titus travelled up and down the country consulting with the editors and directors. His illness was forgotten. Only one thing mattered—to create a single front in the press. Followed everywhere by secret agents, he was advised by friends to be careful but he retorted, "Should I then have sent my friends into the front line while I retired to the positions behind the lines? Never!" On the tenth of January, he reported to the Archbishop and it was decided to issue a joint pastoral letter of the hierarchy in which the Catholic press was expressly forbidden to publish the Nazi propaganda. Quickly the press rallied to the support of the hierarchy. A single front had been created and it now remained for the Press Commissariate to make the next move. Matters were moving to a head, however. "Return as quickly as you can;" ordered his Father Provincial, "the abyss is yawning beneath your feet; one must not rush towards martyrdom." The Archbishop wished him to ascribe everything to the Bishops since they were less liable to reprisals than a Carmelite friar, but Father Titus persuaded him to let him alone stand responsible for his actions. On the nineteenth of January, the Commissariate made its move.   Father Titus was arrested.   After a night in the prison at Arnhem, he was moved to Scheveningen for his trial on the twenty-first before S.S. Hauptscharführer Hardegan.   Let Father Titus' words during his trial speak for themselves!

Hardegan: What was the purpose of your visits to the editors of the Catholic newspapers?

Brandsma: They had to be informed orally that the limit had been reached and that henceforth they had to resist on fundamental principles.   Furthermore, we wanted to learn of their difficulties and opinions so that the Bishops could have their experiences in mind while making their decisions.

Hardegan: Was it the aim of your visits to get a clear-cut idea of what each editor thought?

Brandsma: That was not my primary intention because, even if their opinion had been contrary, the position of the Catholic Church would not have been altered.   Nevertheless, I expected that most of them would agree with the position of the Bishops.

Hardegan: Were the editors of doubtful persuasion to be convinced and eventually won back to Catholic principles?

Brandsma: My answer to this question is that it was not my immediate intention although it had this result.

Hardegan: Was pressure to be brought on the editors to accept the wishes of the Bishops?

Brandsma: On the part of the Church it was emphasized that should the editors propagate the ideas of the N.S.B., they would incur the sanctions they had been told of.   Archbishop de Jong also expressed this consideration in his letter.   During the talks some of them pointed out the danger of financial loss.   But when the Catholic Church upholds her principles, she considers primarily the ideal and only indirectly the material loss to her faithful in defending those principles.   In my opinion, this ideal turned the scale for the majority of the editors.   The Church is strong and powerful through the invincible constancy of her religion.   At all times there have been men who when necessary have given their lives as martyrs for the Church. The Dutch episcopacy is convinced that if the Catholics stand united they constitute a great and formidable political power. In these unsteady times it is the Faith which gives the faithful the courage to bear patiently great material sacrifices.

Hardegan: Does the Church, therefore, knowing the sentiments of the faithful, try to sabotage the decrees of the occupying power and the Dutch government, thus endangering peace at home and preventing the National Socialistic program from finding favor with the Dutch people?

Brandsma: The Catholic Church in the Netherlands observes the decrees of the occupying power or of the Dutch authorities only insofar as they are in accordance with her principles. But if there are basic contradictions to them, the Church refuses to co-operate, come what may. When, through this attitude and her constant action, the political peace at home is jeopardized, the Church certainly regrets it but she does not accept the responsibility for it. She opposes the National-Socialistic ideology for reasons which are rooted in her own ideology and mission. In my opinion it is regrettable that the occupying power is furthering the ideology of the N.S.B., for the Dutch people and especially the clergy wish to know nothing of it. The Catholic Church makes it her task to strengthen the convictions of all Catholics who hold prominent positions.

Hardegan: Before using their influence, why did not the Archbishop and the Catholic Journalists' Association ask for talks as they did later on?

Brandsma: We had no intention of influencing the editors. We were fully aware that with regard to this problem a common attitude already existed. On the other hand, we had expected more from the official governor because of the definite relations we had had with him. In conclusion, I shall again remind you that the Catholic Church observes the laws of the occupying power and the Dutch government only insofar as they agree with her principles. Should one of them, however, take measures which are not in keeping with Catholic doctrine, she, of necessity, is compelled to take no notice of them. They have informed me that I am to remain in prison until this affair is cleared up. I myself adopt the attitude of the Dutch episcopacy.

The following morning he handed to the judge a written statement of the reasons for the Dutch opposition which he concluded by saying, "May God bless the Netherlands; may God bless Germany; may God see them once more united in their faith in Him, those two who live so close to each other and are so closely related." No fresh statement, however, could avert the inevitable. The verdict was a foregone conclusion. Father Titus was found guilty of exerting pressure on the directors of the newspapers and sentenced to imprisonment until the end of the war. Six weeks later, he was moved from Scheveningen to Amersfort and from there to the hell of Dachau where he died on the twenty-sixth of July.

4

DACHAU EYE—WITNESS

Raphael Tijhuis, O. Carm.

FATHER TITUS BRANDSMA came from a very old farming family. He was born on February 23, 1881, the fifth child and first son of Titus Hendrikzoon Brandsma and Tjitsje Annes Postma. At baptism he received the name of Anno Sjoerd. In September 1898 at the age of seventeen, he entered the Order of Carmelites of the Ancient Observance at Boxmeer, Holland. A few days later he was invested in the habit of the Order and received the name of his father and that of the great disciple of St Paul, Titus.

On June 7, 1905, he was ordained priest by the bishop of Herzogenbosch. Soon after his first Mass he was sent by his superiors to Rome. On October 25, 1909, he received his doctor's degree in Theology. He then was recalled to Holland to become a professor in the Carmelite seminary at Oss.

Between the years 1919 and 1923 Father Titus worked on the further development of the Carmelite houses of study at Oss and Oldenzaal. During this time, with the help of other Carmelites, he published the entire works of St. Teresa of Avila in Dutch. He also wrote many articles about Carmelite spirituality in Dutch Catholic newspapers and journals. As a Frisian he endeavoured to introduce again the Frisian language into the schools. He also laboured for the liberty and recognition of the Catholics in that area. Later he himself was to occupy the chair of the Frisian language at the universities of Amsterdam and Utrecht.

In April, 1926, mainly through the preaching and writing of Father Titus, a yearly pilgrimage was begun in Dokkum, the town hallowed by the martyrdom of St. Boniface. Until then Dokkum had been a forgotten town, but now, through the activity of Father Titus, it became a famous place of pilgrimage in that part of Holland. When the Dutch Catholic University was founded in 1923 at Nijmegen, Father Titus was given the professorship of the History of Mystical Theology. During the school year of 1932-1933 Father Titus Brandsma was elected Rector Magnificus of the university.

His lectures at the university centred around the history of spirituality in the low countries. Nevertheless, he did not neglect the influence of the German, English and French mystics. He understood the 'Devotio Moderna' and its crowning glory, Dionysius the Carthusian, as true Low Country mysticism. In 1925-1926 he lectured on the mysticism of Hedwig, a medieval Dutch mystic. At this time he travelled through much of Europe and searched through the archives and libraries for rare medieval manuscripts. He thus laid the foundation for a large collection of microfilms of medieval mystical manuscripts.

A few years later Father Titus began to study the great mystic John van Ruysbroeck. Then he concentrated his efforts on the founders of the 'Devotio Moderna', Gerhard Groote and Thomas à Kempis and the Franciscan preacher John Brugman. Through his study of John Brugman he came in contact with the medieval penitent St. Lidwine of Schiedam and presented special lectures on the mysticism of suffering based on her life.

In 1930 he studied the famous stigmatic Theresa Neumann personally at Konnersreuth. He was not impressed so much by the alleged miraculous in her life as by her nearness to God. He published several studies on Theresa Neumann and on the similar case of Elisabeth Kolb of Hohenmark. As an experienced student of mysticism, Fr. Titus soon realized that the case of Elisabeth Kolb was not genuine.

During this time also he published an article on Carmelite spirituality for the great French theological reference work, *Dictionnaire de Spiritualité Chrétienne*. Moreover he was on the editorial board of the Dutch Catholic Encyclopedia, and wrote over a hundred articles for it. In the Dutch Catholic journal *De Gelderlander* his articles appeared continuously. More than eighty newspapers and magazines regularly published his contributions.

His great interest in the development of the Carmelite Order manifested itself especially in his desire for the return of the Order to its ancient monastery in Mainz. He was the representative of the Order in the negotiations with the Bishop of Mainz, with the city council, and the General of the French occupation forces. Through his efforts the Carmelites again recovered their medieval church in that city. In Holland he helped build the new monasteries at Aalsmer, Amsterdam and Nijmegen.

As a Carmelite, Fr. Titus's way to God was with and through Mary. To be with Mary, to imitate her, meant for him to carry God in oneself and live in him. The Carmelite must with apostolic zeal carry God to the world just as Mary gave Christ to the world. This is the picture of Fr. Titus Brandsma, a true Carmelite. The spiritual life of Fr. Titus was very intense, yet so interior that it did not cause comment among his fellow Carmelites. His interior life was lived in the full and exact observance of community life. In the quiet of the chapel and of his cell he always sought a more interior and closer contact with God. He did not seek any exterior extraordinary mystical experiences in his life of prayer. He lived exactly according to the spirit of the Rule of St. Albert. He often said that interior mortifications were better than bodily mortifications because before all else man must first offer his spirit to God. Everything ordered by obedience he did well and out of a full heart.

His love of his neighbour was extraordinary. He had a good word for everyone and understood no difference in social classes, as in each person he saw the image of God. At Nijmegen, when he used to go every morning to the University, he often saw an old man pushing his heavily laden hand-cart up a certain hill. Fr. Titus would throw his briefcase on the wagon and help push the cart. The poor always came to him and never went home neglected. He used to tell the brother at the monastery door,

> Do not be stingy with giving food and money to the poor for they have a right to them and a right to live. We ourselves live from such gifts. The poor are the friends of God, and as we also want to be God's friends we must love his friends.

His intense activity, before all else as professor at the Catholic University of Nijmegen, brought Fr. Titus into contact with the Catholic press of Holland. Because of the many articles he published he soon became acquainted with the Dutch organization of Catholic journalists. Soon he was elected chaplain of the organization. This duty soon put him on the Nazi black-list in Germany.

After the occupation of Holland by Germany the situation became critical. In August, 1941, the Dutch hierarchy published a joint pastoral letter against the racial theory of the National Socialists. This pastoral caused the Nazis to move into action against the Dutch Catholic Press. Fr. Titus, as spiritual leader of the organization, wrote a special letter encouraging the members of the Catholic press to stand united against the Nazis. He did not conceal the seriousness of this move, but appealed to the ideals of the Catholic press. He wrote: "We are not sure if our adversaries will use force, but if they do, remember that God has the last word and he will reward his true servants."

Now the Gestapo moved in on Fr. Titus. On January 19, 1942, he was taken to prison in Scheveningen, where the reason for his arrest was made known to him: it was because he had tried to organize a united stand of the Dutch Catholic Press against the Nazi-controlled new press.

In Scheveningen prison he found time to write

his long desired biography of St. Teresa of Avila. Because he did not have any paper he wrote this biography between the lines of another book. He managed to finish seven chapters and these were published after his death.

At the command of the Gestapo he had to write his reasons why the Dutch, especially the Catholic Dutch, were against National Socialism. In this report he clearly stated the position of the Dutch against the Nazis but without hate or exaggeration. The end of this report reads like a prayer:

> May God bless Holland and may he bless Germany. Pray God that these two peoples again in full freedom and in full peace may live side by side; that they may recognize him and seek his honor in word and deed, to the salvation of both the related peoples.

After long and tortuous questionings the Gestapo saw that they could not break the prisoner, and he was sent to another prison, the concentration camp of Dachau.

Fr. Titus realized that he would never return from Dachau. Nevertheless, he remained calm and patient. It was the beginning of the end, and he looked upon his time in Dachau as a dark tunnel through which he must travel in order to get to the everlasting light. A few weeks were enough to sap all the strength of the frail sixty-one-year old Carmelite. The hard farm work that he was ordered to do helped to weaken him. Hunger and other frightful conditions in Dachau broke down his weakened constitution. The wounds which festered on his feet were always aggravated by the daily half-mile march to the fields. How painful it was for him! Yet he never complained.

The work area was farmland which was under constant surveillance of guards armed with clubs, who used them on any prisoner who did not keep his eyes lowered. These guards were mostly Communists who had changed over to the Nazis and were known by the Gestapo for their hatred for the Church. The guards, therefore, were not held responsible for the tortures which they inflicted on the prisoners. The cell-blocks where the priests were located had such communist personnel. How paradoxical it was to see Nazi and Communist together, their differences lost in the common hatred for the Church. In all the daily manhandlings and tortures the Communists took over the role of the S.S., and thus the S.S. did not consider themselves responsible for this inhuman treatment.

The farm work affected Fr. Titus's strength greatly. The "easy work" of weeding was tiring for him. Daily on the return march after work two Polish priests used to take him under the arms to lighten the march back to the concentration camp. Fr. Titus was often so tired after this work that he was hardly able to stand on his feet.

A true torture for him, after such hard work, was the evening inspection which often lasted for hours. The prisoners stood in rows of ten for roll-call. Thousands of men, hungry and tired, stood for hours, regardless of weather, summer and winter, rain or snow. Once during an unusually long inspection, I whispered to Fr. Titus at my side to ask just why we were waiting so long. He answered, "I don't know, but we can wait a little longer; we have the time for it!" When at last the inspections came to an end we had to march back to our cell-block, singing loudly by command, so that we had the appearance of happy carefree men!

After returning to the cell-block, the guards then sought reasons for punishing the prisoners. The clergy often had to do punishment marching or running. A hard day's work of thirteen hours was not enough for them. One could not rest either at work or in the cell-block as there were no Sundays or holidays.

The meals consisted of a little thin soup and three or four unpeeled potatoes. After eating the prisoners had to use the little time before line-up in order to clean their plates and eating utensils. These had to be absolutely clean, for just a finger-mark on a spoon was enough to bring down the rage of the ever present guard. If something was not exactly in order the offender would lose his meal and receive corporal punishment.

Immediately after dinner each day the cell-block was cleaned. At a warning call the prisoners had to be out of the cell-block, and if they tarried the head of the cell-block would club them out of the building. One day when we had received such a warning I saw Fr. Titus coming out of the building without his glasses. I asked him where they were and he said that he must have left them in the cell-block. I wanted to get them for him, but if I were caught I would be branded as a thief. Thus Fr. Titus decided to risk the wrath of the head of the cell-block for he was unable to get about without his glasses. He entered the building on tip-toe and managed to get his glasses without being detected. However, on coming out of the building the door creaked. The head of the cell-block heard the noise and turning saw Fr. Titus about to leave the building. He shouted, "What's the matter, Brandsma?"

"I forgot my glasses," he answered.

The head of the cell-block stormed over to him, and with the words "I'll teach you to forget!" hit him in the face with his club. The glasses, in pieces, flew through the door and Fr. Titus followed, under the curses of the head of the cell-block. As I picked up the pieces of glass and returned them to Fr. Titus, I saw how bloody his face was. He did not want any sympathy but said, "If you had gone to get the glasses, you would have got the beating. I certainly should not have forgotten my glasses." He then asked the pardon of the head of the cell-block for his intrusion. He always remained calm, even after such mishandling. Such spiritual strength came only from his close contact with God in prayer.

Before we were called for the morning inspection we had to wait a few minutes on the parade ground. In these few minutes we often sought to speak to the Polish Carmelites who were in a neighbouring cell-block. One Polish Carmelite told me that Fr. Titus always gave the others a sense of peace, as one saw immediately that Fr. Titus was filled with a true interior tranquillity.

The wounds on his feet were a constant torture for him when he walked. One was not allowed to care for one's wounds but had to report to the infirmary which was open three times a week for such care. The medical care there was not too exact, depending upon the particular infirmarian at the time. Thus we sought to care for Fr. Titus's wounds secretly. On unobserved occasions I used to clean his footwounds with a piece of clean paper and then cover them with a piece of clean handkerchief. Only with the greatest difficulty and pain was he able to put on his shoes. Yet he would take this often with humor. Once after such crude care of his wounds, as I picked him up, he tapped me on the shoulder light-heartedly and laughingly said, "Now, I feel like a man again!"

Many times his words would foster in us a mediative thought as we stood on the parade ground. "Mary must help us," he often exclaimed, "and when she is with us, we can bear much." The other Dutch priests were glad to get the chance to talk with him. All liked to be with this wise and sympathetic Carmelite.

How happy he was when I would bring him secretly Holy Communion! Every evening before going into the dormitory there was an inspection of each prisoner to make sure that he had washed his upper body and his feet that evening as commanded. The head of the cell-block would make this inspection, and if a prisoner's feet were dirty he would be beaten for it. One evening as Fr. Titus was being inspected, he was set aide. A few minutes before, I had passed the Blessed Sacrament to him secretly and he had put it in his spectacle case and hidden it under his armpit. The head of the cell-block with one blow laid Fr. Titus out on the floor. He tried to rise, but the continued blows sent him back to the floor. He managed to crawl under the beatings until finally he reached the dormitory door where I picked him up and put him on his bed. I asked him how badly hurt he was, but he only smiled and answered, "Oh, I hardly felt anything, for I was adoring him whom I am carrying." Then he said, "Let us say an *Adoro Te* together." I wanted to kneel, but he said it might attract the attention of the head of the cell-block, so I remained standing and bowed over him. Silently we adored in prayer the hidden God who was in our midst. After this he blessed me with the Blessed Sacrament hidden in his old spectacle case.

The next morning before inspection, we said a short prayer together and he gave me Holy Communion. Interiorly strengthened one could face the day. Fr. Titus used to say that Holy Communion not only was our supernatural nutrition but also our bodily food. How often did we feel this in Dachau!

However, the life in Dachau became too much for Fr. Titus. His strength broke. The nerve-shattering beatings, the hunger, the hard work, and his wounds sapped his physical energy. A council was taken and it was decided that he would have to go to the infirmary. Fr. Titus did not fear the terrible infirmary, even though he knew what would await him there. In the dark tunnel, as he called Dachau, he prayed for strength to the bitter end.

In the middle of July, physically exhausted, Fr. Titus was taken to the infirmary. On July 26, 1942, we received the sad news of his death. At last the carrying of the cross ended for Fr. Titus Brandsma; he had reached his Calvary in Dachau.

Fr. Titus died a heroic death for his religious principles. He was imprisoned because of his unshakable stand on the rights and duties of the Catholic press, on which he could not compromise. Because of this he was condemned to the slow death of Dachau. In the same plight as his fellow prisoners, through his example and unchanging spiritual joy, he was for them before and after his death a shining inspiration.

For Catholic Holland he was considered to be a true martyr who would be officially canonized a saint of the Church. His canonization process was started in Holland. It lasted for two years and over fifty witnesses were interviewed by the ecclesiastical tribunal. Among the witnesses were a Cardinal, two bishops, sixteen priests and religious, among whom five were fellow-prisoners of Dachau. On December 8, 1957, the diocesan process closed formally under the direction of the Bishop of Herzogenbosch and the records were sent to Rome.

5

NIJMEGEN SERMON, JULY 31, 1977

Joannes Cardinal Willebrands

WE are commemorating and celebrating the thirty-fifth anniversary of the death of Fr. Titus Brandsma. Great people are commemorated as a result of their contributions to science, art, religion or in other fields. But it can happen that their importance belongs only to the past without any true or real value for the man of today and his needs. This is not the case with Fr. Titus. Whoever gets to know him, for example from the admirable biography written by his confrere Fr. Brocardus Meijer or from the biography by H. Aukes, but above all from Fr. Titus Brandsma's own writings, begins to know and love him as master and guide. The richness of his spirit combined with great modesty and helpfulness is alive among us and the problems of our times. We are able to commemorate and celebrate Titus Brandsma by bringing alive something of the gift in us that we have received in him from God.

Fr. Titus was a philosopher and a mystic. This was so in virtue of his position as professor at the University of Nijmegen and, if it is permissible to say so, by means of the grace of God. As evidence of this I can cite his well-known lecture on the concept of God delivered on the *dies natalis* of the Catholic University in 1932. Even now I still remember the profound and inspiring impression this lecture had on me, a student of the Warmond major seminary, and on numerous philosophy and theology students. In those days there was a controversy raging over the concept and possibility of a Christian or even Catholic philosophy. Could philosophy have a Christian character and structure? Famous names in this debate were Jacques Maritain, Etienne Gilson and Maurice Blondel. Without touching on this controversy, Professor Brandsma gave an example, a model of philosophical thought about God that embraced the whole spectrum between rational reflection and mystical intuition. His inaugural lecture had a liberating and cheering effect. It was not prepared as a theoretical document dealing with abstract thought but was rather born from a preoccupation for man, from a love for man. He begins, "Among the questions that I ask myself none preoccupy me more than the enigma of how, in the process of development, boastful and proud of its progress, mankind has distanced itself from God in such large numbers." He then asks himself: "Is something lacking only on their part? Or is something required from us so that God will shine again on the world with a brighter light and we can then have the hope that the study of the concept of God will at least alleviate this most pressing need of all men?" His method was that of a liberator: not the negative way of opposition and confutation but rather of understanding and explaining the concept of God in this way: that in the richness of this concept we can see a magnificence which, for us today, causes the greatest fascination in the concept of God. On this point we can hear the word of John (8:32): "The Truth will make you free."

So, Professor Brandsma gave a Christian interpretation of the image of God and how this was developed throughout the different periods of history. The most striking thing about this is the attention he gives to the elements of truth that are present and active in every concept man has formed of God. The title "The Concept of God" leads us to expect a philosophical approach. In fact, he shows how the knowledge of God, once acquired, becomes a call from God who is signalling from afar to come to Him. "In the mystical life there is an ascent of the bride to the bridegroom who is calling and infusing love into the heart." Although only a few chosen people arrive at the heights of contemplation, "all of us should tend towards a contemplation that grows ever clearer. Whoever meets God in the very roots of his existence cannot be considered as one who is apart from life. On the contrary, he has discovered the true reality and the true goal of life."

Professor Brandsma asks that as a consequence of our union with God, we obtain the inspiration to acts of service. That is what we must aim for, in such a way however that the good act has its origin in the awareness that our union with God obliges us to that act. "The action is not sufficient. It must be consciously deduced from the integral presence of God, as though arranged and counselled by Him in the intimate recesses of our being. That will make the action not only strong and irresistible on the outside but also internally strong and a manifestation of a nobler, more beautiful life."

In order to learn this art, Titus Brandsma turned —who would have thought otherwise—to the Dutch spiritual literature. "The mystical works of Ruusbroec in our own Dutch literature could teach us in a fresh way how, by still using the natural gifts of the intellect, we can arrive at a contemplation of God that grows ever clearer. It is a reason for great joy at this time that mystical works are in vogue."

That is all; indeed perhaps I went on too long, on the well-known inaugural lecture of Professor Brandsma. But can we not already see here the most important aspects of his personality and his work, which later became even more developed? He wanted to make the knowledge of God—the supreme complement of which he saw in contemplation and mystical union—accessible and open to everyone. This he did through his articles in the magazine *Carmelrozen*, through his translations of the Spanish mystics into Dutch; through his contribution to the Society of Ruusbroec and to the magazine *Ons Geestelijk Erf*, in creating the Library of Medieval spiritual manuscripts in the Low Countries. Even while in prison he wrote the Life of St. Theresa of Avila. The enormous knowledge that today's man has acquired of the material world urgently requires a deepened knowledge of God. I am speaking of a spiritual need that is being partially voiced in the charismatic movement, in the frequent visits of young people to monasteries, in the desire to model one's life on Christ—what Fr. Titus called the Imitation of Christ. In this Fr. Titus Brandsma is still a master and a guide. His work can even today be a precious help to us: for example, in the preparation of the Dutch breviary if one so wished, there could be an alternative series of readings, chosen from Dutch spiritual literature.

Father Titus has been called a martyr and the request has been made that he be beatified in the Church under this title. It is not very difficult to call martyrs all those millions of innocent people who were tortured and died as a consequence in concentration camps. This is martyrdom in a broad but nevertheless extremely real sense. But it is more difficult to attribute to one of these people the specific title of martyr in the sense of the tradition of the Church: that it was as a result of his faith, his Christian-being that he was arrested and suffered death in supreme union with Christ in faith and charity. In Fr. Titus' case we can say: does not his whole life point in this direction and does not his life find its complement in a lived-out union with Christ, in the imitation of Christ, precisely in his passion and death? For him, the concentration camp was not merely a punishment for his unconditional fidelity to the Church and to his bishop in the task he had received working with the Catholic press. For him it meant much more: it was an entering into the most intimate union with his Lord. This is attested to by his letters, his conversations with his fellow prisoners, the conferences he gave in prison on the mystical life and even the well known poem written in prison at Scheveningen; one verse reads:

> O blessed grief and hallowed pain,
> That leads to thee my Savior slain,
> To suffer now a joy will be;
> It brings me Lord, so near to Thee.

Let us hope, with justified reason, that one day we will be able to commemorate and celebrate Fr. Titus Brandsma in the manner the Church accords to her Beatified and her Saints and that in this day he will be our master and guide.

Translated by Paul O'Brien, O. Carm.

II

SPIRITUAL ODYSSEY

Close to Fr. Titus' heart was his native Frisia: its language, its culture, its mystics.

Fr. Titus played a central role in Dutch ecumenism. Here he is pictured with the Apostleship for the Reunion of Eastern Churches.

1

CATHOLIC SPIRITUALITY

Jacobus Melsen, O. Carm.

It would seem to be taking no small risk to hold up a friar as source of inspiration to laymen at the very moment when they are awakening to a full realization of the calling that is theirs: that of making their own contribution towards the coming of the Kingdom by means of their love for this world. The absolute poverty of St. Francis, for instance, cannot serve as example to a business man, whose vocation consists in building up a loving home-life, in caring for his wife and family and in giving himself whole-heartedly to his work. This in marked contrast to that of the "Poverello" who cast his clothes at his father's feet, that he might stand naked in this world and wedded to poverty.

The situation of a friar, striving after the ideal of contemplation in silence and solitude, also differs completely from that of a Christian layman. Can he really give men and women living in the midst of this world something to hold on to? But the truly great —and I consider Titus Brandsma to have been one of them—the truly great are those who rise above their time and generation. Moved by a deep understanding of the needs of their day, they set up a program which by its breadth of vision retains its value for many years. They are concerned with the very essence of Christianity and help others to find their own direction in at least one section of their lives. Moreover, however divergent the vocations of layman and friar may be, there are many points of contact as the Kingdom is their common goal.

The first years of Anno Sjoerd Brandsma's life differed not at all from those of hundreds of other small boys in the Netherlands. The little Brandsmas, six in all, living under the protection of their parents and in the shelter of Oegeklooster, their farm, grew up in an atmosphere which, though perhaps slightly reserved on the outside, was yet warmly human and sincerely Christian. Mother was perhaps a wee bit over-anxious, father a just man, lord of his pastures and fields. Any infringement of what he considered to be his sovereign rights was taken as a personal insult. Titus' biographers mention an incident of his boyhood, characterizing father and son, and throwing a light on their home-life. One evening a thief out for apples came sneaking into the orchard. Farmer Brandsma, hearing someone moving about, ran out but returned without having caught his man and in a fine fury at the violation of his property: "Just let me get hold of him..." Whereupon little Anno was heard to say: "What a good thing Dad didn't catch him and doesn't know who it is," a remark which caused his father's anger to abate immediately. Even as a small boy, Titus did not keep silent when it was better to speak up. Later on in life too he always spoke his mind and it was this that led him to his death.

Anno Sjoerd never gave a reason for believing himself called to serve God not in the world, but as a friar. Like most Catholic families, did the Brandsma's, with five of their six children choosing the monastic life, consider it the natural thing to do when one wanted "to go the whole way?"

During the last century the mission of the Christian layman was an almost meaningless term. Lay apostolate was practically unknown, Catholics were only just beginning to develop a social conscience, education was exclusively the concern of the religious Orders, as was also the care of the poor, the sick and the aged. Whoever wanted to do something more for humanity, had no other choice but the convent.

Everybody expected Anno Sjoerd to aim high. But what they did not expect was his choice of an Order. People thought Anno Sjoerd would be sure to become a Franciscan. The Franciscans had taught him his catechism and given him excellent guidance during his grammar-school days. But Anno Sjoerd applied for admission into Carmel because—as he was to declare much later—the Carmelites belong to Our Lady and strive after the contemplative life. At the time of making his choice Titus would certainly not have been able to motivate it clearly and comprehensively. And his brother Henry, himself a Franciscan, on being interrogated about Titus' call to Carmel (this was during the process of beatification), still rather marvelled at his decision: "for if anybody led an active life it was my brother." As a well-known Dutch author declared: "He was the only mystic on the European continent to possess a roundabout ticket and to attain beatitude in a railway compartment... And yet when he talked about mysticism one felt that much of it was his own experience."

Titus must therefore have found a synthesis of those two seemingly opposing elements: his manifold activities and the call to quiet and contemplation. Even if his leading position in the Order and his professorship of philosophy and mysticism had not compelled him to, his was far too strong a personality not to search for it and he could never have reached the height he eventually attained without it. The synthesis he arrived at may, I think, be found in an article entitled *Carmes*, written for the *Dictionnaire de Spiritualité*. It is a short but well thought out contribution, giving a theoretical exposition, but also reflecting something of his own attitude:

> The Rule, conceiving of the spiritual life as culminating in active and passive contemplation, takes a different view of the *vita mixta* than the Thomist school of thought. The Thomist ideal is summarized in the formula: *contemplata aliis tradere*; to St. Thomas and the Dominicans perfection lies in crowning the contemplative life by an active one. To a Carmelite it lies in dedicating oneself completely to contempla-

tion. Contemplation should only be interrupted when necessity compels one to go out and speak to men of the things of God. The only motives for leaving God for the cause of God, *Deum propter Deum relinquere*, should be obedience or the love of one's neighbour. As is laid down in the Rule: "To meditate day and night on the law of the Lord and to keep watch in prayer, unless engaged in other justified tasks." The words spoken by Our Lord of St. Mary Magdalene and used by the Church on the Feast of the Assumption of the Blessed Virgin have also been applied to the Order of Carmel: "Mary has chosen the better part and it shall not be taken from her." To a Carmelite contemplation is the better part. In practice the difference between the two points of view is not very noticeable. The Carmelites have realized the necessity of interrupting contemplation for the care of souls and the Popes have called them to the pulpit, to the mission field and to various apostolic activities. Love of their neighbour and obedience to the Head of the Church have made them accept the *vita mixta*; they too are passing on to others the fruit of their contemplation. It is an ideal dictated by circumstances. But the Order has always tried to secure for as great a number as possible of its sons a life according to its ideal proper. Their task in the world completed, they are asked to return as speedily as may be to the first and direct object of their vocation.

Titus is describing the Carmelite ideal mainly as distinct from the Dominican. When obedience or the need of his neighbour calls, the Carmelite can and must leave contemplation and go forth to preach. He may also be compelled to do so by purely human, or even material needs. Thus obedience and the call of his fellow creatures emphatically direct the attention of the Carmelite, contemplative though he be, towards this world. Thus Titus too, for all his ideal of contemplation, had a deep sense of social responsibility, labored hard to establish new grammar schools for the cultural development of Catholics, Frisian in particular and Dutch in general, grudged neither time nor care in order to strengthen the position—and the financial position too!—of journalists, and was tireless in helping the poor, the aged, the homeless, the needy and those in search of a job.

Human among humans

In order to know what sort of people crossed
Titus' path and what was his work, one should have
been able to join him in his travels or to take one's
stand at the convent gate. A seminarian enters with
a tale of woe: he has no money left to continue his
studies. So Titus goes searching for wealthy donors,
till a fixed yearly sum is found. He lets a commer-
cial traveller persuade him to buy paper and pencils,
he draws up new Constitutions for a Superior General, he helps a servant to find a situation. A mother
asks him for particulars of her daughter's patron
saint, a member of a teaching congregation is given a
list of useful books and finds Titus' notes put at his
disposal. During the War a nun complains that she
has no more pressbuttons and Titus answers: "Oh,
just you leave that to me." He listens to the endless
rigmaroles of an old lady as if he had nothing else to
do: "She's such a poor thing and there's no one to
care for her." He advises some boys how to get to
Lourdes, he helps his students, he makes peace
among their professors, he visits sick colleagues and
is always ready to preach at the old people's home.

Lectures over, he sets forth to found new grammar schools, to give talks to non-Catholics, to help
towards the religious schooling of journalists. He is
always at the disposal of his countrymen, the Frisians. He preaches to the University, organizes mis-
sionary exhibitions and supports the ecumenical
movement for all he is worth. Between times he
contributes to papers and periodicals, translates the
works of St. Teresa of Avila and founds and promotes
a Carmelite review.

Though both Brazil and what were then the
Dutch East Indies would have appealed to him, he
was not allowed to go and work abroad, but there
was no apostolic activity in his own country in which
he did not take part. When he was taken captive
and could neither receive visitors nor travel, he
heated stones to warm the feet of his sick fellow-prisoners and even taught them to pray for their tortur-
ers.

79

His superior, amazed at so much activity, says Titus' attitude was the result of his knowing love to be the all-important thing. "The Professor" had time for everything. As a witty fellow Carmelite remarked on the death of Pope Pius XI: "Oh well, the Professor can easily take that on too!"

One might write an elegy on Titus' love for his neighbours, a compendium of the testimonies of his brother, his sisters and his fellow students, of the girl serving in the family whose house he shared for a year, of his colleagues, his brothers in religion and his superiors, of journalists, doctors, pastors, bishops, fellow prisoners and witnesses of his death. According to all these statements, taken down during the process of beatification, Titus' love was without ulterior motives, it knew no envy, ill will or rancor, never did things by halves and was without a thought of self. It was unrestricted, open-handed, helpful, simple, impeccable, patient, careful of his neighbours' reputation, cheerful, steadfast, cordial, meek, unostentatious; joyous, unpretentious, full of comprehension when misunderstood; completely at ease with all men, forgiving, generous; polite, hospitable, obliging; considerate, courteous, unambitious, always available, kind, determined; straightforward, unaffected, willing; disinterested and uncomplicated.

This is how the witnesses, each in his own way, saw and experienced Titus' love. Titus gave his attention to the uncomplaining poor, made no difference between rich and needy, never considered himself, spoke no ill of his neighbours, was completely unassuming, loved to forgive and to make peace, never thought of his own interests, gave away everything, granted help without stinting, never complained, was a pillar of strength to others, never laughed at the failings of his neighbours, had a kind word for everybody, a kind explanation for everything, knew no ambition, radiated encouragement and good cheer, was full of compassion for his jailers and prayed for those who tortured him.

Titus' love had a note of its own. His whole attitude was imbued with esteem for his fellowmen to whom he also gave the chance, one might almost say forced, to love him in return. He noticed people, he also noticed me, then the merest fledgling of a novice. We, newly admitted candidates, looked up to him as "the Professor," so when I saw him coming down the cloisters, I tried to scuttle past with downcast eyes. But this proved impossible, as I was to experience more than once. Titus accosted me, telling me it was time for a shave, and as I was then at the downy stage, I was as delighted at having been spoken to by "the Professor" as at having got hold of a justification for shaving.

The witnesses at the process of beatification clearly indicate the different ways in which Titus' esteem for his fellow creatures showed itself. They had experienced it themselves: "He always had plenty of time for visitors and never gave one the impression of not being welcome. He always succeeded in listening patiently and sent one off with the feeling that he had been the one to enjoy himself." "He would ask other people's advice, he remained interested in them when he was ill and thanked them for everything, even if it was only for an old coat." "He had a kind word for everybody," his sister said. "One could always see he was grateful for a gesture of friendship." "He preferred personal help to organized charity, because of the lack of human contact in the latter." "He saw more possibilities for good in the human individual than most people do." In short: "When the Professor helped one, he always managed to give one the idea of having done *him* a good turn. It was the same thing when he was a prisoner. He often gave away his own meager rations and made it possible, and even easy to accept them by saying: 'Here my boy, you eat this, you need it more than I do.' And if one brought him something from the fields, a leaf of lettuce, some carrots or a potato, he was so pleased that it made one happy merely to watch him."

Titus laicized

When the police arrived, pretending to be students, the doorkeeper of the Carmel at Nijmegen thought it was only a normal case of people coming to appeal to good Father Titus for help. The latter had just got back from trying to find a home for an Armenian orphan. On being called, he got up immediately—Titus could certainly never be held responsible for the well-known complaint of always having to wait such a long time in convent-parlours!—and went to greet his visitors. But any attempt at introducing himself was cut short by Steffen, one of the policemen, telling him: "Brandsma, your recent activities in support of the Catholic press and with regard to the bishops have been watched and it is because of these dangerous political machinations that you are arrested." Back in his room, Titus looked on calmly as the police put his papers together. "Yes, Father Prior, the security police have come to arrest me," he told the Prior, who looked in, nervously scenting something was wrong. His thoughts were still with others, for he especially asked for certain papers concerning an urgent appointment to be sent on. When the Prior was told to go away, Titus—as he always did when leaving the convent—knelt down to ask his blessing. He thanked his brethren for their parting gift: a cake of soap and a pair of scissors. He called Steffen's attention to the red-hot stove which might cause a fire if the room were locked. Saying good-bye, he asked his fellow religious to remember him in their prayers. Then he looked at his watch and urged Steffen to hurry, as the Dutch Railways wouldn't wait, not even for the security police. At the gate he managed to extricate the editor of a daily paper from a situation that might have proved dangerous, by immediately saying that he was under arrest.

During these dramatic moments Titus remained what he had always been: polite without the slightest shade of servility, kind, helpful, courageous. His spiritual balance was not upset. He knew what he had done and for what reasons, and when he embarked on the hazardous attempt to safeguard the Catholic papers and the liberty of the press from the hands of the tyrant he had fully realized the risks involved. When people urged him to flee or to go into hiding his invariable answer was: "I cannot leave my journalist friends in the lurch." Titus must have felt it deeply when on Monday, January 19, 1942, the day of his arrest, he was practically laicized. He had worn his white cloak so proudly, he had entered so deeply into the mystery of the Mass and made the monastic life so completely his own. Henceforth he was no more to wear the habit, nor to endanger the safety of the state by celebrating Mass. In a way he had become a layman, but a Christian layman, remaining dedicated with heart and soul to God and the world. Under the anonymity of the number on his coat, once part of a soldier's uniform, his inner attitude remained unchanged and it was through the vexations of prison life and the martyrdom of the concentration camp that he became fully himself. The whole breadth of the mystical apostolate which was now to be his, is known to the triune God alone.

I'm quite all right

The brother who nursed Titus through a serious illness in Rome, the Prior of the convent where he went to recuperate from his hemorrhages, they seem to remember only one answer that he was always giving: "I'm quite all right." Titus is always "quite all right," always so cheerful, so spontaneous in his sympathy, so naturally obliging—one might perhaps gather the impression that the charity and the optimism which enabled him to interpret the abbreviation of the concentration camp, "P. D. A." (*Polizeiliches Durchgangslager Amersfoort*) as *Probamur dum amamur* (When we are tried, then we are loved) were merely a question of disposition and temperament. But we must not suppose that Titus had got stuck in a certain shallow and good-natured humanitarianism. As is shown by his whole attitude, he certainly valued the world and human beings in themselves, but he dug deeper than that. His very zeal for the apostolate, continually driving him on and never remaining under the surface for long, clearly evinced "where his heart was." In the course of his inaugural address as rector of Nijmegen University (1932) he put it plainly:

We should first of all see God as the deepest ground of our being, hidden in the innermost part of our soul... It is in doing so that we shall always remain in contemplation before him... This indwelling of God and His action in us should not merely be objects of intuition, but should also be made manifest in our lives, our words and our deeds; they should be reflected in our conduct and in our whole being.

Our actions should be consciously derived from the divine indwelling in us, as things commanded or counselled by God Himself in the depths of our soul. Thus they will not only become forceful and convincing in their outward effect, but also filled with inward power as the manifestation of a nobler and more beautiful form of life.

The source of Titus' strength lays in his fellowship with the triune God—everybody noticed how reverently he made the sign of the Cross—and it was this that enabled him always to be "quite all right" while imprisoned at Scheveningen and Amersfoort and even in the concentration camps of Kleve and Dachau where the warders and superintendents systematically deprived the human individual of all sense of his own value.

One of his friends, a parish priest, has given us a description of Titus' first day at Amersfoort:

After hunting around for a bit, I found him in the grey mass of prisoners. He was seated on a bench at the long table between the bunks, crumbling his bread. Without more ado I sat down next to him; he somehow looked even smaller and slighter in his uniform than in his clerical blacks. "How are you, Professor?" "Oh, quite all right." Titus is always quite all right, in spite of a troublesome chronic illness for which he should be treated several times a day. Now this is out of the question, and without saying a word, simply and patiently, he bears the burden of his disease. He is full of courage and confidence, or rather, of trust in God. Fully realizing that the Nazis consider him dangerous, he has not much hope of being released. He is just going to make the best of it. He has looked the fact of being a captive full in the face and is certainly not afraid of the worst. Titus accepts everything so naturally because he has lost all thought of posing and takes things just as Providence thinks fit to send them.

Good Friday, 1942—after an orgy of ill-treatment—a group of men panting with exhaustion are commanded to sit on the cupboards and sing "O Sacred Head, Surrounded by Crown of Piercing Thorn." A crown of barbed wire is placed on a priest's head and a Jew is dragged up to tell what happened at the Crucifixion. To speak about suffering in an atmosphere where such things are possible, means that one must practice what one preaches, and that word for word. At Amersfoort, on that Good Friday of 1942, Titus had the courage to do so, a courage which his audience would have classed as laughable self assurance, if what he said had contained only a single non-authentic statement.

And an eye-witness tells us it proved an enormous event in the life of the camp:

All round him the prisoners were lying about on their bunks, built one on top of the other in three storeys. The whole hut smelt of wooden shoes and rags, of worn out and exhausted humanity. With their shorn heads the men looked unprepossessing and slightly sinister. People were stumbling about and there was a sound of voices, loud and soft, cultured and raucous. At the table a group discussing something. And exactly opposite me, in the narrow space between the bunks, standing on a sort of potato crate in his grotesque grey uniform, Professor Titus, the speaker or rather the preacher of the evening. As was only to be expected on Good Friday, he gave us a talk on the Passion which occupied all his thoughts. The words, welling up straight from his heart, went home. And the whole hut fell silent as the frail little man in grey gently meditated out loud on his box. His eyes were shining behind his big glasses and they made one forget the rest of the shabby little figure. The stillness became almost oppressive. Every man was wrestling with his own problems and his own misery, but here he was being given a key to them: our love towards God.

Titus was "quite all right" even in Dachau, that camp of death. Brother Tijhuis, a fellow Carmelite who was with him there for three weeks, tells us a little about the inhuman treatment he received:

First and foremost among the rules at Dachau came cleanliness; the slightest speck of dust, the tiniest spot of dirt was enough to make the warders furious and then it would rain blows. One evening the head of the cell block, discovering a small stain on the sole of Titus' foot, yelled: "You are another of those dirty swine." A stroke of his truncheon sent Titus flying, and that was only the beginning of a whole series of kicks and blows. As he came crawling into the hut on hands and knees, I picked him up, carried him to his bed and asked him whether he was badly hurt. He looked at me and smiled: "Oh, I knew Whom I had with me," he said and showed me the spectacle case containing the Blessed Sacrament, tightly squeezed under his left arm. Together we said the *Adoro Te* and then he blessed me with the spectacle case. Early in the morning I asked him whether he had been able to sleep: "I have been awake since two o'clock, but was so glad to be able to watch before the Host."

Titus himself, as chief witness, has also put down why he was always "quite all right." As he wrote from prison:

I already feel quite at home in this little cell. Time hasn't been hanging heavily on my hands yet, quite the contrary. It is true that I am alone here, but I have never felt Our Lord so near. I could sing for joy, that He should once again have granted me to find Him so completely, without my being able to get into touch with other people, nor they with me. He is now my only refuge and I feel happy and secure. If it be His will, I am willing to remain here forever. I have seldom been so happy and contented.

2

LIFE IN THE SPIRIT

Aemelius Breij, O. Carm.

FATHER Titus has often been described as God's happy, chosen child, and rightfully so. Everyone who met him went away feeling a little happier, taking with them a portion of that profound peace and intimate union with God in which this priest-professor lived and moved. Father Brandsma was a God-seeker, and every action of his busy life found its motive in one central theme—God. Following the Constitutions of his Order, Father Brandsma made prayer the principle of his life; he made it the beginning, the middle, and the end of his life.

Someone may ask, "Did this Professor of mysticism have personal, experimental knowledge of the mystical approach to God?" It is not ours to judge on this matter yet, as is evident. Nevertheless, his confreres and all who knew him intimately remain convinced that his was an intense spiritual life. They state unanimously that if ever there was a Dutch Carmelite who both knew and led the Carmelite spiritual life, it was Titus Brandsma. For Father Titus in the practical order (as for every Carmelite in the speculative order) prayer constituted the first and principal end of his vocation. Prayer formed the atmosphere apart from which he could not live.

Carmelite spirituality

To evaluate better the spiritual life of Titus Brandsma, it will be helpful to make some introductory remarks about Carmelite spirituality in general.

The vocation to prayer is set forth in the Carmelite Rule in the words: "All must remain in their cells or near them, meditating day and night on the law of the Lord and watching in prayer, unless prevented by other legitimate occupations." Clearly, these few words do not fully describe Carmelite contemplation; they merely give its general outline. A detailed exposition of the Carmelite life of prayer, together with the way in which the Carmelite must embrace such a life, is found in the many beautiful traditions of the Order, in the writings of Carmelite friars and nuns.

The most ancient traditions of the origin and purpose of Carmel are recorded in the *Book of the First Monks*. It is true that the contents of this book are a mixture of history and legend; yet the very legend itself is important, because it reflects the spirit and the atmosphere in which it developed. What is more, this book, dating from the thirteenth or fourteenth century, is, as it were, the *Magna Carta* of Carmelite spirituality. It describes the spiritual framework of Carmel, the search for God through an Elijan-Marian contemplative life. It points out that the crown of this life is a mystical grace—a pure gift of God. And yet this crown is the fruit of an apostolic zeal manifested in prayer and sacrifice or, when charity and obedience demand, in the care of souls.

Carmel thus presents to us a twofold end: the first we try to reach by our own efforts in the practice of the virtues with the help of divine grace. This end is to offer God a holy heart, a heart purified from every actual stain of sin. We attain this goal when we are perfectly hidden in *Cherith*, that is, in charity. Since God wanted Elijah to reach this end, he said to him: "Hide yourself in the torrent of Cherith."

The second end is a pure gift of God to us. It consists in this: that we may taste in our soul and experience in our mind the power of the divine presence and the sweetness of heavenly glory—not only after death, but even during this mortal life. So we are to drink from the torrent of the divine pleasure, the Cherith of divine love, as did Elijah before us. "Yahweh, the God of Israel, lives," said Elijah. "And I stand in his sight."

In an extensive article on Carmelite spirituality, Father Titus himself observed:

Not only the ways of purgation and of illumination, but the ways of union and infused contemplation also are clearly proposed to Carmelites as the goal to be pursued, the ideal to be reached, even though such union and such participation in the celestial life is called a pure gift of God. As far as I know, there is in no Order a book which determines the norm of that Order's life, and which has in so emphatical a manner proposed the vocation to the mystical life.

But Carmelite contemplation is Marian as well as Elijan. The author of the *Book of the First Monks* records the Marian tradition of the Order by a beautiful allegorical interpretation of 1 Kings 18: 44. While Elijah prayed for rain to relieve the country of Palestine, parched by three and a half years of drought, a small cloud appeared to announce the answer to his prayers. Then a heavy rainfall refreshed the dry earth. In the small cloud, the author comments, the future Mother of the Saviour was foreseen by the Prophet. Elijah transmitted this conviction to his followers who continued to pray for the Incarnation throughout the centuries. When Mary lived in the world, they conversed with her as with a sister. And after Christ's death, they joined the infant Church where the Apostles baptized them on the first Pentecost. As early as the year 83 A.D., the Carmelites had erected a chapel in Mary's honor—and in this way the Carmelite Order became the first Marian Order, the Marian Order par excellence.

Elijah standing in the sight of Yahweh and Mary in her divine Motherhood form a symbol of the Carmelite vocation. As Father Titus put it, they form "the mystical orientation of Carmel."

Prayer

Such teaching we see clearly reflected in the life of Titus Brandsma. His prayer, for example, was not restricted to the hour of daily meditation, holy Mass, or to the Divine Office, for he never considered prayer as a mere part of his daily duty. Rather, for him prayer filled every moment of life. We find among his notes these profound words: "Prayer is life, not an oasis in the desert of life."

He was convinced both in theory and in practice as well that prayer is better than knowledge, and therefore he looked upon study and science as means to better prayer. Hence he did not permit his extensive activity to detract in any way from his intense interior conversation with God. Instead, he elevated his own field of activity to the level of solitude with God; he tried ever "to see the world with God as its foundation so that he is not contrasted with it.".

Father Brandsma's prayer was a simple consideration of God's love in order to increase his own love for God and man. He wished not to approach God sorrowing, but preferred to rejoice because he saw in all things God's goodness and omnipotence. He thought of God not as greatly removed from him, but as intimately close in the deepest and most interior part of his being. He knew that the contingency and helplessness of the human being should unite itself with Being itself, Being that finds in itself the sufficient reason for its own existence. He recognized God present within him in his life of grace, and by constant effort he sought to increase his union with him.

Titus realized also that reaching God costs sacrifice, that the spiritual life does not consist in a growth of sweetness or sensible emotion. On the contrary, he once remarked that when God sought union with us, he sought it by suffering, contempt, and death, a way radically opposed to modern naturalistic standards. He condemned the complacency of those who, seduced by quietism, do nothing but dream of a sweet, restful mysticism. He saw clearly that the genuine spiritual life leads to Calvary: one finds rest only in the cross, in death close to the wounded heart of Christ. He taught that a spiritual life without asceticism, without mortification and self-denial, is nonsense, or at best fanaticism which disappears before its solidity can even be tested.

Father Brandsma certainly perceived the inherent beauty of true sanctity, and yet he sadly admitted the futility of expecting all men to strive for it, because the ideal of sanctity will never succeed in pleasing the world. But he warned that asceticism should not be viewed as something negative. Rather it is a liberation of the spirit by which one begins to live the Christ-life, to radiate the divine goodness. Consequently, he taught that we must not mourn too much in our ascent to God by seeing in the cross only forbidding sacrifice.

We all know how pleasant it is to deal with a person who is never troublesome. And such a person was Father Titus. In the morning, when asked how he had passed the night, he would sometimes mention that it had been sleepless, that he still felt the sharp headache which had robbed him of his rest. Yet during the day no one could detect in him any ill effects. Often he reached home late in the evening or perhaps past midnight after a long tiresome journey. But late or not, five-thirty the next morning found him in chapel with his confreres. As a rule his afternoon nap was disturbed by students or other visitors. But he always went to the parlor with his usual unfailing kindness, and with a box of cigars under his arm whenever possible. His motto was: "It must be a feast wherever we are."

Positive spirituality

In all phases of the spiritual life Father Titus emphasized positive elements. For example, consider his remarks on the three religious vows. Obedience for him was not compulsion by command or prohibition; it meant to strive fruitfully in the position in which God's Providence places one. Obedience is at once a positive and a social virtue. Father Brandsma compared the human race to a flower bed. Which are the nicest flowers? No one knows and no one cares. It is the total effect that makes beauty, the variety merely setting off the whole. And thus a good porter is important, as is a good cook. Important, too, is it that education be excellent. All things are necessary. And there is no one less happy than a discontented religious: the enjoyment of the world is not lawful for him, and the enjoyment of the religious life he cannot appreciate.

In the same light Father Brandsma considered chastity. He lamented the fact that this beautiful virtue is commonly considered negatively: avoid violations. We did not make our vow of chastity, he points out, in such a frame of mind. Our chastity must be founded on love, on the highest love. Therefore, its most dangerous enemy is mundane love, either of oneself or others. Yet chastity is by no means anti-social; rather it must ennoble and sanctify social life. We must ever see in our neighbor the image of Our Lord and serve him in the person of his creature. This relationship of creature and Creator alone must be the measure of our fraternal love.

Regarding religious poverty Father Brandsma was not content with mere abstinence, he wanted to be truly poor. Usually the prior himself had to send Titus to the brother tailor to be measured for a new habit. And when his superiors, because of financial needs, had to reduce the long list of his subscriptions to scientific periodicals, Father Titus simply submitted. From then on he happily went to the University library, if need be, to find the exact places for a comma or a period. Once the prior wanted to replace Titus' wooden bed and straw mattress with a spring-bed. But Titus insisted that he slept more soundly in his wooden box on the straw mattress and hard planks.

With unusual sharpness he defended the sincere practice of poverty.

> Without it the religious is a Pharisee—a gentleman in the monastery dressed like a poor man, but without a true love for poverty. Here in Holland, more than anywhere else, we are too much attached to all kinds of things and used to comfort. We want everything put in order under the pretext of Dutch solidity, cleanliness,

and neatness. We seek the rich and give more honor to them, even in our heart. The poor are of us, but we do not wish to be of them. We thereby make ourselves ridiculous before God who accepted our vows.

Yet it was characteristic of Father Titus that he preferred to go to a poorer shopkeeper than to a more prosperous one, even though he could buy at a lower price from the latter. His love for man superseded his love for poverty.

The ascetical life

Father Titus was surely an ascetic, but not an ascetic with a sour face, not a monk whose very aspect makes one think of judgement day. Everyone felt at ease with him, and no one so much as suspected that this happy, mild Carmelite kept his discipline and hair shirt hidden in his desk drawer. In such a way did he try to realize the first goal of Carmel—to offer God a holy heart. He freely offered himself to be united even here on earth as closely as possible with God, and thereby to possess heaven during his mortal life, and to bring heaven to his fellowmen. Nor did God spare his generous servant. From the very beginning of his religious life, God purified him spiritually and corporally. And by such purification Father Titus learned early to overcome the natural tendency to sadness when he was given no consideration by his brethren—when, so to speak, he was put in the background. He learned to act as if nothing had happened. Notice how remarkably often Father Titus speaks in his meditations and conferences about the great saints of suffering: St. Teresa, St. John of the Cross, St. Mary Magdalen de' Pazzi. When Titus' own sufferings reached their climax in the concentration camps of Amersfoort and Dachau, when he was deprived of everything, when he remained a broken body covered with a few rags, then he could still smile because he then belonged completely to God.

The spiritual life of Father Titus could, properly speaking, be summed up in two words: *seeking*

God. Men and things, he saw them all in their proper relation to God, for all things reminded him of God. Once on a cold winter evening, without scarf or gloves and with valise in hand, Father Titus left the train and climbed toward Merkelbeek. On the hilltop he turned around. Far in the distance he saw the many twinkling lights of the coal mines of Limburg, of the Hendrick and Emma. And he began to reflect how every light there was a weak image of the sun, from which it finally derived all its light and warmth. Those lights reminded him of the souls of men—all made in God's image, all fed by the divine light itself.

One of Titus' convictions was that we must study if we are to better our prayer constantly. Himself a professor of the history of mysticism, he overlooked no opportunity to use his rich knowledge of mystical theology and of the great mystical authors for his own spiritual benefit. For his own meditations and in his conferences he enjoyed using the writings of St. Teresa, and of the Dutch mystics Beatrijs and Hendrick Mande. And following their example, he often likened the soul to a garden which must be made as fertile as Carmel, a spiritual orchard of the Child Jesus and his Mother Mary. In this garden each man should sow and cultivate the grass of humility so that all others may tread on it with easy conscience. There he should also plant the lily and the sunflower. The latter, for instance, teaches both active and passive recollection.

We can seek God, with our own eyes, or God himself can appear in so overpowering a manner that we cannot miss him—the sunflower always turns towards the sun. The red rose, symbol of ardent love, image of the soul living, growing, and flowering in Christ, should also be in the garden. The rose pleases all eyes; it is a delight, a consolation. Roses mean a feast, and it must be a feast wherever we are—always a happy face, always helpful. The Little Flower, that full-blown rose, not wavering on its stem, but proudly spreading its petals to be cast before the Blessed Sacrament, is an image of our task of preparing the way for our Lord in the hearts of men. He must increase; I must decrease, says St. John. We must dread all personal honor and glory, claim nothing for ourselves in order to win souls for Christ. Our love must be extreme, excessive: the foolishness of the Cross. We must not let ourselves be surpassed in love by anybody, for love is the first, the greatest, the most divine virtue. Our example is Christ—bleeding on the cross from a thousand wounds. Our symbol is the red rose among the thorns: at the end a full-blown flower for our Lord.

In such sentences we see the complete Father Titus; we feel something of his deepest nature. Titus lived by love, almost never occupying himself with sin. The fear of the Lord may be the beginning of wisdom, he thought, but it is only the beginning. For him, love was at once the starting point, center, and goal—there was no place left for fear. When God's love covers our sins, then alone will they be forgiven and their memory need never again trouble us.

The Marian life

Titus' spiritual life was penetrated by one great ideal: to form Christ, the Son of Mary, in himself. Just as Christ was formed in the bosom of Mary, and under her guidance grew in grace before God and man, so Titus wished to place himself under her protection in order to be, like Christ, ever more completely her pupil, and thus be united to her Son. Moreover, as a child of the Mother of Carmel, Titus wanted to have her life as an example for himself and to reflect her virtues in his own life. Here we can also see that his aim was to form Christ in himself—to be regenerated and live only the Christ-life. In short, Father Titus wanted to be a *theotokos*. For him, God's activity and life within us was the starting point of the life of love, and Mary was the Mother of that life.

In this divine activity within us we have to see the continuation of creation, the continuation and the further revelation of the eternal birth of the Son from the Father. The consciousness of this life of God in us, of the indwelling of the Blessed Trinity, must be revived. God has to live again in us, or to be born once again. God's Son assumed our human nature that we could again have a share of the divine nature. We must, on our part, unite ourselves with Christ, and in and through him with the whole Trinity. And no creature participated more fully in this grace than Mary. She, the Mother of all men, is the example of how God must be born again in us, how he must live in us. We must acknowledge ourselves as her children because her Son is our Brother and because she will teach us how to receive Christ, bear him within ourselves, bring him forth again to the world. Therefore, Mary is the Mother of the spiritual life, the Mother of the life of the consciousness and experience of God.

Father Titus finds his ideas affirmed by Ruusbroec, St. Teresa, St. John of the Cross. He finds them presented in the most ancient commentary on the Rule of Carmel, written by the theologian John Baconthorp, and in the *Book of the First Monks*. Titus' environment, therefore, was that of the great prophet Elijah, the man of God, who from Carmel's heights saw the small cloud which announced to him the coming of Mary Immaculate and the birth of the Savior.

Furthermore, Father Titus disliked narrow-minded individualism in the spiritual life. He lamented that we are always so occupied with ourselves that we so easily forget how all of us are united together in and through God. And he noted emphatically that our highest value, our force and our dignity, consists precisely in this union. This idea should also color our understanding of Mary. We must not consider Mary as alone, for she is the Mother of God only to unite us closer to God: God seeks us through Mary. And we must also remember the doctrine of the communion of saints.

God united himself with Mary in order to unite himself with and through her with each one of us: with the Church which embraces all of us in one mystical body. In the communion of saints Mary occupies a very singular, high, and sublime position. Of course, we cannot raise ourselves to that height, but that does not mean we do not share in her glory, that we are not one with Mary. "He who does the will of my Father in heaven, he is my Mother..." Thus we should be united with Mary, the Mother of God, because God made Mary his Mother and ours at the same time.

Communion of Saints

Father Titus clearly did not want a private place near our Lord. He lived in the great family of men, in the Communion of Saints. Praying his office, he felt himself standing in the ranks of Carmel's saints, one among the many who form the whole praying Church. He did not want to become a saint in solitude, but together with all other men. He even could go so far as to rejoice in the penances of his fellow-men when he himself was unable to perform them and yet wished to share in them in some way. He realized that many good things effected by himself were the fruit of others' prayers.

"Communion" for Father Titus meant primarily love and service. There was for him no doubt that man's intentions are much better than his works, and therefore his love wanted to suffer everything. Father Titus wanted to look upon men and things as our Lord did, and to love them with him. "We must study," he said, "to serve one another; in this way we may create a sphere wherein all will become saints."

Father Brandsma had a particular love for many saints in heaven because they made him live more intimately in the great communion of souls, more closely united with the Head of the Mystical Body, Christ the King. He loved St. Teresa, about whom he wrote innumerable times; he loved St. Liduina of Schiedam; he loved St. Boniface, at whose shrine Titus built a park for processions. Father Brandsma also loved deeply the holy *poverello* and the energetic, hard working Father Brugman. When a German soldier came to take away Father Titus' pipe and tobacco in prison, he yielded them generously, thinking of the feast day of St. Francis de Sales.

The apostolate

In Carmel the apostolate is the fruit of prayer, the love of God. There the love of God is the starting point, the center, the purpose of zeal for souls. This zeal manifests itself first in prayer and sacrifice, but also in the direct care of souls. It is the ardor and the fire of love that engulfs everything around it, and wants to attract everything toward itself and God. Thus it is understandable that St. Teresa of Avila and the Little Flower both sighed that they wished to be men in order to go to souls as priests. Both remained in their cloisters. Yet today we share in the fruit of their lives of love.

Father Titus lived by love. Prayer is love at rest; the care of souls is love in action. Prayer and activity permeate one another till the distinction between them becomes vaguer and vaguer, and they finally coalesce into one fervent ardor of love. Then it is that one reaches the summit of Carmel; then one is ready for the final flight to God, accompanied by the legions of souls he has saved.

In Carmel's coat of arms is the hand of Elijah holding a flaming sword, and the motto reads: "I am consumed with zeal for the Lord God of hosts." Just as Elijah had often to leave the solitude of Carmel in Palestine to convert his people to Yahweh, so Father Titus had often to leave Carmel in Nijmegen to bring God to men. As he poignantly expressed it: "to leave God for God." In reality he simply left God in the solitude to find him again in man. He labored for every man because every man is a member of the mystical body of Christ, or is potentially a member. He was deeply conscious of the responsibility of a Christian, and still more that of a priest.

Let us consider it well, just as every day hundreds of people are brought to the Church by the heroic life of some of us, so hundreds every day are repelled from the Chruch by the non-Christian life of many who call themselves Christians, even Catholics. If we consider the intercession of a saint or the influence of a soul favored by God as a special grace from heaven, then we can equally consider it a disaster if such saints do not cross our path of life, if we miss the sweet influence which a chosen soul could exert on us. All Catholics should be so saintly that God through them could sanctify millions, just as He would have saved cities like Sodom and Gomorrah for a few just men.

Father Titus was heart and soul an apostle. More than once he worked until he collapsed. In the first years of his priestly life the prior sometimes had to carry Titus to bed because he had so exhausted himself on his journeys of mission propaganda that he could no longer stand on his feet. He asked his superiors to send him to Brazil, to Java. And when he was not sent, he helped his confreres there with the money he earned by mission exhibitions. In all ways, great and small, he tried to help others. Always and everywhere he was primarily a priest, a religious, a seeker of God: overflowing charity. His guiding principle was: all that is good must be done. Any easygoing in the field of the apostolate he called negligence.

But by no means did he lose himself in his work. From a train passing by a church he greeted Jesus. A visit to a city could not be called such if he did not first kneel down, at least spiritually, before the altar.

Conclusion

Clearly, the secret of Titus' fruitful life was his great love for God and man. He was everyone's friend and wished all men to be friends with one another. Innumerable times he reconciled quarreling people, resolved conflicts. He did admit one conflict, but in it he knew the victory of love for Christ.

Whoever wants to win the world for higher ideals must have the courage to come into conflict with it... The conflict with the world is hard. But Christ died on the Cross and was victorious.

This small brother of our Lady experienced this conflict to the full in Dachau, and his death in union with Christ's death on the cross marked his final and complete victory over the world.

Translated by Otger Steggink, O. Carm.

3

MYSTICISM: THE AIM IN LIFE OF FR. TITUS BRANDSMA (1881—1942)

Jacobus Melsen, O. Carm.

> People have to see God again and live in contemplation of God. This is called mysticism. So be it. I can even applaud this usage if in it I can find the expression of the truth that in mysticism we have to see the progressive and highest development of what has potentially been posited in human nature. It is a great pity that this is no longer understood.
>
> (Fr. Titus Brandsma, *Godsbegrip*, 32)

DURING his lifetime, Fr. Titus Brandsma was already called "a mystic immersed in everyday life," who could be "serene and yet restless" because of his inner experience of God. This testimony was repeated after his death. "He was the mystic on the Continent of Europe who had a season's railroad ticket and who became holy in train compartments... When he talked about the history of mysticism, you felt that much of this had been experienced personally," wrote Godfried Bomans, a pupil of Fr. Brandsma. Fr. Titus' colleague, Prof. J. van Ginniken, remarked the same thing on occasion of the Carmelite friar's discourse on the concept of God: "If I am not mistaken, there too Brandsma's mystical experience shone through." And Titus' successor, Smits van Waesbergen, wrote in reference to his life's work:

> His solid naturalness, his balanced character, his theological schooling, the tradition of his Order, made him fully realize that mysticism is the freely bestowed development of the interior life, which is at once grad-

ual and organic, and by no means rare. And may we speak in this context of his personal experience? We think so. Much, or rather everything justifies this conjecture. His person and life's work would otherwise remain inexplicable (*In Memoriam*, in *Ons Geestelijk Erf* 16 [1942], 178-179).

A mystical outlook on life

These testimonies are not groundless. But in Fr. Titus' case one will not see mysticism in the classical sense. He was not a monk who lived withdrawn from the world, and so could not dedicate his full attention to his personal conversation with God nor have time enough to reflect on his experiences in order to formulate them clearly. We have no diary of his, no doctrine, no description of his experiences. His personal views hide themselves within historical studies. He did not write or speak about his intimate experiences. As Father Sassen observed:

> Only to a very few was it given to penetrate his inner self, but the nobility of his character became clear to everyone who approached him. One did not have to penetrate his inner self... to know that all of him was genuine, because all his thinking and acting was based on firm principles and on a deep and strong faith (*In Memoriam*, Amsterdam, 1942, 6).

Yet his inner self has not remained totally hidden, as is already evident from the above testimonies. His very appearance spoke about his personal relationship to God.

Even though Fr. Titus himself left no clear testimony about his experience of God, in whom all is one —an experience that surpasses all images and concepts—from his studies, retreats, sermons, etc., from his outlook on life and from the orientation he chose in his work, at least from these elements his mystically oriented outlook can be clearly read. His was a very strong, all pervading passion to seek God in order to live united to him. Only God could fascinate him and only the highest form of union with God could satisfy him.

> To consider life as a march through the desert to Horeb in order to see God there and in the contemplation of God to give a totally new dimension to life. To make of life a foretaste of heaven by already here seeing God united with us as much as possible, God living and working in everything (*Notes for a Retreat*).

> There is no more urgent need than total surrender to God, putting oneself totally in his hands. In his infinite, and therefore in his incomprehensible love,... He wishes to fill us with himself, if only we wish to be filled by him and do not close our hearts to him by filling them with things that are not him. If we know how to empty our hearts from all this and to detach ourselves from all that is not God, then we shall remain astonished about his work within us. If man were deeply penetrated by this truth, he would be totally absorbed in God (*Introduction* to A. Groenevald, *Carmellicht*, Sittard, 1939, 9).

Inspired by conventual life

The starting point for Titus' "seeking out the ultimate reality" was not, as happens with so many in our day, the voiding of a culture in which God is no longer present in any way. The search was no battle in the wilderness of life with a God one does not know. For Fr. Titus, the starting point was a definitive choice of "God alone," made in his far-off youth, but constantly reaffirmed by his conventual life and developed into a complete commitment to him. He was seeking God to whom he had already given himself definitively by his vows.

This starting point was reinforced by his being bound to the Order of Carmel, whose primitive eremitical inspiration exercised a strong attraction on him. Personal intimacy with God alone was something primary for him. This was not cultivated for the sake of the apostolate, but as a value in itself. Openness to man and to the world he saw as a value contained within this (*Dictionnaire de Spiritualité*, II, col. 156).

102

Not to divide our hearts between God and the world. See the world with God in the background, so that He does not create a contrast with it (*Notes for a Retreat*).

His driving passion

This passion radiates through all the writings of Fr. Titus. He never passed by an opportunity to press for a more intense seeking of God, for a new life with him, for becoming more aware of his presence, for seeking his image anew, for striving after mysticism as the aim of one's life.

His love for God alone drove him to an intense solidarity with the world, with "the great confusion in the realm of thought." He had little sympathy for the concept current at that time, that "there we stand in the whirlpool of life... as the unshakable rock," but neither did he end up in the "desert of freedom" where one loses his human moorings. Within himself he possessed an interior resting place which was open to the great world and at the same time was anchored in God, "the rock in its varied forms, which do not touch the essence, and yet alter the perspective in no small way" (*Godsbegrip, 22*).

The closed, the hardened and the calculated found no mercy in his otherwise mild eyes, because these extinguish the Spirit who within a man inspires to new forms of life.

He who does not see the manifestation of the Holy Spirit in the Church, does not fathom its essence. The awareness of that fact is the safest warranty of the Church's flourishing... We must therefore broaden our hearts and leave our narrow boundaries, within which our life is lived. God's Spirit must have his own way with us, to blow through us, that he fill us as broadly and abundantly as our hearts, created for the infinite, permit... The fresh breeze is directed at the doors and windows of the stuffy dwelling of our soul, we suffocate in the choking atmosphere of our worldly existence, but we fail to throw aside the barriers and to let the breath of the Holy Spirit pass through our hearts... We know we are not one with Him and don't live through Him, in Him, with Him. And yet, that is the first requisite in order to be a real Catholic. The awareness of this has faded in too many people. If it lived on in its broadest horizons, we would see other things. We do not pray without meaning that God send his Spirit and that all be recreated and the face of the earth be renewed. This is of vital importance for the Church (*Introduction* to M. Meschler, *De Heilige Pinkstergave*, Weert, 1928, 10-11).

Let us not enslave the Spirit and harness him with our formulas (*Liturgisch Mishoren*, in *Ned. Kath. Stemmen* 19 [1919], 226-241).

His inborn gifts

In a certain sense Fr. Titus had an easy time of it. He had a sharp intellect, a serene emotional life, he was by nature an optimist, he sought automatically, as it were, balance and synthesis.

"Easy" however applies only up to a certain point. When it is question of one's personal attitude face to face with God, the question applies equally to all: "What did you do with the talents given you?" and not "How difficult a time did you have of it?" Fr. Titus could have developed his rich talents for himself. This was certainly not a farfetched danger; however, he avoided it because of his passionate love for God, in which he found a support—and no more—in his religious vocation:

We have not been called, in our public appearances, to do magnificent and much talked about things. That would go against simplicity as we should practise it. But it is our duty to do the ordinary things with greatness, that is, with a pure intention and the application of our whole personality. We don't desire to stand in the forefront and be applauded for achievements which people in the world look up to. We wish only to be conspicuous by our simplicity and sincerity. Cardinal Gasquet once said about the Carmelites that they were distinguished for their natural and sincere appearance: they are 'simple and sincere,' unsophisticated and straightforward in body and soul. I consider this to be the finest thing that can be said about our spiritual attitude and about our apostolate among people (*Notes for a Chapter*, Nijmegen).

His natural gifts brought him to God in a unique way. The joyful acceptance of suffering, from which he was not spared, characterized him.

> Don't serve God with many sighs. Gladly and courageously show how true it is that: My yoke is sweet and my burden is light... Have a smile on your face and see suffering in a higher light in which it becomes God's choice for you and a motive for gladness. Happiness is not a virtue, but an effect of love (*Notes for a Retreat*).

> Christ cannot live in us. We don't permit it... Because we do not have that love which keeps us really united with the Beloved... We Dutchmen have to be doubly on the alert in this matter. We have as our watchword, 'Don't exaggerate.' And therefore we suppress all spontaneity. We don't call it that. We speak of carefulness... We will keep our heads cool. There is so much reserve, so much cool calculation, that love and sacrifice and courage are totally missing in us (*Talk on Heroism*, Oct 28, 1936, to students in Tilburg).

Through his sound humanity he personally experienced that a mystical vocation activates and makes everything unfold in man. With predilection he sought a confirmation of his experience in the works of mystics:

> The higher the soul stands on the ladder of mystical union, the more harmoniously will her faculties work together... What she (St. Teresa of Avila) stressed in the beginning as strongly as possible, namely, that the ascent to God has to be a perfecting of man's nature, she maintains as well in her description of the higher degrees with even more emphasis if that is possible. Here human nature appears in all the splendor of an harmonious development...

> And I am glad to be able to draw your attention to this, because the notion is rather widespread that mystical grace destroys nature...

> Nature is not annihilated. God who created us to

his image and likeness, will see that likeness made as striking as possible, not by having it absorbed into his essence, but by leaving it be itself and united with him, resting in him in the highest development of its being (*Ons Geestelijk Erf* 6 [1932], 362-363).

He was therefore aware that love does not consist in being absorbed but in a free and autonomous abandonment:

To be autonomous by surrendering oneself. Autonomous in relationship to God. Hypersupernaturalism. God wills that we also act and be ourselves. Our autonomy is not abolished, not even in the most intimate union with God (*Notes for a Chapter*, Nijmegen).

In his writings he often returned to the importance of not presenting mysticism as inaccessibly high. He was deeply convinced that the development of man requires mysticism as its final scope. Not that everyone would reach its highest forms, but certainly that every sound spiritual life must allow itself to be determined by mysticism as its directive.

He was confirmed in this conviction by his study of the *Devotio Moderna*:

The *Devotio Moderna* had overstressed human receptivity and the necessity of practising virtue in preparation for the coming of the Bridegroom, who alone determines the person to whom he wishes to descend, so that we need not speak about that, since we cannot contribute anything to it. They attached more value to social works in imitation of Christ's life than to mystical grace, to the exterior side of the spiritual life than to the interior. Thus the spiritual life lost its deepest inspiration and force and was not able to keep a happy balance in the trend towards exteriority (*Godsbegrip*, 12).

Therefore, he repeatedly pointed out the danger that we commit the same fault in our own days:

Already once in the history of our spirituality we have seen how a one-sided practice of virtue has led to an externalism in the spiritual life. So we have to be on our guard that unconsciously it does not go that way

106

again... Action is not sufficient, it has to be consciously deduced from God's interior inhabitation, as commanded or recommended by Him in the depths of our being (*Ibid.*, 35).

He did, however, appreciate the practical attitude of the *Devotio Moderna*.

His path to mysticism

Fr. Titus has been called "a practical mystic." He himself often expressed his appreciation for mystics such as Ruusbroec and St. Teresa "so sober and matter-of-fact, so real and practical," with "a strong pedagogical character." It is as if he were speaking about himself:

They are both masters of the spiritual life, who did not in the first place express what made them write, although both concede that now and then it was this force from within that made them do so. They wrote especially so that others would know the ways which God uses to conduct souls to union with himself (*Ons Geestlijk Erf* 6 [1932], 368).

Again and again, Fr. Titus indicates the way as being rather simple:

We must indeed go out of ourselves, we must do all we can to go out to meet him, but it is He who comes. The person who does not withdraw himself from his embrace, by constantly wandering among earthly things and not opening his heart to him, will finally experience his love, his superabundant love... The way to this grace consists in increasing our receptivity... Then God will not withhold from us the pleasantness of being aware of union, nay of unity with himself (*Ibid*).

To be in constant quest of God is, according to Fr. Titus, alternately active and passive, a desired and very conscious seeking with heart and intellect, *and* a being captivated.

We can look for God with our eyes. God can also act so overwhelmingly that we have to see him. He can determine our gaze. If we use our intellect to full advantage and do not remain hanging back at the mere surface of things, then we shall ascend from the finite to the Infinite... If we seek this, we shall find it. For if we adjust ourselves to this Object, then it determines us, fascinates us. And so there is continuous interaction between the passive and the active in the process of recollecting ourselves, which we could also call a turning towards God (*Notes for a Retreat*).

With regard to this active recollection, he lays a strong accent on becoming aware of it:

Don't live in a haphazard way. In your activities, think that God sees you, but people do too. In your activities do remember not to let intimate love for God and people fail.

Live in the awareneess of living in God's presence. Keep in mind ever more clearly its basis, not only in faith, but also by reason... In our piety we should rise above the merely sensible.

Realize and use better the gift of acting with awareness (*Notes for a Chapter*).

For Fr. Titus, using the intellect consciously is the first step towards the intuitive contemplation of God and towards mystical union, in which the divine light penetrates the being of man without images and concepts:

This light becomes fuller and deeper still, if it illumines not only the senses and the imagination, not only the higher faculties of memory, intellect and will, but the soul itself... Although that mystical union surpasses by far the intellectual contemplation of God as Creator and Provider by way of abstraction, still it remains for him the first disposition, the foundation, the point of departure (*Ons Geestelijk Erf* 6 [1932], 355-356).

To turn actively into oneself "by means of the abstracting intellect to the point where one meets God in the roots of his being" (*Godsbegrip*, 29), in Titus' vision, however, also included the affections. Thinking of the sunflower as an image of this turning in on oneself, which is at the same time a turning towards God in the depths of one's being, he meditates aloud:

> Image of recollection, which must be the first flower that we must allow to blossom in our hearts. We must keep our hearts directed to God and make ourselves receptive to the rays of light of his illumination and the glow of his fire of love (*Notes for a Retreat*).

Fr. Titus speaks very little about the negative side of our turning to God. For him asceticism consists in the positive concentration of all one's faculties on God. He teaches that this process has to coalesce with mysticism "insofar as they are ordered to each other and lead to one another" (*Ascese* in *Kath. Enc.* 3, col. 135).

About self-denial he remarks:

> It is desirable to see self-denial in as positive a light as possible, that is to say, as the positive will to do what love requires with the sacrifice of oneself (*Zelfverloochening* in *Kath. Enc.* 24, col. 252).

The way to God is simply to direct oneself to him and—still more importantly—to let oneself to be captivated by him and risk the consequences of this.

Vital, all embracing contemplation

As with St. Therese of Lisieux so also with Fr. Titus much of his inspiration hides itself behind the imagery of contemporary artificial flowers. His language is alternately flowery and scholastic.

Within the scholastic framework, where the faculties of man were neatly distinguished, he looks in vain for a correct formulation of the synthesis which nevertheless peers through: to love God with all the faculties—with reason, intellect, imagination and affection, that is to say, intuitively and dynamically.

He speaks about our abstractive faculty "which must conduct us to the delightful contemplation of God." This faculty and intuition are practically identical in Titus' mind, if by intuition we do not mean a blind feeling, but rather the result of strict attention which does not withdraw in the end from the control of the man who is reflecting (*Godsbegrip*, 23, 26, 31). On this path of the concentration of intellect and love which result in an intuitive penetration of one's own experience of being, we can contemplate the one Ground of all things in our own inner depths:

> We must see God first of all as the deepest Ground of our own being... and adore Him not only in our own being, but just as much in all that exists, first of all, in our fellowman, but also in nature, in the universe, as He is omnipresent and permeating everything with the work of his hands (*Ibid.*, 26).

This contemplation is a vital contemplation; life itself is directly involved in it:

> This indwelling and impact of God must not merely be the object of intuition, but must manifest itself in our lives, express itself in our words and deeds, irradiate from our whole being and in our actions... From the intuition of God within the inner make-up of all things there then easily follows the inspiration that flows from it into action (*Ibid*).

> ... not seeking Him in places and in streets, but in the depths of our being, so that we see Him there with our intellect, love Him with our will, hold on to Him with all our faculties, that He might live in us, evermore... He is at the same time the strongest warranty of your solidarity, for in all of you lives the one Lord (*Mystiek en pseudomystiek* in *R.K. Artsenblad* 8 [1929], 283).

> We go on living our own lives and think much too little of how in God we are united with each other and all together are united with Him.

> Our presence everywhere must be a treat, a feast, a comfort for other people.

> All things for all men. Solidarity with one another, interest in each other. No prying interest. Taking into account the introversion of some characters. People often mean to do better than they actually do. Therefore, love puts up with everything. What

does Our Lord put up with? How He sees things dif-
ferently than we. To see men and things with God's
eyes. Love them with Him. Reflect on how to serve
others. Detachment and humility are companions of
love. All three are a preparation for a life of prayer
(*Notes for a Chapter*).

All embracing love

What a person writes and what he experiences
and thinks do not always coincide. In this sense, Fr.
Titus could have written and preached about mysticism, for instance, in order to be a good Carmelite. The writings that we have condensed above, are
confirmed however by his life, and vice versa, his life
is explained by his writings. His union with God embraced everything in a dynamic love: the world in
development, the various movements and Church-
building organizations, the great but also the concrete, little events, mankind as well as the concrete
man as he presented himself to Fr. Titus at a given
moment.

From the many witnesses from all sorts of positions, functions and places, we can distill a hymn like
that of St. Paul to the Corinthians. In him they saw
a love that was:

openhanded, generous, helpful,
simple, correct, patient,
sollicitous for the good name of others,
cheerful, firm,
without secondary ends,
cordial, gentle, unpretentious,
full of understanding when misunderstood,
completely at ease with high and low,
forgiving, magnanimous,
hospitable, obliging, considerate, courteous,
not jealous, not ambitious, without rancor,
not preoccupied with self,
sincere, unsophisticated, adverse to minimalism,
uncomplicated.

He liked personal help more than organized charity because in the latter, personal contact was lacking.

He had all the time in the world when someone came for a visit; he never gave the impression that your coming was not welcome. He always had time to listen patiently and gave you the feeling that he found it congenial.

By his appearance you could see that he was thankful for friendship shown him.

In short:

When the professor helped you he did it in a way that gave you the impression that you had provided pleasure *for him*.

And further:

At the moment sometimes they talk about an accumulation of positions in the business world; compared with Titus these seem paltry. The remarkable thing, however, is that this man did all extremely well, though he himself was far from being of a strong constitution (F. Oudejans in *De Tijd*, 28-12-1961).

His proverbial charity was not a humanitarianism whose ultimate source is the human ego. To give love in order to become a respected person can be one of the most refined forms of using a fellowman for your own purposes. Fr. Titus however loved his fellowman for his own sake; his ultimate motive was not for his own ego but for God.

During his life this love had already been proved by its inner strength, but the definitive proof came only when he had to make good on what he had said in a sermon in Dokkum in 1939:

Christianity with its preaching about love is called out of place and must be replaced by old Germanic force. Though the new paganism does not want love any more, we shall—mindful of history—overcome that paganism and not give up our love. Love will conquer once again the hearts of the heathen for us.

The strength of this love not only found expression in an admirable attitude, but also in the refusal that cost him his life... "A man who among us students at Nijmegen was known as one who was not able to refuse what we asked him, yet gave his life for what he refused to give up" (G. Bomans, *In Piam Memoriam* in *Elseviers Weekblad*).

The experience of God in the final trial

When he was deprived of everything—needed medical help, protection of an academic and cloistered environment, work, religious symbols, his hope in life—he remained the same joyful man, emptying himself for the sake of others. In the camp of Amersfoort, on Good Friday, 1942, he had the courage to talk about mysticism, about experience of God and the "glad, thankful feeling" that the thought of a suffering God rouses in us. Every unauthentic word would have been noticed. An eye witness describes the atmosphere of human misery on which these words fell and still had meaning:

> All around the prisoners were leaning, sitting or lying on the bunks, three rows high. The smell of clogs and rags, of worn-out and tired people hung over the whole barrack. The close-shaven heads deprived them of any individuality and even gave them a somewhat sinister outward appearance. There was a cluttering about, a murmuring with both hard and soft voices, refined and screaming voices. Several sat at a table talking. Just opposite me in the corridor of bunks, Professor Titus, the orator or rather the preacher that evening, stood on a kind of box for potatoes in his ridiculous, drab uniform. It became—how could it be other on Good Friday—a meditation on the Passion of Our Lord, of which his heart was full. Spontaneously the words welled up from his heart and hit target. In the barrack, you could have heard a pin drop. There in his grey togs, standing on a box was that short man meditating aloud for us. Behind his oversized eye-glasses his eyes sparkled; they made a person forget the rest of his miserable figure. It was oppressingly quiet. Each was struggling with his own problems and misery. Here a key was being offered: the love of the Lord.

Straight from his heart, relying on his rich experience, Fr. Titus provided warm human comfort in this desert of modern civilization right up to his last day. And in the short period in which he was allowed to be alone with God, locked up in his prison cell at Scheveningen, where no one could come to visit him any more, he wrote some lines which finally betray a bit more of his inner self. Here we can see how little he needed people *for himself*.

> I could shout for joy because He made me find Him again entirely, without me being able to go to see people, nor people me. He is now my only refuge and I feel secure and happy. I would stay here forever, if He so disposes. Seldom have I been so happy and content (*My cell*, memoirs).

Three weeks later this exaltation took spontaneous poetic form:

> O leave me here but quietly alone,
> let it be chilly and cold around me,
> and let no people come to me,
> being lonely does not tire me,
>
> For you, O Jesus, are with me.
> Never was I so near to you,
> Stay with me, Jesus, stay with me,
> Your nearness makes all up for me.

*Translated by Adrian Staring
and Redemptus M. Valabek, O. Carm.*

4

THE MYSTICISM OF THE PASSION

Adrianus Staring, O. Carm.

Was Titus Brandsma a mystic?

This question has been often raised already, in the Process of Beatification as well. The late Father Jacob Melsen dedicated an article to it: "Mystiek als levensdoel" (cf. previous chapter).

> But in Fr. Titus' case one will not see mysticism in the classical sense. He was not a monk who lived withdrawn from the world and could dedicate his full attention to his personal conversation with God, nor did he have time to reflect on his experiences in order to formulate them clearly. We have no diary of his, no doctrine, no description of his experiences. His personal views hide themselves within historical studies. He did not write or speak about his intimate experiences. Only to a very few was it given to penetrate his inner self. But the nobility of his character became clear to everyone who approached him. One did not have to penetrate his inner self... to know that all of him was genuine, because all his thinking and acting was based on firm principles and on a deep and strong Faith (*In memoriam T.B.*, Amsterdam, 1942, 6).

Titus Brandsma was a professor of philosophy and the history of mysticism, namely of Dutch mysticism. He did not teach mystical theology, but the history of mysticism as a part of Dutch literature. He knew Saint Teresa of Avila, Saint John of the Cross and other mystics of his Order as no one else in Holland, and in his lectures on philosophy man's relation to God was his favorite subject. The famous Latinist, Prof. Christine Mohrmann who was his pupil, testifies:

I never heard him lecture *ex professo* about mysticism, but in his lectures about philosophy he spoke repeatedly about mysticism. From the manner in which he spoke about mystical subjects in my opinion it was clear that, to say the least, he felt for the mystics an affinity which he did not feel for the philosophers. He was himself, not in the field of philosophy, but in that of mysticism.

In the years that I as a student had a regular contact with him, I have always had the impression that with him it was the question of a *"présence de Dieu"* (living in God's presence). This appeared from numerous brief spontaneous remarks he almost unconsciously made in his lectures and which did not properly pertain to the subject. He would drop for a moment the rigid line of abstract argumentation, to give a spontaneous close-up of his own spiritual life (*Beatification Process*, qq. 19, 67).

Many who have known him were of the opinion that he also had personal experience of mysticism. His brother Henricus Brandsma said: "Without doubt he was mystically minded" (*Beatification Process*, as also the following citations). Others: "My personal conviction is that he also experienced mysticism himself" (Mathias Arts, O. Carm.). "He was not only an expert in mysticism, but I am convinced that he experienced it too" (Othmarus Lips, O.F.M. Cap). "From his writings and from testimony I think I may conclude that he also experienced mysticism" (H.W.F. Aukes). "I can confidently declare that he also experienced mysticism, that is, that he had a close conversation with God" (P. Verhulst). "I am convinced that he was not only an expert in mysticism, but that he also lived it or tried to live it" (Bonaventura ter Ellen, O. Carm.). "I believe that the Servant of God also experienced it. His talks were often about it. Extraordinary gifts he did appreciate, but he did not find them the main thing in the spiritual life" (Borromaeus Tiecke, O. Carm).

Simple people, for whom the term mysticism was perhaps too highflown, formulated it in their own way: "About this I cannot testify. But I know indeed that he lived in very close union with God" (Richardus de Groot). "He was an extraordinarily spiritual man" (Anna Kersten).

A Lutheran physician and psychologist says: "I had the strong impression that he not only knew but also experienced mysticism." And to the question "What do you understand by mysticism?" he answered: "A profound conversation and union with God" (Dr. Pieter Herman Ronge).

The Dutch humorist Godfried Bomans, who was a pupil of Fr. Brandsma, expressed it in his own way: "He was the only mystic on the continent of Europe who had a season's railroad ticket and who became holy in train compartments... When he talked about the history of mysticism, you felt that much of this had been experienced personally" (*Op de keper beschouwd*, Amsterdam, 1963, 58).

His colleagues come to the same conclusion. Prof. J. van Ginneken remarked on the occasion of Fr. Brandsma's discourse on the concept of God: "If I am not mistaken, there too Brandsma's own mystical experience shone through" (*Herden Kingsrede*, 23 Sept. 1947). Prof. Regout, who also died in Dachau: "He was serene and yet restless: a mystic immersed in everyday life" (*Album amicorum Titi Brandsma*, 1939). And Titus' successor, Smits van Waesberghe, wrote in reference to his life's work: "And may we speak in this context of his personal experience? We think so. Much, or rather everything justifies this conjecture. His person and life's work would otherwise remain inexplicable" (*In memoriam*, in *Ons Geestelijk Erf* 16 (1942), 178-179.

Certainly it is true that one need not be a mystic to talk about mysticism. One can be an expert in the paintings of Rubens or Rembrandt without being able to paint a stroke. But in Titus there was something more: his absolute honesty and sincerity. His actions corresponded to this words: "Everything about himself was real." He did not speak about himself but about that of which his heart was full: God and his fellowman.

Another indication that he was a mystic himself we can see in the fact that he was convinced that all Christians, and certainly all Carmelites, are called to the mystical life. About the blind mystic John of Saint Samson he writes:

> As emphatically as possible he rejects the idea that the mystical life—which does not consist essentially in sights and visions, stigmata and levitations, but simply in seeing God before us and in us, being consumed through love for Him, knowing the divine fire within us and only wishing with God that it burn and consume us —that this mystical life is not for us, for every one of us (*Carmelite Mysticism*, Chicago, 1936, 95).

He did not oppose mysticism to asceticism or to the abstracting intellect.

> And it is this abstractive faculty that must conduct us to the *visio Dei*, to the delightful contemplation of God that one day will constitute our eternal felicity in heaven... Only a few of the elect may arrive at the highest contemplation; to an ever clearer contemplation all of us must bring ourselves. Let the highest contemplation remain the privilege of a few, who, to use medieval terms, have practised the dying and illuminating life and thereby have acquired the requisite receptivity for the contemplative life and are proportionately favored with it (*Godsbegrip*, Nijmegen, 1932, 28).

> What I therefore defend and consider as necessary for these times, is the contemplation of all that is in its dependence and origin from God. Therein—and first of all in ourselves—we must see his work, distinguish his being, recognize and adore him. God is there and He reveals Himself to us there. There He wants to be seen and recognized. He is after all nowhere better knowable for us than in the ground of our being... People have to see God again and to live in the contemplation of God. This is called mysticism. Be it so. I could even approve, if I might see it a manifestation of the truth that in mysticism we have the further and highest development of what human nature is capable of, even though this potentiality is realized only through special divine grace (*Ibid.*, 31-32).

> We must see God first of all as the deepest ground of our being, hidden in our inmost nature, yet able to

118

be seen and contemplated there; knowable at first by reasoning, then by regularly focussing on him without each time applying our reason and as it were by intuition, so that we find ourselves continually contemplating God and adoring him not only in our own being but in all that is—first of all in our fellowman, then in nature, in the universe, present everywhere and penetrating everything with the work of his hands. This indwelling and penetration of God must not be the object of our intuition alone, but should reveal itself in our lives, express itself in word and deed, shine forth from our being and conduct (*Ibid.*, 26).

Mysticism is God touching us, and reciprocally man touching God. It is not something totally new, but a further blossoming and development of God's presence in each one of us in the ordinary order of nature, knowable and visible for our abstracting intellect, a further blossoming and development of God's special presence in the children of His Church in the order of grace, knowable through divine revelation, given to the Church and conserved in the Church, an object of faith. In a third state of the abundant and overpowering love of God for man the divine no longer hides behind the human, and the divine presence becomes the object of immediate inner experience. A deep inwardness is necessary to see and really know what is visible and knowable in us in a hidden way. To that inwardness we ourselves can contribute very much. God, the subject of our knowledge and love, can also on his part engross our faculties and compel us inward, that is, toward Him (*Mystiek en pseudo-mystiek*, in *R.K. Artsenblad* 8 [1929], 266-283).

Meditation and reasoning are thus the point of departure for mysticism, as in the first Mansions of Teresa of Avila's *Inner Castle*. But Fr. Brandsma also warned against the use of the word "intuition."

Many take for intuition what is the result of reasoning that has become unconscious... So we have to be careful with the word intuition, certainly when used in connection with contemplation of God; on the other hand we need not be afraid of people who use the word, but because of too little introspection they take for intuition what is nothing else than the result of ordinary and thus unconscious reasoning and... abstraction (*Godsbegrip*, 31).

That contemplation of God in nature is not yet mysticism we see in a remarkable meditation he wrote at Niagara Falls, one of the few writings in which he speaks about himself.

The question, whether the summit of mystical experience is to be found in the enlightenment of the intellect or in the love of the will, is to my mind, best answered in the school of Carmel, in this sense, that first of all one must not separate too sharply what in human nature is most intimately united and what also in God's nature—in the image of which man is created—is one, although there is a distinction between them.

The school of Carmel sees in the mystical union more the perfecting of man's nature than the special perfecting of its faculties. The school of Carmel likes to take over a number of theses from the school which claims the enlightenment of the intellect to be the highest; but with the same eagerness the Carmelite school accepts several opinions of the school which places the greatest emphasis on satisfaction of the will. The Carmelite school sees, especially in the highest phases of mystical life, both faculties intermixed, so supporting each other, in such continuous, close cooperation, that the question, which of the two stands highest, to which of the two should go the crown, makes a somewhat unpleasant impression on her.

While I am writing this, I listen to the roaring and rushing of Niagara Falls. This cataract demonstrates beautifully how water, subject to the laws of gravity and according to the nature of a fluid, flows down to the lowest parts on the earth... Full of admiration I gaze at the roaring masses of water, which continuously plunge down from the high channel into the suddenly many meters lower bed of the river. What is really the most beautiful aspect of this phenomenon?

Someone, who is metaphysically minded, will probably get lost here in contemplation of the wonderful potentiality of water, being attracted through the so much greater mass of the earth. Suppose water had not this potentiality, this urge towards the centre of gravity of the earth, then there would not be a cataract. Suppose the water was not a fluid, then it would not break into millions of drops, which make it look like an avalanche of snow.

Had not its particles the faculty of absorbing and reflecting the light, the masses of water would not glitter like crystal, and the rainbow would not be there at our feet. Had the water not that power of resistance, it would not thunder in our ears, when we venture to its proximity.

But not everybody regards the Falls in this way. Thousands of people admire them, without thinking about the potentialities of the water, without ever having heard about that. They do not come here to see the beauty of the water and to admire its nature, but to watch the magnificent sight of those ever approaching waters, suddenly falling down plump with a thundering roar, bursting asunder into clouds of foam, which rain down far away, to fall back into the fast fleeting river. They listen to the roaring river and cannot get enough of that wild music. They enjoy watching the blending of colors in the water, not only the rainbow which stands in the middle, when the sun shines over the falls, but also the colors the water shows, according to the volume in which it tumbles over the rocky sides. Here it is green, there white like silver, somewhere else the color of mother of pearl.

Now one could say, that the first manner of contemplation of this famous cataract stands much higher than the second one, that the intellectual contemplation gives a much nobler satisfaction that the last, which is more a sensitive one, but we stand there simply as human beings, who possess both these faculties and in whom these faculties help and support each other wonderfully. We would prefer these two manners of approach to flow together and unite, so that they strenghten each other.

Both the subject and the object here demand union, not separation. There is no doubt about it, that the less opposition we make here and the more we let the faculties cooperate with each other, the higher and nobler and more perfect our enjoyment will be.

One may say, that I have been using a wrong simile here. We were considering the cooperation between will and intellect and now I give an example in which is shown the cooperation between senses and intellect. But first I am of the opinion that this example teaches us much also about the relation between will and intellect. We learn from it that we have to consider more the unity between our faculties than their opposition.

But there is something more. I go back once more to the water of the Falls. It is also an image of our human nature. This wonderful cataract is being visited by millions of people for its matchless beauty. I, personally, meditate rather about what lies behind this beautiful phenomenon: not only eye and ear are here fascinated, but much more my intellect, which ponders over all God has hidden in the water. I see not only the beauty of nature, the immeasurable potentialities of the water, but I see God at work in His creation, in His revelation of love. Nevertheless my eyes and ears are also captivated and time after time I return, to see and hear. Many a time this last pleasure even predominates. (*Professor Titus Brandsma, a True Representative of Carmel*, in *Analecta Ordinis Carmelitarum*, 14 [Roma, 1949], 3-26, 15-18).

He certainly was often totally absorbed in prayer, not only during meditation, but also in the Divine Office and especially when he said Mass. "I sometimes thought: if a bomb fell on the church, Father Brandsma would not notice it at all" (H. Aukes, *Het leven van T.B.*, Utrecht, 1962, 162). This fact, observed by many others, is the strongest indication that Titus Brandsma knew the higher degrees of mysticism, even from experience.

Mysticism and Mystical Phenomena

Generally mysticism in the strict sense is seen as the immediate experience of God ... characterized by passivity.

Basically, we consider 'mystical' every *psychological* reality, in which man believes that he reaches God directly and immediately, in one word, 'that he experiences God.' ... It would not be in the least out of order to reserve the word 'mystical' strictly speaking to mystical realities of the second category (passive mysticism) (*Mystique*, in *Dictionnaire de Theologie Catholique*, X, Paris, 1929, col. 2600).

This phase is often characterized by ecstasies, visions, revelations, to say nothing of stigmata and other phenomena. But do they belong to the essence of mysticism? It is a fact that in the later life of

122

such great mystics as Saint Mary Magdalen de' Pazzi and Saint Teresa of Avila, they often disappear.

Titus Brandsma draws attention to another fact. About the letters and ecstasies of Gemma Galgani (she had not yet been beatified) he writes:

> Mystical life one could describe as so close a union of God with our weak human nature that the divine no longer hides behind the human, but irradiates outwardly in glorious splendor. But this does not mean that the divine in the mystical life totally supplants and suspends the human, that there does not remain very much that is human in the mystical life... To overlook the individual personality of the mystically gifted one in mysticism is to obscure her most beautiful glory.

> Many are inclined to recognize mystical action only where the mists have been as good as totally dissipated. They are too much inclined to forget that in mysticism, aside from the divine element, the human element, the mystic's own personality has to be taken into account (Introduction to: Bonifacius, C.P., *Brieven en extasen der Dienaresse Gods Gemma Galgani*, Eindhoven, 1927, iii-xi, iv-v and vi).

Many times he returns to this point.

> Many regard mysticism so highly that they totally idealize, nay divinize man, forgetting that this union of God with man is something that takes place in human nature, received into it according to the nature and condition, the capacity and adaptability of that nature (*Mystiek en pseudo-mystiek*, p. 266-283).

So man is not totally passive in mysticism, and the immediacy of the mystical state lies perhaps more in love than in intellectual knowledge.

About visions of the Passion and stigmata Father Brandsma was very reserved. He visited Theresa Neumann in Konnersreuth.

> In Konnersreuth I remained rather indifferent to Theresa Neumann's stigmatisation, bloody tears and even abstinence from food, but a deep impression was made on me by the fact that one could live so totally with God (Lecture, cited by Meijer, *T.B.*, 151).

He also examined the case of a Protestant girl in whom stigmata were provoked under hypnosis:

> I readily concede that in otherwise equal circumstances one has to be more prepared for hysterical phenomena among Catholics than in other circles, certainly Protestant circles... but though I take this into consideration, I must still declare that in my opinion the facts of Konnersreuth so far surpass what is known up to now, that they cannot *as yet* thus find a satisfactory explanation (*Wondtekenen en lijdensvisioenen* in *De Maasbode*, May 6 - July 21, 1935).

> Whether or not such phenomena are of a supernatural kind is a matter of indifference to me (typed article, *Bij een nieuw geval van stigmatisatie*).

Many have taken Titus Brandsma's reservations about the marvelous character of stigmata as a doubt about the genuineness of these phenomena. This was not so. He hoped that these phenomena would be explained in a natural way from psychology, and one would not immediately have recourse to a miracle. But, as he let it be known in his lessons, even if they were not "supernatural" in the sense of a miracle, one could call them supernatural in another sense, if they sprang forth from the divine virtues of faith, hope and charity (Notes by students of Fr. Titus' lectures).

Mysticism of the Passion

Especially after 1930 Father Brandsma devoted himself to the study of the mysticism of the Passion, not only in Theresa Neumann and other stigmatics, but also in such medieval figures as Saint Lidwina of Schiedam and the Franciscan Johannes Brugman. (*Van ons Geestelijk Erf*: weekly page in *De Gelderlander*, 1938-1940. *De H. Lidwina van Schiedam*, 11-2-'39; 18-2-'39; 25-2-'39. *Een niet uitgegeven werk van Pater Brugman over het H. Lijden*, 11-3-'39. *Pater Brugman's beschouwingen over het Lijden*, 18-3-'39; 25-3-'39; 1-4-'39; 8-4-'39; 15-4-'39; 22-4-'39; 29-4-'39. *Een nieuw ontdekt werk van Pater Brugman*, 10-6-'39; 17-6-'39. *De woestijne des Heeren*, 9-3-'40; 16-

3-'40).   With Saint Teresa of Avila he knew that mystical union with God does not exclude the human, but that union with God traverses the humanity of Christ and that all grace comes to us through Jesus.   Thus he wrote about Gemma Galgani:

> Meditation of the Lord's Passion has found here a response in words that not only vividly present to the mind the scene of the Passion of Jerusalem, but also excite to a response of love, to devotion to that Holy Passion. . . So many rather dream of a mysticism full of sweetness and blissful rest, without reflecting that God who seeks our union followed the way of suffering, contempt and death.   True mysticism leads to Calvary, only to rest dying in the embrace of the Cross upon the bloodless heart of Jesus (*Introduction* to *Brieven*, vii).

> From the crib to the cross suffering, poverty, misunderstanding were his portion.   His whole life was directed to teaching people how differently God sees suffering, poverty and misunderstanding on the part of people from the false wisdom of men.   Suffering is the way to heaven.   Oh, that we would realize this very day, the value God has included for us in the sufferings he sends upon us, He who nevertheless is the All-bountiful" (Introduction to: Ad. Tanquerey, *Het lijden vergoddelijkt*, vertaald door Elias Theelen, O. Carm., Parijs-Doornik-Rome, 1934, i-ii).

Father Titus had experience of suffering and not only during his last six months of captivity.   He had a very weak, ailing constitution.   Four times he had severe stomach hemorrhages; two of them brought him to the verge of the grave.   The last years of his life he continually had to contend with illness.   What was remarkable in him—and that for a gastric patient—was the great gladness and joy which always irradiated from him, in prison and in the concentration camp as well.   This gladness sprang from his love for Christ who suffered out of love for us.   Thus he was wont to console his fellow prisoners: "Our Lord suffered still more for me" (*Beatification Process*, Raphael Tijhuis O. Carm).   "That is only a trifle compared to what Our Lord suffered for us" (*Process*, Richardus De Groot).

He never wearied of recommending this view-point to others at retreats:

> The folly of the Cross. Our love has to become proverbial. We must not let ourselves be surpassed in love by anybody. It is the first, the greatest, the divine virtue. Our example is Jesus, bleeding on the Cross with a thousand wounds. Whoever wants to win over the world to higher ideals, must have the courage to come into conflict with it. (The world) in the end runs after him who has the courage to do that which it lacked the courage to do. But this conflict with the world is hard. It caused Christ to die on the Cross (Notes for a Retreat).

> Consider life as a Way of the Cross, but take the cross on your shoulders with joy and courage, for Jesus with his example and grace made it light (Retreat *Naar Jezus met Maria*, 1939).

> Let us follow Jesus on the royal way of the cross, not with repugnance like Simon of Cyrene, but with joy and gladness, for we are royal children (Way of the Cross).

> Do not serve God with sighs. Gladly and of good heart show the truth of the words: My yoke is sweet and my burden is light. Be of good cheer and see grief in a higher light, in which it becomes a free choice and a motive for gladness. Joy is not a virtue, but an effect of love (Notes for a Retreat).

His example was Mary.

> As children of Mary with the desire to be similar to her and thus become similar to God, we are driven to God like her, we stay with her at the foot of the Cross to participate in the sacrificial death of Our Lord and, dying to ourselves and to the whole world in the company of our Mother and led and helped by her, to live only in and for God (Introduction, *Carmellicht*, 1935, p. [12]).

In his testament he had written:

> I unite myself in my death with the death of my Savior and I place myself with Mary at the foot of the Cross of My Lord. *Forever will I sing the Lord's mercies* (Meijer, *T.B.*, 459).

What he preached to others he realized in himself. In the prison of Scheveningen he could write:

My vocation to the Church and to the priesthood brought me so many wonderful and beautiful things that I willingly accept some unpleasantness in return. I repeat in complete agreement with Job: We have received good things at the hand of God, why should we not receive the evil He sends us in His Providence? The Lord gave, the Lord hath taken away; blessed be the name of the Lord. Apart from that, I am not so badly off. And although I do not know what will become of me, I know myself to be wholly in God's hands. *Who will separate me from the love of God?* (*My Cell*, Jan. 23, 1942).

Beata solitudo. I am quite at home in this small cell. I never get bored here—quite the contrary. I am certainly alone, but never was Our Lord so near to me. I could shout for joy that He has again allowed Himself to be found by me, without my meeting people or people me. He is now my sole refuge and I feel safe and happy. I am willing to remain here always, if He will allow me to. Seldom have I been so happy and content" (*Ibid.*, Jan. 27, 1942).

And in his first letter of February 12, 1942, he wrote:

I am already at home here. I pray, I read, I write, the days are too short. I am very calm, happy and content... Would you be so kind as to inform Dr. de Jong (the Archbishop of Utrecht) that he should not worry or reproach himself on my account. I suffer here with joy and I am quite all right (*Beatification Process*, doc. 68).

In his well-known poem written in the prison he could say:

Though that requires of me more courage in suffering,
Oh, all suffering is well with me,
Because through that I am like You,
And this is the way to Your Kingdom.

I am happy in my grief,
Because I know it is no more grief,
But the most elected lot,
That unites me with You, O God.

On Good Friday, 1942, in the concentration camp of Amersfoort, Fr. Titus gave a lecture. Officially it was named: "The Place of Gerhard Groote in Dutch Literature," for religious subjects were severely forbidden, but the sub-title was: "Dutch Mysticism of the Passion: Its True Nature," and it became a sermon about the Passion of Christ. In the notes he prepared beforehand we read: "On this day, glad, thankful feeling with vivid imagination of the Passion of Christ, in union with *our* suffering. God for us, God with us, God in us, our strength." It became a lecture which made upon all, Catholics and others, the deepest impression, a lecture spoken from the heart (Aukes, *Het Leven*, 260-262).

In all the prisons and camps he made the deepest impression by his gladness and joy, the grateful acceptance of all suffering. Even to the doctor and the nurse in the hospital of Dachau where he was to die he was always friendly and cordial. At the hands of this doctor he had to undergo a terrible degrading experiment, but he prayed like Jesus: "Not my will, but thine be done." To the nurse who was to administer him the deadly injection that put an end to his life and who once said to him that most priests are good for nothing, "he answered with a saying of Saint Therese, that the best priests are not always those who stay in the pulpit and preach beautiful sermons, but the best priests are those who have to suffer much and offer up their sufferings for sinners. He added that he was glad to be allowed to suffer" (*Beatification Process*, "Tizia").

This joy in suffering, the total acceptance of the worst suffering out of love for Christ and for sinners: is this mysticism? It is not a passive experience of Christ's Passion, but an active participation in his Passion, consciously and to the last consequences. Thus did Christ suffer for us, so did Mary suffer with Him. It was a union with God in love, in the highest love. Perhaps we may not call this mysticism in the strict sense: it was more than that (cf. I Cor 12:31 and 13:1-13).

5

THE BEATIFICATION PROCESS

Adrianus Staring, O. Carm.

A well-known professor of Nijmegen University once asked about Fr. Titus, "Would there ever have been a question of beatification, were it not for the circumstances of his imprisonment and death?" A no less known colleague answered that this was the wrong way to pose the problem. A person's life has to be judged in its entirety and as it actually was; it is not fair to leave out part of it.

When we ask ourselves, 42 years after the death of Fr. Titus Brandsma, how he came to be proposed for beatification, we can concede without a qualm that his imprisonment and death in a concentration camp, or rather the manner in which he underwent these, influenced this initiative to a considerable degree. But we cannot isolate his death from his previous life. A Lutheran doctor who became acquainted with Titus at Amersfoort already remarked that such a person must have been far above the average even in civilian life. There were a number of people who called Titus a "saint" even before his imprisonment. More than through his unequaled charity—already then proverbial—this impression was strengthened by his profound reverence at the altar and by his life's ambition, expressed in his every word and deed, to make God known to men. For to be holy means to be intimately united to God. Others, in spite of their reverence and esteem for Titus, never thought of him as a "saint," because this word suggests one far removed from ordinary life, a performer of miracles. After all, one often forms an idea of holiness after one's own image and likeness;

that is why some individuals, such as the professor mentioned above, could hardly appreciate why Titus should spend himself and his precious time on people or things which did not interest *them*.

Biographies of Father Titus

In the fall of 1942 the writings of Titus in prison found their way back from Dachau; they created a deep impression on the narrow circle of readers to whom they became known. They inspired the Protestant minister, Dr. Wumkes, to write a "short life of a saint." The well-known poem of Titus was copied and during the war was even printed illegally. Meanwhile Fr. Christopher Verhallen, O. Carm., collected the testimony of witnesses who had known Fr. Titus during his imprisonment and received reports of favors received. After the liberation of the southern Netherlands in September of 1944, Fr. Titus' writings in the prison at Scheveningen, *My Cell*, *Daily Schedule of a Prisoner* and *The Last Writing*, an essay about the opposition of the Catholic population to the N. S. B., the Dutch version of the Nazi party, were published with a short introduction by Fr. Brocard Meijer, O. Carm. In spite of restrictions on paper, 50,000 copies of each were printed within a few months. In 1946 Spectrum published *The Great Saint Teresa of Avila*, an unfinished biography written in the prison of Scheveningen, completed and published by Fr. Brocard Meijer.

Titus becomes known

The prison writings not only caused devotion to Fr. Titus to increase continually; they inspired a demand for a biography. In 1945 the Carmelite clerics of the house of studies at Merkelbeek presented a study of the life and writings of Titus Brandsma to his close friend Fr. Hubert Driessen, O. Carm., on the occasion of the latter's golden jubilee of the priesthood. Fr. Brocard Meijer was given the task of writing a biography. During the war H. W. F. Aukes, who became acquainted with Fr. Titus in connection

130

with his work on the journal *Frisia Catholica* and as an employee of the library of the Catholic University of Nijmegen, also began to collect material on his life. In 1947 W. ten Have published his pamphlet, *Prof. Dr. Titus Brandsma*, and the same year Spectrum published his large biography *Titus Brandsma*. This biography, which the writer announced to be "provisional," is based on an exclusive study of the sources. The author writes with respect, one might almost say with reverence, without in the least embroidering the truth the way certain hagiographers do. The book describes Titus especially as a defender of the faith and a hero of the resistance, stressing his many activities. The book was exceedingly well received, even in the non-Catholic press. Dr. J. Tesser in *Streven* and Dr. M. Smits van Waesberghe, S. J., in *Ons Geestelijk Erf* expressed the desire which was already shared by many: that Titus would be eventually canonized. In 1951 Paul Brand of Hilversum published the large volume, *Titus Brandsma*, by Fr. Brocard Meijer. This book, based on an even wider documentation, concentrates on Fr. Titus' activities as a Carmelite and professor. The style, however, is sometimes too exuberant. This book was also well received by the press, among others by the Protestant professor, G. Gosses in *De Linie*, and it led to greater esteem and reverence for Fr. Titus.

Innumerable articles about Fr. Titus have appeared in newspapers and magazines, casting light on one or other aspect of his personality and activities. Outside Holland these appeared mostly in Carmelite magazines, but also in others. For the benefit of the English-speaking public Fr. Albert Groeneveld, O. Carm., in 1954 wrote a pamphlet, *A Heart on Fire*, reprinted a year later. From the books by Aukes and Meijer, Josse Alzin wrote a French biography, *Ce petit moine dangereux*, published in Paris in 1954. This little book was translated into Spanish, *Ese frailecito peligroso* in 1956, into Portuguese in Brazil, *O crime de um frade*, the same year; into English, *A Dangerous Little Friar*, Dublin and London, 1957. A pamphlet by Fr. Aquinas Houle, O. Carm., *Titus Brandsma*, appeared in Chicago in 1956. The same year in Australia, Fr. C. Shortis, O. Carm., wrote the booklet,

Father Brandsma, Carmelite, Educator, Journalist, Nazi Victim.

Dick Hendrickse included Fr. Titus among the heroes of the resistance in his book, *De dag waarop mijn vader huilde* (The Day My Father Wept), Haarlem, 1960, pp. 109-116, as did the well-known American weekly, *Time*, on March 9, 1962 (p. 33).

Meanwhile the voluminous biography by Fr. Brocard Meijer had been long sold out. In his monumental work *Kardinaal De Jong* (1956), Aukes discussed the figure of Titus at length and succeeded in drawing a more accurate picture of the relationship between the Cardinal and Fr. Brandsma in the matter of their intervention in the Catholic press. Since Fr. Meijer, who had become provincial of the Carmelites in the Netherlands, had no time to revise his book completely, Mr. H. Aukes was asked to write a new life of Fr. Brandsma. For this purpose he now had at his disposal a rich mine of new information which had come to light in the course of the process of beatification. In 1961 Spectrum published *Het leven van Titus Brandsma* (The Life of Titus Brandsma) reprinted in 1963. It is more than a revision of the "temporary" biography of 1947. It is completely rewritten and penetrates more deeply the real being of Fr. Titus: his relationship with God as it shines forth in his life. This book received favorable reviews in the non-Catholic press as well.

Based principally on Aukes' book is the fine English biography by Joseph Rees, *Titus Brandsma. A Modern Martyr*, London, Sidgwick & Jackson, 1971.

An Italian biography

In Italy Msgr. Fausto Vallainc, like Titus himself an ecclesiastical advisor to Catholic journalists, had been working on a biography for several years. For this purpose he visited the Netherlands twice. As sources he used an Italian translation of the book of Fr. Brocard Meijer, Alzin's *Ce petit moine dangereux*, an additional manuscript by the same writer and finally a translation of the accounts by witnesses in the process of beatification. *Un giornalista martire, Padre Tito Brandsma* appeared in October, 1961 (a second printing in 1963). It treats Fr. Titus primarily as a journalist and a martyr of this profession. The style is somewhat oratorical, though less so than is usual in Italy. In due course the book was presented to the Holy Father. Pope John XXIII told the present writer as well as a number of other persons that he was deeply impressed by the book, that he had begun to read it one night and had not been able to sleep before he finished it. He promised to speak of it again and did this in an audience for the foreign press held in Rome on October 25, 1961. The following is the literal text: "A recent book, presented to Us a few days ago, was written by a journalist and about a journalist. We cannot tell you the whole story: only that it treats of a Dutch journalist who had a weak constitution, but who became a Carmelite and who even as a young man gave evidence of extraordinary qualities. He distinguished himself especially in the study of social questions. We speak of him also because he was born in the same year as We: he in February and We in November. He would thus have been of the same age as We. His was truly a beautiful life, which became the glory of his country, where he became ever more famous according as his articles were published, read and admired. The war came, the terrible image of which is still before Our eyes. He ended up in prison, was mistreated, and one may truly say was martyred. His story awakened such respect in Our heart because it is a question of a man who in the midst of immeasurable trials always kept with him the practice of brotherly love, of heroism of the highest degree."

In more than fifty newspapers and magazines reviews of this book appeared: not only in the Catholic but also in the non-Catholic press, reviewers expressed admiration of Fr. Titus. Raimondo Manzini, editor-in-chief of the *Osservatore Romano*, wrote the introduction to this book and in January of 1962 spoke in Naples and Milan about the life of Fr. Titus as an example for journalists.

The writings of Father Titus

Much of what Fr. Titus published during his lifetime was connected with the concrete circumstances of his time. The large edition of the *Works of St. Teresa*, begun in 1918, was revised by his confrère, Fr. Thomas Keulemans, in 1948-49, and republished by Paul Brand in Hilversum. His own life of *De grote heilige Teresia van Jezus* (The Great Saint Teresa of Jesus) which he wrote under the most difficult conditions in the prison of Scheveningen, without sources and without the Saint's writings, and which in 1946 was added to and published, is too weak as a biography to be considered for republication, especially in view of the fact that so many excellent lives of the Saint have in recent years been translated into Dutch. His inaugural speech as rector of the Catholic University of Nijmegen, *Het Godsbegrip* (The Concept of God, 1932), is still worth being read and pondered. The conferences which Fr. Titus gave in America in 1935, and which were published the following year in Chicago under the title, *Carmelite Mysticism: Historical Sketches*, may admit improvement in certain sections in view of more recent studies, yet they remain in the opinion of the present writer the best synthesis of the spiritual life of *both* Carmels published to date. This same little book was published unchanged in Dublin, 1955, under the title, *The Beauty of Carmel*, with a short life of Fr. Titus by Fr. Jerome O'Dwyer, O. Carm.

A German translation and adaptation with a short biography was edited by Fr. Christophorus Verhallen, O. Carm., *Das Erbe des Propheten. Geist und Mystik des Karmel* (Köln, Wienand-Verlag, 1958).

In the field which was so dear to him—the spiritual writings of the Low Countries in the Middle Ages—Fr. Titus published a number of scientific studies and from 1938-1941 a series of weekly articles entitled "*Van ons geestelijk erf*" (Out of our Spiritual Heritage) in *De Gelderlander*. These articles are an excellent popularization of the subject. "A selection of the best parts of this serial with perhaps the addition of a few other writings, would be more than welcome," H. Aukes commented in his book (1961). An anthology of Fr. Titus' writings on mysticism is being prepared by Bruno Borchert, O. Carm.

The Process

Although pressure was exerted on all sides to begin the process of beatification, the Dutch Carmelites thought it wiser not to initiate such an action themselves. On January 31, 1949, it is true, Cardinal de Jong was asked what his attitude would be toward an eventual process. He answered that he would heartily welcome it. After the appearance of the major biography in 1951, the general request was ceded to.

On January 11, 1952, Rt. Rev. W. Mutsaerts, Bishop of Den Bosch, was asked permission to begin preparations for the process. Permission was granted in principle. Fr. Peter Starmans, O. Carm., was given the task of answering the ever growing volume of mail, of giving lectures and preparing the process. Memorial cards with Fr. Titus' picture and the text of his poem had already been printed; now new ones appeared with a prayer for his beatification. After one year hundreds of thousands had already been distributed; then translations were made into French, German, English, Polish, Italian, Spanish, Portuguese, Javanese and *bahasa Indonesia*.

From the very beginning this literature emphasized the figure of Fr. Titus rather than favors granted. He must live on among us not as a sort of miracle worker, but as a person who inspires. The novena booklet by A. Groeneveld, *In Pater Titus' leerschool* (In the School of Father Titus), achieves this aim and it has been in great demand ever since its first appearance in 1957. Fr. Starmans gave more then 500 talks illustrated by slides on the life of Fr. Titus. In 1957 Fr. Felix Wezenbeek took over from Fr. Starmans and has since given 2,000 talks. The priest who was supposed to help in preparing the actual process had been given another assignment, so Fr. Adrian Staring was appointed for this work when he returned from Rome in 1954.

Fr. Staring's first task was to begin new research on Fr. Titus' life, not from a biographical viewpoint but with an eye to presenting his case for the process. The question immediately arose: should the process be drawn up to present Fr. Titus as a martyr or as a confessor? There was no doubt that he was a martyr in the same sense as were the other victims of the Nazi regime, but could one speak of martyrdom in the sense in which the word is used by the Church? *"Non poena sed causa facit martyrem."* It is not *what* he suffers but *why* he suffers that makes the martyr. Did Fr. Titus undergo death as a witness to and on behalf of the Catholic faith? The faith involved here need not necessarily be an article of faith or a point of moral doctrine; it may be a means which is necessary in safeguarding, spreading or illustrating Christian faith or morals. Was the Catholic daily press, as it existed in the Netherlands, such a means? This question was unprecedented in the processes in Rome.

Another problem which the Roman process would raise was that of the nature of the persecution carried out by the National Socialists. The processes of many of the victims of Communism—considered as martyrs—were already under way. Fr. Titus, however, would be the first victim of Nazism to be put forward as a martyr. Rome would thus have to answer the following questions: was the resistance of the Catholic and other Christian churches in the Netherlands of a religious or political nature? Were the motives which led to the prohibition of the N. S. B. simply "Catholic politics" or were they part of the Christian world outlook? And finally—another unprecedented question—could death in a concentration camp be considered a form of martyrdom?

Besides all this, the investigation would have to decide whether Fr. Titus had willingly accepted death —and that as a witness to the Catholic faith.

The investigation begins

Investigation showed that there was enough evidence to warrant setting the process for martyrdom

in motion. By making it impossible to refuse advertisements for the N. S. B. *on grounds of principle*, the
Nazis themselves had made the affair a question of
religious principle, as Fr. Titus himself brought out in
his circular to the newspapers.

For safety's sake, however, it was decided to investigate the process not only from the angle of martyrdom but also from that of sanctity of life. If the
fact of martyrdom were not accepted in Rome, then
the last six months of Fr. Titus' life would count and
be reckoned as telling proof of his heroic faith, hope,
charity and fortitude. Proved holiness of life would
have great value in the final judgment, because a
martyr bears fuller witness to the Church when his
previous life has been one of heroic holiness.

On January 13, 1955, the diocesan court was in-
stalled first at 's Hertogenbosch and a few days later
at Amersfoort. Cardinal de Jong was the first witness. In the course of that year the vice-postulator
worked at the *Stellingen en Artikelen* (Theses and Articles) in which he briefly explained what he was trying to prove and chose a number of witnesses. Besides the process about the reputation for sanctity
and martyrdom, two others were conducted. The
first concerned "non-cult," in which proof had to be
given that no official or ecclesiastical cult was being
shown to Fr. Titus—the Church does not want to
have her judgment anticipated—and the second, the
"collection of writings." On December 8, 1957, the
final solemn session terminating the three diocesan
processes took place in the Carmelite church of
Nijmegen. In 80 sessions 50 witnesses had been
heard, among them three bishops and four non-Catholics. About half of the testimony concerned the
martyrdom and the circumstances surrounding it.

The writings of Fr. Titus were gathered into 136
volumes and then—together with the three processes—were sent to Rome. Before the end of December, 1957, they were turned over to the Congregation of Rites. In the following years, under constant
pressure from the postulators, much preliminary
work was quietly done in Rome. (Every year 50 pro-

cesses come in, while at the most only five are completed. The number of processes actually being handled is over 1,000. The testimonies concerning the reputation for holiness and martyrdom were translated, the translation was revised and recopied by hand, this copy was compared with the original, declared authentic and bound.

Then the advocate of the process, Carlo Snider, prepared a selection of the testimonies and documents, printed as the *Summarium* in 1965.

The writings of Fr. Titus were divided among eight Dutch theologians who had to determine whether they contained anything contrary to faith and morals and in what ways they revealed the virtues or faults of the servant of God. When these examiners had finished, the writings were redistributed in such a way that each one was examined independently by two experts whose printed opinions were handed over to the consultors of the Sacred Congregation of Rites in 1962, and the final decree of the Congregation approving the writings, was published in 1964.

The final decree regarding "non-cult" was given only in 1975.

Meanwhile the process dragged on; without going into details, we can say that there was a strong disagreement between historians and theologians on the one hand, and some canonists on the other. These latter saw martyrdom only as a juridical formula, without any connection with changing historical circumstances, and without a clear idea about the true nature of National Socialism. On the 22nd of May, 1984, the Cause of Martyrdom was discussed by the consultors of the S. Congregation for the Causes of Saints: the result was unanimously in favor.

Devotion to Titus

Before and during the II Vatican Council petitions were gathered from ecclesiastics and laymen from all over the world; these were printed in 1965. Among them were 34 cardinals, 600 bishops, 41 superiors of religious orders and hundreds of priests and religious, among them more than 250 who had been in Dachau. One of these letters was from Cardinal John Baptist Montini, the future Pope Paul VI; another was signed by Carolus Wojtyła, the present Pope. In most of these letters the bishops see Fr. Titus as a forerunner of all the great themes that were then discussed at the Council.

In their petition the German and Dutch bishops wrote, among other things: "Brotherly love between the peoples of the Netherlands and of Germany would be greatly advanced by the beatification of this man who effectively promoted devotion to St. Boniface, the apostle common to both peoples and who— even in the midst of suffering and injustice inflicted on him by his enemies—begged God's grace that these people might stand side by side in peace and perfect freedom."

From ancient times one of the most important criteria for recognizing an individual as a saint has been the devotion attached to a place connected with him—usually his grave. In Rome at the Congregation of Rites it was frequently asked if this existed in the case of Fr. Titus. Immediately after the war it was suggested that a statue should be erected in the Netherlands and one was actually erected at Oss. At Nijmegen, however, in 1955, the plan matured of dedicating a chapel to Fr. Titus because his ashes rested in a common grave at Dachau among those of more than 50,000 other victims.

Under the sponsorship of Cardinal Giobbe, a commission was founded in 1959 which consisted of the dean and mayor of Nijmegen, university professors and personnel of the Catholic press. By the end of 1959 the money had been collected through an appeal made in the Catholic newspapers and on July 24, 1960, the chapel was solemnly dedicated by the Rt. Rev. Constance Kramer, O. F. M., bishop of Luanfu and a relative of Fr. Titus.

The severe, sober lines of the chapel are reminiscent of a concentration camp's bunkhouses and barracks. In front of the chapel is a tall pylon with a symbolic reconstruction of the cross, symbol of suffering and victory. The interior of the chapel, however, has an intimate air about it and a great urn, with ashes of the victims of Dachau, visibly links this monument with the place where Titus died.

Fr. Titus today

"Among the many questions I put to myself none occupies me more than the enigma that developing man, proud and priding himself in his progress, turns away from God in such large numbers." This is how Fr. Titus began his famous 1932 talk on the Concept of God. In a sermon about Sts. Boniface and Willibrord, pronounced in July, 1939, shortly before the German invasion of Poland, he expressed it so: "How we, who live in these lax times, have to look up to both those men. Both of them, knowing that speaking about God would probably cost them their lives, still try to bring another people to God, because they know and believe that this is what will make the people truly happy. Even if the new paganism no longer wishes love, we shall overcome paganism with this very love. Love will conquer the hearts of the pagans for us."

The burning questions of Fr. Titus' time are still with us today, even in a more urgent form. Over and above the open battle against faith in God and the subsequent persecution of believers, there is the continued progress of secularization, even among Catholics, even among priests and religious. It seems that the world does not need God any more. And when it does not need God, it needs no one. "Let each person be as strong as possible. Let the weak perish. Christianity, with its message of love is called out-of-date and has to be replaced with old German force." This is a formulation of Nazism, and is the practice of many today.

This is what Titus Brandsma became a witness against. He witnessed to his faith in God by his deeds, especially by his love, which he extended even to his enemies, and also by his glad giving of his life for God and for his fellowmen, just as Christ did for us.

Fr. Titus was never aloof from the world; on the contrary, he was fully involved in modern life. The problems of his time are still with us. His answer to them has to be ours as well.

III

ASPECTS OF HOLINESS

In the spirit
of Carmel
Titus preached
the role of
Mary in bringing
Jesus to man

A view of the Marian Congress promoted by Fr. Titus at Nijmegen, 1920

1
TRUST IN GOD

Adrianus Staring, O. Carm.

Hope and trust

Trust, as a Christian virtue, is part of the theological virtue of hope. It is a "more resolute hope." Supernatural hope has two objects: its own happiness in heaven and the divine help of grace. Hope proceeds from faith and animates faith; it also proceeds from love because it strives towards God as its ultimate end and supreme good.

Eternal happiness is beyond our natural forces and, like grace, is a free gift from God himself. For Christians, hope in God is hope in Christ who merited heaven for us and gives us his grace by means of the Church.

Trust in God does not exclude trust in oneself. God also created our natural forces, our gifts and our faculties. In man there is always a danger of attributing everything to himself, but this is not so with the saints. During the period of Quietism there was an attempt to exclude the will and personal interests and actions from the spiritual life so as to reach the level of "pure" and disinterested love. Exaggerated expressions of a total diffidence towards human nature and its faculties can also be found in certain orthodox spiritual authors of the seventeenth century.

Hope refers to the future and this future is to a large extent unknown. Trust therefore involves both magnanimity and strength of spirit. People who are anxious, fearful and fainthearted don't get very far in the spiritual life, whereas those with strong wills and magnanimity do. These are the people who venture to undertake and realise great works and carry on despite difficulties and obstacles. They know that they are running risks but they are trusting and don't allow failures to dishearten them. They have a broad vision, they are tenacious and persevering even in difficult situations that appear desperate. Weak and fearful people hold on to them because they know how to give reassurance and encouragement.

Titus Brandsma's trust

Titus Brandsma was such a person—a man of many initiatives and undertakings, even if they were to cost him his life. His trust, even in the things that had nothing to do with eternal happiness and divine grace, was trust in God, because he was always aware that everything he was able to do was a gift from the God who created us and who gives us the necessary faculties and help. When a mission on the island of Java was offered to the Dutch Carmelites, Titus wrote to his friend Hubert Driessen: "*Audaces fortuna adiuvat*—fortune helps the bold—so goes the proverb, but I would put it this way: *confidentes Deus*—God helps those who trust" (Letter of December 17, 1920). His brother Henry says; "He had a great trust in God. In all of his undertakings he counted above all else on the help of God. He often said: 'God will see to it.' He saw no difficulties; he was a great optimist and often used to say: 'There's still the Lord'" (*Summarium* of the process, p. 43, nn. 75, 78c and 80). His sister Gatske says the same thing:

> He always trusted in God. He often spoke about the goodness of God. He also stimulated other people to trust in Him. He used to say: 'We must leave everything to Our Lord... pray and trust in God.' Often he used to repeat the words of St. Paul: '*Omnia possum in Eo qui me confortat*.' He also stimulated others to trust in God: 'The Lord is so good.' he used to repeat often. He used to say: 'Do your best and God will do the rest.' Even in difficult matters and undertakings he trusted in God and asked that we pray to Him (*Summ*., nn. 75, 76, 77, 79, 80, pp. 32-33).

His classmate, Aloysius van der Staaij: "He had a great trust in God. In all his undertakings he counted above all on the help of God. He didn't see difficulties; he was a great optimist and often used to say:'There's still the Lord!' Also, 'God will look after it'" (*Summ.*, nn. 75, 80 and 78c, pp. 75). Another schoolmate, Fr. Adalbertus Lokkers: "Toil never caused him any fear; difficulties just didn't exist for him because he trusted in God" (n. 80, p. 59). Fr. Bonaventure ter Ellen:

> His trust in God was unlimited. This trust proceeded from his faith and was exceptional. In himself he was an optimist and had a great deal of trust in the goodness and grace of God. He also stimulated others to trust in God and used to say: 'Don't worry, everything will fit into place.' Even in difficult undertakings he showed trust in God yet at the same time he himself continued to work for the successful outcome of his project (*Summ.*, nn. 75, 76, 79, 80, p. 65).

He remained the same when he was a professor at the University of Nijmegen: "He was full of trust in God, he was never alarmed or frightened. I am convinced that he possessed the virtue of hope in an exceptional manner. He always used to say: 'Don't be frightened, everything will fit into place.' He also prompted others to put their trust in God. 'Look upwards. There's a Father up there who is looking out for us" (Anna Kersten, *Summ.* nn. 75 and 79, p. 67). "He certainly had an immense trust in God. The principal virtue was trust in God and in the power of prayer" (Fr. J. S. van Rooij, O. Carm., nn. 76 and 78c). Fr. Borromeus Tiecke, a student of Fr. Titus says:

> I have the impression that the Servant of God trusted in God more than normal. This was particularly evident in many of his undertakings—including his activity as a professor. He didn't place too much trust in himself but, following the example of the great St. Teresa, he placed his trust above all in God. By pointing out the goodness of God, he encouraged others;... he used to say that God would have looked after us if we had been faithful to the Rule and Constitutions. The Servant of God also stimulated others to place their trust in God. I'm of the impression that in

many aspects his life was heroic even before his martyrdom, especially, his trust in God (*Summ.*, nn. 75, 76, 19, ex off., pp. 89, 90, 95).

Brother Joseph Pelgrin is of the same opinion:

> I believe that he was full of trust in God. He had an absolute trust in God. He even used to ask for our prayers. He prompted others to have faith in God and used to say: 'Everything will be put right.' In the retreat too, he exhorted us to leave everything and place our trust in Jesus alone. Even in difficult moments he was confident that everything would come out right with the help of God (nn. 75, 78c, 79, 80).

His university colleagues express the same judgement: "He prompted others to place their trust in God and used to say: 'There's still Our Lord!'" (Prof. Frutten, n. 79). This optimism was certainly linked with his trust in Divine Providence. "I have the distinct impression that this wasn't just a natural virtue. He trusted in God even in University affairs and its future and used to say: 'We'll get there all the same'" (Msgr. C. Bellon, nn. 75 and 78c). The well-known Prof. Christina Mohrmann:

> It was constantly clear from his lessons that for him Christian hope was an ever present reality, and that was beyond the ordinary. In that he was without complications and simple in the extreme. For him it was a habitual and normal expression: 'As you know... later on in heaven we'll...' Plainly such Christian optimism—which at times could appear to secular outsiders as reckless trust or levity—flowered from his continual and general union with God. One of his habitual expressions was: 'Our Lord will see to it.' In his great optimism and trust in God he used to burden himself with excessive work but that didn't seem to disturb his tranquillity and his serenity (*Proc.* nn. 75, 76, 77, 80, 84).

His student confreres give us a more theological vision. "His most eminent virtues... his unlimited trust before God. I am under the impression that he had a supernatural trust in God to a degree higher than normal, because in everything he aimed at union with God. His trust in God was based on this. He stimulated others to have the same trust in God" (M. Arts, nn. 64c, 75 and 76).

He was inspired by the supernatural virtue of hope to a degree much higher than normal because he firmly trusted that he would be saved thanks to the love of Christ. He expressed himself in this sense more than once. He often used to say: 'Act out of love for God and for Christ and then Paradise will come by itself.' He often said: 'The Lord will look after this.' He also brought others to place their trust in God and to pray—not just prayers of petition but prayers of resignation. More than once he showed his trust in God when there were difficulties. He expected everything from Providence (B. Meijer, nn. 75, 76, 78c, 79, 80).

Fr. Titus' biographer H. Aukes puts it this way:

From his writings and from investigations it appears that hope was the basis of his spirituality. From this derived his encouraging of others and his continual concern for others. This was the atmosphere of trust in God by which he penetrated my soul and the soul of others (*Summ.*, n. 76, p. 152).

Some people were of the opinion that Titus Brandsma had too much trust in men, that he was too ingenuous to judge people. He used to help many people who did not merit help and sometimes his charity was abused. Fr. Titus knew this but despite it he was not deluded or exasperated. The heavenly Father too causes the sun to shine on the wicked and the good alike and the rain to fall on the just and the unjust (Mt. 5:45). Fr. Titus was convinced that there was something good in even the worst men. One of his prison companions recounts: "He used to say that the men of the S. S. were at Himmler's service and were obliged to carry out his orders. About Himmler he used to say that although he was possessed by German instincts he still remained a human being" (C. de Graaf, *Summ.*, n. 60, p. 319). In the camp at Dachau:

He used to speak very naturally even with the head of the block Becker who belonged to the S. S. and who often used to insult him and beat him. Sometimes I used to say to Fr. Titus, 'Don't talk with those men, you won't get anything out of it—at the most blows.' Fr. Titus then replied: 'That's why we mustn't give up. Who knows that there isn't something left in them' (*Summ.*, n. 60a, p. 354, R. Tijhuis, O. Carm.)

Who knows? Before his execution in 1946 Fritz Becker was reconciled with God (P. Lenz, *Christus in Dachau*, 1956, p. 400).

His trust in defence of the faith

In May, 1940, Holland was occupied by Germany and at once restrictions were imposed on the Churches to favor and propagate National Socialism. In February, 1941, measures were taken against religious and priests involved in teaching. Titus Brandsma was President of the Federation of Directors of Catholic Schools at Middle School level and Upper and Lower School level and he organised a general protest.

At the moment I'm the lawyer of these schools and for now we're only dealing with priests and religious but who knows what'll happen tomorrow. If we don't take up a position we'll be trampled on. In any case, they have to know what we consider to be our right. Whatever happens we'll try to remain calm and resigned to the inevitable. God will have the last word. We shall be secure in his hands. No one can resist his way of ordering things (*Summ.* p. 418: Letter 8-3-1941).

He said to his co-workers in the secretariate of the Middle Carmelite schools: "Leave everything to God, trust in Our Lord, everything will fit into place" (P. Flor. Haagen, n. 77). "You must put more trust in the Providence of God" (P. Raphael Gooijer, n. 78). "He was a man of unlimited trust in God" (*Ibid.*, n. 75-77).

His companion in the struggle for the defence of Catholic teaching, Doctor J. de Boer says:

Even in an unconscious way we were stirred by this behaviour to place our trust in God. He was certainly suffering as a result of his initiatives for the Catholic press and especially for Catholic schools, but he trusted in God to guide everything for the best. My first wife and I were edified by his joyful trust in God (*Summ.*, nn. 79-80, p. 201).

Fr. Titus showed the same trust in defence of the Catholic nature of the newspapers which was to lead him to martyrdom as testified by the journalist H. Geise: "He trusted in God and in the power of prayer. Often he stimulated us to pray for something. Whenever he undertook some activity he often used to say 'We can't do anything else but pray.' Action in favor of journalists was a difficult undertaking. On that occasion he showed a great trust in God" (*Proc.* nn. 78c, 79 and 80). The journalist F. Frequin: "He also stirred others to place their trust in God by his writings and by his own mouth as we can see from the last sentence in his letter to journalists: 'God has the last word and He rewards the faithful servant.' These words, in a dangerous moment of the war, were an inspiration for us" (*Summ.*, nn. 79-80, pp. 212). His companion in the struggle, the director of the newspaper *De Gelderlander*: "In fact I have the impression that in this he trusted in God and in the power of prayer. It is clear from all his letters that he stirred others to place their trust in God" (G. Bodewes, *Summ.*, nn. 78c and 79, p. 222).

The Martyr in prisons and concentration camps

In isolation in the prison of Scheveningen (Jan. 20 - March 12, 1942), Fr. Titus wrote in his diary of the first days: "Even though I don't know how this is going to end I know very well that I'm in God's hands. *Who will separate me from the love of God?* He is my only refuge and I feel protected and happy. I will stay here for ever if He wishes it so. Seldom have I been so happy and content" (*Summ.* pp. 500 and 502).

But especially in the tough camp of Amersfoort (March 12 - April 28, 1942) we can see his joyful trust animating the other prisoners.

He used to affirm that we were all in the hands of God and had to leave everything to Him. In his conversations with us he displayed his hope in eternal happiness: encouraging us and stirring us on to putting our trust in God. He drew his trust and his strength from his hope in God, in Jesus and in his cross. He trusted completely in God and in the power of prayer. He was a stimulus and an encouragement for me too. Among other things he told me that we are in the hands of God. I can declare absolutely that he gave evidence of a great trust in God (Fr. Verhulst, *Summ.* nn. 60b, 76, 78c, 79-80, pp. 263-264).

Another companion:

I consider his most eminent virtues: his goodness, his piety and his unlimited trust in God. His trust in God was quite considerable and stemmed from deep inside him. He also drew attention of others to the divine goodness and more than once he told me: 'We have a Father in Heaven who is so good.' He never spoke about failures and disappointments and often he used to repeat: 'Put your trust in God, everything will fit into place.' He had trust in God and in the power of prayer. He also stimulated others to place their trust in God, inducing them to pray. He once took me by the shoulder and said: 'Don't worry: we have a Father in Heaven who is so good. Don't think about it any more' (T. van Mierlo, *Summ.*, nn. 64c, 75-77, 78c, 79, pp. 271-272).

Fr. J. Aalders confirms this: "He was a symbol of trust in God for us and he instilled courage in the other detainees. Everyone, even the non-Catholics, clung to him. Although he was forever optimistic he was convinced that they wouldn't release him. He used to confide in God and in the power of prayer about this. He was full of courage and trust or, to put it better, trust in God" (*Summ.*, nn. 76, 78c., pp. 285 and 289). "He placed himself completely under the Will of God. He trusted in God and in the power of prayer and also spurred others to pray" (L. Siegmund, *Summ.*, nn. 77 and 78c, pp. 311-312).

Non-Catholics too confirm this. Colonel A. Fogteloo: "His great strength of spirit and his joyfulness revealed a great trust in God" (*Summ.*, n. 64, p. 260). A Lutheran doctor: "He spurred on others to place their trust in God and he had a lot of influence in the camp. In everything he gave proof of his trust in God" (P. H. Ronge, *Summ.*, nn. 77 and 80, p. 299). A non-believing professor: "He left everything to God" (G. Borst, n. 75, p. 394).

Back in Scheveningen prison (April 28 - May 16, 1942), where he learned of his destination for Dachau, Titus Brandsma shared a cell with two young Protestants. One of these testifies:

> His trust in God was immense. He trusted in the cross of Christ and in grace. He was convinced that in a short while he would reach Paradise: this was his hope. He also gave us encouragement and pointed out the future happiness to us. He was completely resigned to the Will of God and used to say that nothing would happen without his Will. He trusted in God and in prayer. Sustained by his trust in God, those days were unforgettable for us (C. de Graaf, *Summ.*, nn. 75-77, 77c, 80, pp. 320).

Another prison companion: "He had a great trust in Heaven. He certainly trusted in prayer and even got me to pray. He was full of trust in God: everything was more difficult for him than for me" (H. van Nieuwenhoven, *Summ.*, nn. 76, 78c, 80, pp. 326-327).

The next step towards Dachau was the prison at Kleve in Germany. According to the prison chaplain Ludwig Deimel: "He practiced trust in God to an extraordinary measure. When all attempts to free him had failed he didn't express the slightest sign of disappointment, discouragement, depression or desperation, but instead remained serene, joyful and full of trust in God" (*Summ.*, nn. 75 and 77, p. 336). A Dutch prison companion:

> He displayed a great trust in God. He always used to speak about Heaven. More than once I heard him say: 'We're in God's hands.' He was always happy and in good humor. He trusted in God and in the power of prayer. He used to say to me: 'De Groot, you've got to pray; all of this will come to an end. I don't get bored here even for a moment' (*Summ.*, nn. 75-77, 78c).

In the camp at Dachau (June 19 - July 26, 1942)

A German priest, Heinrich Rupieper, was with Fr. Titus on the seven day journey from Kleve to Dachau, and he was also in the entrance block in Dachau for ten days. "He gave me the impression of being a special person, submissive to the will of God and tranquil. He used to say: 'We're in Our Lord's hands.' Fr. Titus was completely calm and resigned: 'Don't let things bother you; Our Lord will provide and will put everything into place'" (*Summ.*, nn. 55 and 62, nn. 347-348). His confrère Br. Raphael Tijhuis: "His habitual pet phrase was: 'We're in God's hands!' I believe that I'm in a position to affirm that the Servant of God exercised the virtue of hope to a degree greater than heroic. He trusted in God and prompted others to trust in the power of prayer" (*Summ.*, n. 77, and 79b, p. 362). His other priest companions say the same thing: "He certainly had a great trust in God and openly showed it. He was resigned to the will of God" (J. Lemmens, *Summ.*, 64c, p. 370). "He said to me: 'We hope to pass from this life to life with the Trinity.' He trusted in God and in the power of prayer. He even spurred me on to trust in God" (O. Lips, *Summ.*, nn. 76, 78c, 79, p. 375). "Trust in God: this was apparent in his happiness, his good humor and his admirable patience and tolerance" (J. R. Rothkrans, *Summ.*, n. 64, p. 390).

The last week in the camp hospital, where he was on the point of death, Titus Brandsma conserved the same attitude. The nurse who later would have to administer the fatal injection testifies:

> He even gave me his rosary to get me to pray. I replied that I wasn't able to pray so the rosary was of no use to me. He said that even if I didn't know how to pray, I could at least recite the second part of the rosary: 'Pray for us sinners.' I laughed at that. He told me that if I prayed a lot I wouldn't be lost (*Fasc. reserv.* n. 60b, p. 4).

According to all the witnesses, a joyful trust in God, even in the most difficult and dramatic circumstances, was a characteristic of Titus Brandsma's spiritual life. Right from his youth his example was St. Teresa of Avila who, while trusting in her own actions and in human means, waited for everything from Divine Providence. Later on, the 'Little Way' of St. Therese of Lisieux. a total abandonment to God, exercised a strong influence on his spiritual life. When his sister Maria, a Poor Clare, asked him: "Brother, what must I do to become perfect," he always used to reply: "Carry out your daily duties punctually, even in the smallest things. This is so simple! Follow Our Lord like a young girl and skip about behind Jesus; leave all your worries to Him: this way you're doing enough, this is perfection— don't tire yourself out, surrender yourself."

Translated by Paul O'Brien, O. Carm.

2

LOVE OF NEIGHBOR

Adrianus Staring, O. Carm.

The love of God was the most important commandment already in the Old Testament (*Dt*
6:5). Jesus joined to it another commandment
which would be its equal—the love of neighbor (*Mt*
22: 37-40). At the same time he extended this love
not only to those who are near but also to those far
off, and even to one's enemies (*Mt* 5: 44-45).

It will always be difficult to judge concretely
whether we love the Lord with all our heart, with all
our soul and with all our mind. But Jesus taught us:
"If you love me you will keep my commandments"
(*Jn* 14: 15). Love for one's neighbor, or as St. John
puts it, for one's brothers, is the "new" commandment which Jesus gives his followers (*Jn* 13: 34-35; *1
Jn* 2: 7-8).

"God is love" (*1 Jn* 4: 7). "In this was God's love
for us revealed: God sent his only begotten Son into
the world that we might have life through
him. Love consists in this: We did not begin loving
God, rather He loved us and sent his Son as a victim
of expiation for our sins" (*1 Jn* 4: 9-10; cfr. *1 Jn* 2:
2).

God's love for us was revealed in the love of his
Son, made flesh for us. Our love for Christ will be
revealed in our love for neighbor. "No one has seen
God; if we love one another, God remains in us" (*1 Jn*
4: 12). "The person who does not love his brother
whom he sees cannot love God whom he does not
see" (*1 Jn* 4: 20). We have not even seen Christ: but

in love for neighbor our love for Jesus and for God the Father is revealed.

The love of Titus Brandsma

Of the most important virtues which characterized Fr. Titus Brandsma, almost all the witnesses at the Process for Beatification indicated his charity as the first of all. "His great love for God expressed itself in love for neighbor. All are in agreement that he shone with great love for neighbor and that he repeatedly put into practice the teaching, 'Love knows no limits'" (Brocard Meijer, O. Carm. *Process*, n. 64c; *Summarium*, n. 86).

His sister Gatske said:

He sought perfection especially in love. He was good to everyone and wished to help them all. His most noteworthy virtue was his love for God and for neighbor, his goodness, his simplicity in his relationships with others. His whole life was love. If he could do something for another, he did it. This is why he was loved by everyone, because he had a good word for everyone. Love of neighbor was his most conspicuous virtue" (*Summ.*, n. 64a, 64c, 81, 85).

His brother, Henry Brandsma, said the same thing: "His charity was extraordinary. He wished to help everyone" (*Summ.* n. 81). "The Servant of God practiced the virtue of charity to a heroic degree. He always sought to make himself useful to everyone" (Aloysius van der Staaij, O. Carm., *Summ.*, n. 81).

The majority of witnesses uses the word "goodness" which they describe as "exceptional," "the most noteworthy, perhaps even heroic, factor," "exceptionally good to everyone," "what struck a person the most," "his most eminent virtue," "visible to everyone," "in the concentration camp of Dachau he showed his heroic charity especially through his goodness" (*Summ.*, *passim*).

Titus, however, was certainly no "softy." His character was strong, ardent.

His charity was expressed especially in his eager and ready availability to help others on both spiritual and material levels, or as St. John writes: "My children, let us not love with words or mere talk, but with authentic works" (*1 Jn* 3: 18).

He showed very great solicitude for the poor. While we thought he was going around asking for financial help, in reality he was giving it. At times he looked for work for housemaids. When he was Prior many poor people came to the door of the monastery. He wished that everyone be given something; he did not know how to refuse anyone" (A. van der Staaij, *Summ.*, n. 87).

"He left no stone unturned in favor of the health of others. 'Our love for neighbor should be proverbial,' he used to say" (Bonaventure ter Ellen, O. Carm., *Summ.*, n. 85).

"His personal tendency was more towards personal help rather than organized charities because in the latter case, personal contact is lacking" (Borromaeus Tiecke, n. 88).

"All are in agreement that he shone with great love for neighbor and that he repeated and put into practice the teaching, 'Love knows no limits'" (B. Meijer, *Summ.*, n. 85).

His long-time Prior, Fr. Christopher Verhallen, provides a substantial description:

I know by personal experience that many people appealed to him for material aid; he tried to help as much as he could. He asked others for help in the case of ecclesiastical students. I also know of one instance in which he materially helped a poor family. I have also heard of other instances in which he helped the poor. After the 1914-1918 War, he attempted to have German children re-settled in Oss. I also have indications of the way in which he supported various initiatives such as the charitable work "Used paper."

The vast number of people who came to him—either for advice or for aid in desperate, important or futile matters—was simply staggering. His availability, both calm and eager, was the most evident and the most attractive of all his good qualities. When asked, he helped and intervened with a cordiality that never offended. He often foresaw a request, and spontaneously provided help. Professor Sassen has declared: 'He did favors with such generosity that the person who was appealing to him felt that he was doing Fr. Titus a favor.'

He himself put into practice what he indicated to others. Once at a house Chapter he stated: 'We should study how to help others.' He was naturally disposed to help others, but the extent of his aid and the way in which he gave it cannot be explained on a natural level. It made no difference to him whether he was asked for help on a spiritual or temporal level. Even in the latter case, by means of a simple word or by his altruistic and kind goodness, he knew how to attain a spiritual effect. Once a seminarian who was studying abroad came to tell him his troubles, in that he had no money left in order to continue his studies. Father Titus asked how much he needed *per annum*, and then spent most of the day visiting well-off people, trying to persuade them to donate a sum for this good work. At the same time, Fr. Titus asked them to make the same contribution every year; otherwise, he considered that he had done only half the job.

A travelling salesman of writing paper and pencils used to come to him, recounting his tale of woe about his family difficulties; Fr. Titus would always buy some materials from him. The Superior General of a religious congregation asked him to look over and complete, if need be, a plan for new Constitutions. Fr. Titus had to make time in order fulfill this task with precision, a task he had taken on voluntarily. A mother asked Fr. Titus for further details about the Patroness of her daughter, Hermieneke, in order to provide a model for her. He immediately responded to her request, even though he was busy with many other things. While he was visiting the Sisters of Rijkevoort, he heard that the sisters who worked in the laundry room needed snap-on buttons. Fr. Titus remarked: "All right; I'll take care of that," and he did.

Fr. Titus would never refuse help. Even when the matter was not to his liking, he was equally prompt in the aid he provided. An old, rather eccentric lady used to visit him, talking to him about her material difficulties and other preoccupations. Fr. Titus obtained a subsidy for her from Social Services; he patiently heard her out about her other worries, although it took a lot of his time. On occasion, when Fr. Titus was out, I spoke to the woman, and later told him that I could not understand how he could take up his precious time patiently listening to those interminable tales about insignificant troubles. "If I were you, I would have shown her the door long ago." Fr. Titus replied: "But she's only a poor old lady; otherwise she'd have no one to pay attention to her." The limitless availability of Fr. Titus became well-known. As Prior he used to tell us, "We should do all we can to make our love of neighbor proverbial;" this is practically what happened to him.

Despite his many commitments, when his help was requested, he never gave the impression of being badgered, or of losing too much time. On the contrary, he gave the impression that he had nothing else on his mind and that he was glad to give the help requested of him.

He wrote letters to help others find a job. Religious and priests asked Fr. Titus to help them get transferred when this was necessary for their vocation or for perseverance in it. In these cases he used to write to Bishops abroad and even was ready to go abroad to make a personal appeal in their favor.

Once two youngsters came asking him for a plan to make a bicycle trip as a pilgrimage to Lourdes. Although Fr. Titus obviously had no personal experience in the matter, he drew up a detailed itinerary for them, pointing out the best places in Belgium and France. This certainly must have cost him much time.

He never wasted a moment of time. In my opinion, in certain cases he could have limited himself in order to dedicate himself to his other duties the better. This can be explained by the fact that he maintained that it was more important to do an act of charity, or rather that he believed that he could do one and the other (*Processus*, n. 87-88).

He did the same for the jounalists. "He helped jounalists in person, acting as an intermediary, and looking for a job for them when they were out of work. He also offered aid when they were in financial straits" (Louis Frequin, *Summ.* 88).

Fr. Titus continued on the same path in prison and in the concentration camps. His help was primarily in the spiritual sphere, although spiritual ministry was forbidden with strict sanctions. While everyone was suffering severe hunger pangs, he secretly used to share his ration with others. "He was very detached; for example, he once gave me a portion of his all-too-meager rations, because he realized I was very hungry" (Theodore van Mierlo, *Summ.*, n. 78b). "He was not one who gobbled up his food; on the contrary, he even gave away some of his own portion" (Cornelis de Graaf. *Summ.*, n. 107). "When he had to go to Dachau, I gave him a so-called traveler's packet of food, and he immediately gave it away to a hungry fellow prisoner" (Henry van Nieuwenhoven, *Summ.*, n. 52a).

In Dachau: "Even though our portion of bread was very small, more than once I saw Titus give his away to a hungry companion, with the comment, 'Here you go, my friend, eat it, you need it more than I.' He also often gave away his soup bowl; he would drink the water, but then give away the beets or carrots that were in it" (Raphael Tijhuis, *Summ.* p. 357). And even during the last week of his life, in the hospital: "The other prisoners often came to blows over a piece of bread; the Servant of God gave some of his bread away to others" (Tizia, n. 118).

He paid special attention to the sick (B. Tiecke, n. 90). "He took care of the sick in the barracks; he comforted them and was of service to them, even though he needed help more than others" (John Aalders, n. 90). "Even when he himself was ill, he took care of the other sick men. He would heat up stones on the stove and place them by their frozen feet, he arranged their so-called pillows, he would tuck in their blankets, bring them water, recite evening prayers with them, without any distinction of persons or of religion. He showed a real motherly care for the sick" (Leo Siegmund, *Summ.*, n. 90). "Regularly (twice a day) he paid a visit to the sick bay, even though for a period this was strictly forbidden; he was always successful in entering" (T. van Mierlo, *Summ.*, n. 90).

Characteristics of his charity

In his hymn on love St. Paul writes: "Love is patient, is kind; love is not jealous, nor vain; it is not puffed up; it is not lacking in respect; it does not see its own interests; it is not irascible; it does not keep an account of evils inflicted; it does not take delight in injustice, but rather in the truth" (*1 Cor* 13: 4-5).

In the description of Fr. Titus' charity, these characteristics have been evident.

Fr. Titus was "kind, courteous and hospitable; perhaps a little too much so," says his brother (*Summ.*, n. 89). "He was always affable," is the witness of the domestic helper at the Pensione where Fr. Titus resided during his first four years at Nijmegen. "He was exceptionally affable with the students" (Christine Mohrmann, *Summ.*, n. 80). "I think 'kindness' is the way to describe his basic attitude in life" (Hendricus Aukes, *Summ.*, n. 64c). "He was exceptionally courteous and affable; he had a kindly smile for everyone" (L. Frequin, *Proc.*, n. 90). "He was courteous with everyone, even with non-Catholics... even with members of the Gestapo" (Peter Verhulst, *Summ.*, n. 89, 91).

His courtesy was not the condescending type. He would always greet the novices with a courteous bow, while the other fathers and the master generally treated them like a sergeant with new recruits for the army. "The way in which he welcomed everyone with a heart-felt and understanding smile warmed up icy souls" (Anne Fogteloo, *Summ.*, p. 259). "He exuded an affability that won over even his enemies. He knew how to win over people with his affable candor, or I would call it, his limitless goodness" (J. van de Mortel, *Summ.*, p. 520). During his last days in the Camp Hospital, "Fr. Titus was always kind and cordial even with the doctor" (Tizia, n. 56b), the doctor who killed him.

Love for his enemies

Jesus extended love of neighbor to love for one's enemies: "But I say to you: love your enemies and pray for those who persecute you, because you will then be sons of your heavenly Father, who makes the sun shine on the good and evil, who makes it rain on the just and on the unjust" (*Mt* 5: 44-45).

Christ died for sinners, "enemies of God," so that they might be converted and become friends and brothers. This is why Fr. Titus could at times be indignant: "The Lord has forgiven everything; what is it that people still have to talk about!" (Gatske de Boer Brandsma, *Summ.*, n. 91a).

Before the War Fr. Titus had no personal enemies. "After the occupation of Holland by the Germans, he accepted this injustice with more resignation than his confreres" (C. Verhallen, *Summ.*, n. 91a). During the Nazi occupation not only were the nation and fundamental human rights trampled on, but also the Church and religion were persecuted. Anyone who lived through this experience knows how difficult it is not to give vent to one's feelings. "In the case of Fr. Titus, I never heard a harsh word, not even about the Gestapo" (Verhulst, *Summ.*, n. 60b).

"I never heard him speak with the minimum of disdain for the Germans and for the camp guards. He had no harsh words even for his enemies" (van Mierlo, *Summ.* n. 91). "He never showed feelings of revenge or hatred towards the guards or towards the Germans. About the Gestapo, he said they were in the service of Himmler and had to follow his orders. Even about Himmler, for instance, he would say that even though he was obsessed with German instincts, still he was a human being" (de Graaf, *Summ.*, n. 61a). "I never heard him inveigh against the Germans. He would get much less riled

163

about the Occupation than other people did. Leaving aside his attitude on questions of principle, Fr. Titus' conduct towards the occupation authorities was very correct" (Verhallen, *Summ.*, n. 58, 59b).

But he showed his love for his enemies above all by praying for them and by forgiving them. All the witnesses are in agreement on this point.

> He used to pray for the enemies of his nation: "he used to pray for his enemies and for his executioners; "he was ready to forgive and he never spoke badly about others:" "he was disposed to forgive them and considered them as people who had been led on the wrong path;" "from my talks with him, it was obvious that he did not exclude them from his prayers." "He was always ready to forgive and he pointed out occasions when I used too harsh expressions about the guards." "Once when the guards had yelled at him very rudely, I said to him, 'Ah well, Father, it's been a bad morning.' He smiled and said, 'Lord, forgive them because they know not what they do.'" "He urged us to forgive and to pray for them. He was big-hearted in his pardon." "How many times he prayed the Rosary (on his fingers) precisely for those who were persecuting him. 'We want to pray for them,' he would say." "He willingly forgave all those who had harmed him in any way." "He forgave his executioners and his guards, he used to pray for them and he also invited us to pray for them."

Fr. Titus remained true to himself in his rapport with the nurse who administered him the fatal injection in the Dachau camp hospital. "I immediately noted that he had great compassion for me. He was very clement even though he knew that we—the doctor and I—controlled his life and death. The Servant of God had a great deal of compassion for me. Once he took me by the hand and said, 'What an unfortunate girl you are; I will pray for you'" (n. 56a, b).

Greatest love

"No one has greater love than this: to give one's life for one's friends" (*Jn* 15: 13). "He gave his life

164

for us, so we too should give our lives for our brothers" (*1 Jn* 3: 17).

In 1947, when the first notable biography of Fr. Titus was published by H. Aukes, in which his many activities were described, the Carmelites said, "He was one of us!" Nijmegen University declared: "He was ours." Frisians said, "Ours." A journalist wrote "But he gave his life for us."

In fact, when Fr. Titus undertook his dangerous mission regarding the Catholic press, he did so as Church advisor, responsible for the Christian conscience of his friends, the journalists. Even in Amersfoort Camp and Kleve Prison, when certain death was a definite alternative, he declared that he was ready to do it again, if it were necessary.

With these convictions, after the example of Christ himself, Fr. Titus suffered "the slow martyrdom" of concentration camps for his friends, for journalists.

Translated by Redemptus Maria Valabek, O. Carm.

3

SIMPLICITY

Adrianus Staring, O. Carm.

It's not an easy task to write about simplicity: it seems that a lot of effort is required to be a simple person. In a beatification process when the virtues are discussed, they are generally divided into the traditional scheme: the theological virtues: faith, hope and charity; the cardinal virtues: prudence, justice, temperance and fortitude. Under which virtues should we put simplicity? St. Thomas Aquinas places it along with truth, i.e. with a virtue akin to justice (S. Th. II-II, 109). Perhaps we could also place it along with temperance as a virtue akin to humility.

Simplicity is a characteristic of a person—it is a part of his character.

We can describe simplicity as an absence of complexity; in a moral context it is contrasted with duplicity or hypocrisy.

The simplicity of Titus Brandsma in the testimonies of the beatification process

In the diocesan process of beatification there was a global question on the virtues of Fr. Titus: "How did the Servant of God strive for perfection? and, "Which of his virtues do you consider most outstanding?" (*Summ.* q. 64 *a* and *c*, p. 11). Practically all the witnesses mention, among other virtues, his simplicity. The well-known Latinist Professor Christine Mohrmann states: "In that he was devoid of complications and simple to the utmost" (Int. 76). Bishop Huibers: "His efforts in everything he did were in the most simple manner possible, spontaneous, natural and disinterested" (Int. 88, p. 244). His brother Fr. H. Brandsma testifies:

> He was extraordinarily simple. He always remained simple, even when, later on, he occupied a superior position. His extraordinary simplicity... struck the Carmelite Sisters at Drachten. They always said, 'How simple this man is!' He didn't feel lost in the highest social circles but was very simple with simple people. He knew how to be simple with simple people and cultured with cultured people (*Summ.*, Int. 78, p. 43).

Fr. R. Gooijer, O. Carm: "Once after having met him here in the Carmel of Nijmegen, my parents said: 'One wouldn't guess that he was a university professor'" (Int. 106).

Others say: "He was always simple" (F. Haagen, O. Carm., Int. 105). "He was very simple. His simplicity was surprising. He was fascinating even for his adversaries" (P. Verhulst, Int. 105c and 106). "The incredible charm of his personality lay in his great natural and genuine simplicity" (T. van Mierlo, Int. 106). Fr. J. Aalders who was with Fr. Titus in the camp at Amersfoort says, "I was always struck by his simplicity: he never used learned words. Everything in him was simple and without any ostentation and for this reason people took him to be a very common man, whereas in reality he was extraordinarily far from being common. Titus' simplicity was extraordinary, but one had to be aware of it. His transparent simplicity bore the stamp of truth" (*Summ.* p. 287 and 292). Doctor P. Ronge: "He was simple in all things. There was no pretence about him" (*Ibid.* Int. 106, p. 300). Professor J. Borst: "Without exhibition, simple, modest" (Int. 64, p. 314). C. de Graaf, a Protestant prison mate, testifies: "In my opinion his most outstanding virtue was simplicity" (Int. 64, p. 314). Another prison mate, H. van Nieuwenhoven: "One thing he absolutely wasn't, was haughty. He didn't attract attention as being a professor" (Int. 105b, p. 328). The prison chaplain

L. Deimal says: "His manner of speaking and his behavior were natural; there was nothing affected about him" (Ibid. 106, p. 337). His prison mate at Kleve, R. de Groot: "He wasn't at all haughty. I found out he was a professor from the other prisoners. He was simple, without affectation and affable with everyone" (Int. 105b and 106, p. 343). Br. Raphael Tijhuis: "His most notable virtue was his simplicity and his readiness to pardon. He spoke to me and the others with a lot of simplicity. At Dachau too, he spoke with everyone without showing off his culture and didn't even use difficult words" (Int. 64c and 105b).

Fr. O. Lips, O.F.M. Cap., says: "The general opinion was that he was very simple in his behavior" (Int. 106, p. 376). Fr. H. Kuyper: "More than anything, his simplicity was extraordinary; he never let himself be influenced by the conditions in which he was compelled to live. Very self-possessed and simple, he was full of courage" (Int. 64, p. 382).

Simplicity in relations with other people

Simplicity is seen first of all in relations with other people: in his dealings with his neighbours we can see no self-interest, affectation or hidden motives but rather disregard for himself. Simplicity is especially seen in relations with people who are themselves simple or come from a humble social condition.

Many witnesses connect Fr. Titus' simplicity with his goodness. His sister says: "His goodness, his simplicity in his relationships with other people. He was simple with everyone, with our staff too." (G. de Beer, Int. 64c, p. 31; 106, p. 35). His brother Henry Brandsma: "Helpfulness and simplicity. He didn't feel lost in the highest social circles but he was very simple with simple people. He knew how to be simple with simple people and cultured with cultured people" (Int. 64 and 78a, p. 43). Others say: "He was always simple, always affable" (A. Kersten, Int. 64). "The Servant of God sought after perfection in simplicity and in cordiality with his neighbour,"

(Dott. Woltring, Int. 64). "Professor McGuire of the Catholic University of Washington replies that 'Titus gave him the impression of being an extraordinarily good, simple and kind person'" (C. Mohrmann, Int. 121b, p. 77).

"The Servant of God sought after perfection in simplicity and in goodness" (J. S. van Rooij, O. Carm., Int. 64a). "He was exceptionally good with everyone... and he was also very simple" (J. Pelgrim, O. Carm., Int. 64c). Professor Rutten: "In his relationships with other people he was always simple. Even when speaking he was very simple and not haughty" (Int. 105). Professor C. Bellon: "His goodness, his simplicity and his helpfulness. He was simple in himself and in his relations with other people" (Int. 64c and 106). His confrère M. Arts: "As regards people: his great love for his neighbour, his goodness and his simplicity" (Int. 64c). Bishop M. Jansen: "More than anything else I was struck by his simplicity and his readiness to help out" (Int. 64 etc.). His prior, C. Verhallen, states: "He was simple in his relations with other people, he never spoke with a haughty air and he established cordial relations even with the most simple people. As I've heard it from others, his simplicity lay in the fact that he greeted even the poorest people. He chatted spontaneously with the domestic staff in the University" (Int. 105b and 106b). H. Aukes says the same thing: "In his relations with me—I was an assistant in the University Library—he was always very simple. He had a generous nature, simple and full of understanding for other people" (Int. 105 and 106). His confrère F. Haagen: "In all his actions he was extremely normal and simple, ready to help everyone. He was very simple and knew how to get on with everyone" (Int. 64c and 106). Father Gooijer, O. Carm.: "In his relations with others he was very simple. He never hid anything whenever he knew something about the meeting of the Definitory" (Int. 106). "He was simple in his relations with other people as I myself was able to notice when I went to him" (J. de Boer, Int. 106, p. 203). "In his relations with other people he was simple. He was always cordial, simple and correct in his relations with other people" (G. Bodewes, Int. 106 and 109).

In the concentration camp Fr. Titus remained the same. "He was simplicity personified. In the sick-hut he was just as cordial with the ill-treated occupants of the wagons from Limburg as with the others" (A. van Mierlo, Int. 105b, p. 275). His companion L. Siegmund: "He knew how to get on even with illiterate people and there was nothing 'put on' in his words and conversations" (Int. 106, p. 314). His cell-mate C. de Graaf: "He was simple and relaxed in his relations with his neighbour" (Int. 106, p. 319). H. van Nieuwenhoven, another prison companion: "He was very simple in his dealings with other people and he was very relaxed with everyone" (Int. 105b, p. 328).

At Dachau too, Fr. Titus appeared the same. Fr. O. Lips, O.F.M. Cap., says: "He was simple in his relations with other people" (Int. 105c, p. 376). Fr. J. Rothkrans: "He was gentle, good and truly simple. He wasn't at all haughty, but very simple in his relations with others" (Int. 64 etc., p. 390).

Simplicity and modesty

Some witnesses see a connection between Fr. Titus' simplicity and his modesty or humility. It's obvious that a proud or vain person cannot be simple.

Fr. Titus' brother, Fr. H. Brandsma, O.F.M., says: "His humility is a result of his simplicity" (Int. 105, p. 44). Colonel A. S. Fogteloo: "Very gentle, modest and simple" (Int. 64 ecc., p. 260). Professor Borst: "Devoid of exhibitionism, simple, modest. He was a remarkably modest man" (Int. 64 and 78a). And in the camp at Dachau the parish priest J. Lemmens: "He was simple and humble. He had absolutely no airs" (Int. 64 ecc., p. 371). The parish priest H. Kuyper noticed the same thing in the camp at Dachau: "He was modest and exceptionally simple: he didn't do anything to draw attention to himself" (Int. 64 ecc., 883).

When his sister, Maria, a Poor Clare nun at Megen, asked Fr. Titus:

> Reverend brother, what must I do to become perfect? he always replied, "Carry out your duties punctually every day, even in the smallest things. Oh! This is so simple! Follow Our Lord like a little girl and skip about behind Jesus; leave all your troubles to Him: in this way you are doing enough, this is perfection, don't tire yourself out, give yourself up instead (*Proc. dioc.*, doc. 12).

Doctor B. Woltring says: "As I've already said, he was very simple and ingenuous and in all of his actions he demonstrated that he wanted to follow the Will of God" (Int. 93a). Professor C. Mohrmann: "He sought after perfection... with a very sincere devotion—sometimes even like a young boy" (Int. 64a, p. 75). And his prison companion C. de Graaf: "Important as he was, he always felt small and modest" (Int. 78a, p. 328). His confrère M. Arts says: "Generally speaking the Servant of God was always in the same happy mood. He displayed a youthful simplicity and joy and stimulated others to have the same confidence in God" (Int. 76).

Simplicity and the Little Way

Our Lord told us: "Be cunning as serpents and yet as harmless as doves" (Mt. 10:16). Certainly Jesus was not recommending deceit, which is the opposite of simplicity, nor what the manuals termed "carnal prudence." But Jesus also said: "Anyone who does not welcome the Kingdom of God like a little child, will never enter it" (Lk. 18:17). Jesus is not recommending just any kind of ingenuousness, nor childishness, but the trusting simplicity of a child.

In the Middle Ages we come across the term: "*simplex idiota*": the word "*idiota*" means: illiterate or unlettered. But even an illiterate person can be very crafty and cunning. Simplicity is naturally more striking in a university professor. Professor Mohrmann says: "My initial judgement on the first lesson he gave at the university was that here we're

dealing with a man who has accepted an appointment, in all simplicity and humility, which he himself
considered very difficult" (Int. 15).

Simplicity of intention

Simplicity is seen in words and acts but these are
manifestations of the interior life. A simple person
seeks the direct way in his interior life—proper intention and no complications. He seeks after God in
everything with an undivided heart and is open to
grace. From the external manifestations we can dis-
cern the intention, as Fr. Titus' confrère A. van der
Staaij has done: "He was simple in his intentions and
in his relations with others" (Int. 106, p. 54). His
confrère J. S. van Rooij says: "He was very simple in
his intentions and his relations with others" (Int.
106). His prior, Fr. C. Verhallen: "He was simple in
his intentions and completely disinterested" (Int.
106). His companion in the camp at Amersfoort, L.
Siegmund, says the same thing: "He was very simple
in his intentions and in his relations with his neighbour" (Int. 106, p. 314).

We pointed out at the beginning of this article
that the system of virtues seems a very complicated
thing, but simplicity reduces everything to a unity. A
simple person is the opposite of a fanatic who has but
one determined aim and sacrifices all the other aspects of life for that aim. Simplicity, on the other
hand is connected to all the other virtues—above all
to charity, as we have seen above in Fr. Titus' simplicity in his relations with other people. It is charity that forms the unity of all the virtues.

Translated by Paul O'Brien, O. Carm.

4
JOY

Adrianus Staring, O. Carm.

"Joy is not a virtue; it is an effect of love."
— Titus Brandsma, *Notes for a Retreat.*

A French proverb has it: "A sad saint is an unlikely saint." As a child, Titus Brandsma's health was very precarious. Four times he suffered stomach hemorrhages; as a result he was twice at death's door. In the final years of his life he was afflicted with various serious sicknesses. Usually stomach sufferers become hypochondriacs; none of this for Titus Brandsma. Many witnesses attest to this. His sister says: "During his illness he was always happy and in good humor" (*Summarium* I, p. 33). While studying in Rome he also hemorrhaged. His fellow student, Fr. Louis van der Staaij asserted: "In Rome he was a very happy patient and spoke as normal" (*Summ.*, I, p. 48). His friend Fr. Alberto Grammatico put it: "He would smile at me serenely, like a saint" (F. Vallainc, *Un giornalista martire*, p. 66).

"He had self-control not only in daily life, but also in sickness and in physical suffering. Even then he showed good humor" (*Summarium*, I, p. 203). A fellow Carmelite affirmed: "Even when faced with failure and opposition, he remained joyful and serene" (*Ibid.* p. 65).

In his daily life, people always found him the same. Professor Christine Mohrmann asserts: "This gratitude for the faith revealed itself in a constant joyfulness" (*Processus*, n. 66). "He was always in good humor; he was cordial and spontaneous" (*Ibid*). "He was always in good humor" (*Ibid.*, n. 77). Joseph de Boer left this testimony: "I was particularly struck by his joy. His gratitude for the faith revealed itself in a great joy, even though by nature he did not possess a very happy and witty character" (*Summarium*, p. 100). Bishop Martin Jansen has this to say: "Above all his great joy and his incredible optimism" (*Processus*, n. 116).

Fr. Titus' joy revealed itself particularly in his cordiality and affability. "He was always cordial and kind when we visited him. He was cordial, spontaneous and very simple" (*Summarium*, p. 34: G. de Boer). "The Servant of God sought for perfection in simplicity and in cordiality with his neighbor" (*Processus*, n. 64a: Bernard Woltring). "He was always affable" (*Ibid.*, n. 64: Anna Kersten). "He was exceptionally affable and courteous" (*Ibid.*, n. 89: Florentius Haagen, O. Carm.). "His outstanding virtue was his amiability" (*Ibid.*, n. 64c: Raphael Gooijer, O. Carm.).

Fr. Titus' biographer, H. Aukes, paints the following portrait of Fr. Titus: "Above all I consider him a man of Gospel spirituality: joyful, loyal, charitable... It seems to me that 'benignity' is the expression that describes his approach to life. He reminds us of the first Frisian Saint, Ludger, whose second *Life* depicts him thus: 'Pleasant in his ways and with outstanding humanity, making his teaching acceptable everywhere'" (*Summarium*, p. 150-151).

Joy in prison

All the above-cited testimonies related to Fr. Titus' life before his martyrdom. But such joy and happiness characterized Fr. Titus during the six months of imprisonment and life in the concentration camps as well.

A Protestant Colonel, A. F. Fogteloo, who was with Fr. Titus in the prison of Scheveningen and in the concentration camp at Amersfoort, first described the harsh conditions of prison life, and then continues: "I was greatly amazed when the door of Brandsma's cell would open, to find a happy man inside. His whole face was radiant; his grateful and kindly gaze struck me with particular force. I always saw him in radiant humor" (*Ibid.*, p. 258). Giving an over-all view of his behavior in both prison and Amersfoort concentration camp, he expressed himself so:

> What was most noticable was his goodness, his meekness, his radiant face. When someone, in such surroundings, is like him, he must be a man spiritually out of the ordinary. His eyes were extremely gentle; he had great joy. He was very well mannered, given his priestly formation and his delicacy of character. The way in which he greeted anyone who came to him, with a cordial and understanding smile, provided new warmth to frozen souls (*Ibid.*, p. 257).

Another companion said: "With regard to his stay in Scheveningen, I can testify that the Servant of God always had a very joyful and contented attitude" (*Ibid.*, p. 262: P. Verhulst).

The same witness recalled Fr. Titus' behavior at the Amersfoort concentration camp (March 12 - April 28, 1942): "He was always content; I never heard him grumble or complain" (*Ibid.*, p. 264). All the prisoners agreed on this point: "The Servant of God always had the same good humor and never talked about himself. As a good Catholic, Titus had a natural and sincere joy about him" (*Ibid.*, p. 270, 271). The priest, Fr. Aalders, stated: "His appearance too witnessed to his intimate joy, as I myself was able to verify. He was the most affable man in the camp and accessible to everyone" (*Ibid.*, 285-286). "During that fleeting greeting, he would be smiling and was very happy. Behind the large lenses of his glasses, his eyes were sparkling, full of goodness, cordiality, merriment. He retained this serene amiability the whole time he stayed in Amersfoort." A Lutheran doctor, P. Ronge testified: "His tranquillity was plain to see. He was always in good humor" (*Ibid.*, p. 298). A doctor without any religion stated: "In all circumstances, he preserved a joyous tranquillity" (*Ibid.*, p. 304: J. Borst). Another fellow prisoner commented:

He was grateful for his faith and for his vocation. I deduce this from the fact that he was always happy and in good humor, and I never noted a single sign to the contrary. He was always happy and in good humor. He gave a more supernatural meaning to our imprisonment" (*Ibid.*, p. 310-311: J. Siegmund).

That Fr. Titus had his difficult moments was not lost on his companion Jan van de Mortel:

He was never in bad humor, was very balanced, he did not pose difficulties for others. Physically he suffered greatly because of the harsh life of the Camp and because of the inhuman treatment. He tried to hide it, but many times he was intensely sad. Not for himself, but because men were doing this to one another. His humor remained stable. Actually, he became more meek rather than more severe. He remained an optimist (*Summarium* II, p. 521).

The same in the prison at Scheveningen (April 28 - May 16, 1942), where Fr. Titus shared a cell with two Protestant young men: "He was grateful for his faith and was content" (*Summarium* I, p. 320).

It was the joy which shone on the face of Father Titus that impressed the guards and myself too. He was always in good humor and full of interest for the other prisoners. I was struck most by his serenity and joyfulness, his modesty and his goodness. His joy always made the deepest impression on me. He knew quite well that he would never regain his freedom, but he was resigned and at times even content (*Ibid.*, p. 325-327).

In the prison of Kleve, Germany, where Fr. Titus waited for his transfer to Dachau (May 16 - June 13, 1942), he remained the same. The prison chaplain, Ludwig Deimel testified:

His attitude was calm, serene, joyful and kind. That merriment and that patience did not demand an effort on his part. During his stay at Kleve, when all the attempts to free him from prison failed, he did not show the least sign of delusion, of discouragement, of depression or of desperation. He remained serene, merry and full of trust in God" (*Ibid.*, p. 325-327).

And a Dutch fellow prisoner testified:

> He was always in good humor, content and full of resignation, to an extent that I thought: 'If that man is not a saint, no one is.' The most notable virtues in him were joy and the spirit of prayer. His gratitude for the faith revealed itself in the fact that he was happy to be able to undergo all those sufferings for Our Lord. More than once I heard him say: 'We are in God's hands.' He was always happy and in good humor (*Ibid.*, p. 341-342; R. de Groot).

In Dachau: June 19 - July 26, 1942

In the concentration camp of Dachau, Fr. Titus met Brother Raphael Tijhuis, O. Carm. Even in those circumstances, Fr. Titus still could be in good humor:

> If anyone asked him whether he had been beaten, he would answer smiling: 'For that fellow beating seems to signify his morning prayer.' When I had finished (tending to his swollen feet) and helped him to get up, he would tap me on the shoulder with a smile and say to me: 'Now, Brother, I'm a gentleman again.' His gratitude for the faith was evident in his constant joy and merriment. I never saw him angry or in tears, notwithstanding the terrible treatment he had to cope with. He was always merry and in good humor" (*Ibid.*, p. 356, 362, 364).

His fellow prisoners are in agreement: "He was always merry and in good humor" (*Ibid.*, p. 370: Rev. J. Lemmens). "I never heard him complain. He was always merry and in good humor and was a support for the others" (*Ibid.*, p. 372: the Capuchin O. Lips). "However, he was always in good humor, balanced and merry, full of internal tranquillity and of equilibrium. He was serene, balanced, merry and in good humor, full of spiritual serenity. He had a sense of humor; he was a mild joker" (*Ibid.*, p. 382,

177

383: Rev. H. Kuyper). "But he was always in good humor and always happy. His trust in God was revealed in his joyfulness, in his good humor and in his wonderful patience and tolerance" (*Ibid.*, p. 390: Rev. J. Rothkrans). J. Overduin, a Protestant minister, attested: "I still can see Professor Brandsma. our sincerely dedicated brother in Christ, as he was in the bathhouse for the last time. Tired out and exhausted in body, emaciated, with his legs puffed up with water, but strong in spirit, always kind and joyous in the Lord" (*Ibid.*, II, p. 546).

Even during the last week of his life, in the camp hospital, he remained calm and serene, as witnessed by the nurse who administered the fatal injection to him: "He was always happy. For the greater part, sick prisoners were preoccupied with themselves and thought only of themselves, but the Servant of God was always in good spirits and was a support to everyone, and particularly to me" (*Fasciculus riservatus*, p. 5, n. 61, 62b).

Joy in the writings of Fr. Titus

This joy in suffering already appears on the pages of his diary written during the first week of his detention in Scheveningen prison (January 23 - 28, 1942):

There exists a contrast in principles, but to defend them, with joy I will suffer whatever is necessary. My vocation for the Church and my priesthood have enriched me with many pleasant and joyful things; willingly do I accept everything that might appear unpleasant. O blessed solitude, I feel at home in this cell. Up to now, I have not been bored, quite the contrary. I feel like shouting for joy because again He in his fulness has allowed me to find him, without my being able to go to men, nor men come to me. He is my one refuge; I feel protected and happy. I will remain here always, if He wills it so. Rarely have I been so happy and content" (*Summarium* II, p. 500, 504).

In his well-known poem of February 12-13, 1942, he could write:

> A cup of sorrow I foresee,
> Which I accept for love of Thee,
> Thy painful way I wish to go:
> The only way to God I know.

In the first letter he wrote from prison, written on February 12, 1942, he explained: "I am very calm, happy and content and I become used to things. Please let Dr. de Jong (the Archbishop of Utrecht) know that he should not be concerned nor go to any trouble over me. I suffer here with joy and I am well" (*Ibid.*, 511-512). On March 5, he wrote: "I don't have to cry, I even sing a bit in my own way, and naturally not too loudly" (*Ibid.*, p. 513-514).

The secret of his joy

In some people to rejoice in suffering could be a masochistic tendency; from the above citations it is clear that in Fr. Titus was a question of something entirely different. Fr. Titus accepted sufferings, he did not seek them out: he accepted them from the hands of God for another purpose. In the poem he wrote in Scheveningen prison he turned his gaze on Jesus:

> My soul is full of peace and light:
> Although in pain, this light shines bright.
> For here Thou keepest to Thy breast
> My longing heart, to find there rest.

His joy derived from his love for Christ, who suffered out of love for us. This is how he consoled his fellow prisoners: "This is only a trifle compared to what Our Lord suffered for us. What we suffer is merely a trifle when compared to what Christ suffered for us" (*Summarium* I, p. 340, 342: R. De Groot). "Our Lord suffered more for me" (*Ibid.*, p. 363: R. Tijhuis).

God's love for us was expressed in the Passion of Christ because of our sins. Our love for God is expressed in our love for our neighbor, even of our enemies, even of sinners, and in bearing all sufferings in union with the Passion of Christ. Joy does not derive from the suffering, but from love itself. This was the reason for the joy and happiness which Fr. Titus always showed his neighbor, the reason for his cordiality and affability even towards his enemies and towards the harsh guards. "He was the most affable man in the whole camp and accessible to everyone. He was the most amiable man towards everyone in the camp. He did not speak ill of the Germans" (*Ibid.*, p. 286, 284: Rev. J. Aalders). "At Amersfoort he was deemed the most amiable man in the camp" (*Ibid.*, p. 153: H. Aukes).

The reason for his joy Fr. Titus had expressed in some of his writings:

The folly of the cross. Our love should be proverbial. We should not allow anyone to surpass us in love. This is the first, the supreme, the divine virtue. Our model is Christ, bleeding with his thousand wounds on the cross. The person who wishes to conquer the world for superior ideals, has to have the courage to engage in battle with it. In the end, the world follows the person who has the courage—despite the world—to do what it doesn't dare do on its own. But the battle with the world is hard: it led to Christ's death on the cross" (*Notes for a Retreat*).

Consider life as a Way of the Cross, but take the cross on your shoulders with joy and courage, because by his example and by his grace Jesus made it light" (*Ibid*).

Let us follow Jesus on the royal road of the cross. Let us carry his cross, not unwillingly as did Simon of Cyrene, but with joy and gladness, because we are royal sons" (*Via crucis*).

Don't serve God with sighs. Let it be apparent with gladness and good spirits that it is true that 'my yoke is pleasant and my burden light.' Show a glad face; see sorrow in a higher light, in which it becomes something choice and a reason for joy. Joy is not a virtue, but an effect of love" (*Notes for a Retreat*).

From crib till the cross, suffering was Christ's lot, as well as poverty and misunderstanding. The thrust of his whole life was to teach men how God values suffering, poverty and the misconceptions of men, just the opposite of the false wisdom of the world. Suffering is the road to heaven. Ah, if we just had, even today, the awareness of the value which God enclosed for us in the suffering that He sends us, He who is infinitely good! (*Introduction* to the book *Het lijden vergoddelijkt* of A. A. Tanqueray).

On Good Friday, 1942, in the Camp at Amersfoort, Fr. Titus gave a conference on the mysticism of the Passion which left a lasting impression. In the brief notes he had prepared we read: "On this day: a glad and grateful attitude with a living representation of the Passion of Christ in union with our suffering. God for us, God with us, our example. God in us, our strength. I can do all things in Him who comforts me" (H. Aukes, *Het leven van Titus Brandsma*, p. 240-241).

The priest, J. Aalders, left a description of the conference:

> After an instructive presentation, Titus began to speak of other, very deep arguments, which moved our hearts. The conference became—and it couldn't be otherwise on Good Firday—a meditation on the Passion of Christ, of which his heart was full. 'Heart speaks to heart:' there, heart touched heart. The words sprang up spontaneously in his heart from the love for his Savior which burned there and they hit the mark. You could hear a pin drop in the barracks. Even the Communists were listening with interest. Had love ever been preached to them with so much ardent conviction? (*Summarium*, p. 293-294).

During the last days of his life, spent in Dachau's hospital ward, the nurse who gave him the *coup de grace* injection stated that the majority of priests were not worth anything. Fr. Titus "replied with a saying of St. Teresa, that the best priests are not always those who are in the pulpits and who deliver the most beautiful sermons, but that the best priests are those who have to suffer and who offer their sufferings for sinners. He added that he was content to be able to suffer" (*Fasc. riservatus*, p. 4, n. 60b).

Many people maintain that Fr. Titus Brandsma was not only an expert on the history and doctrine of mysticism, but that he himself knew the mystical life and the delights of mystical union by personal experience (cf. A. Staring, *Titus Brandsma and the Mysticism of the Passion*, in *Carmelus*, 28 [1981], p. 213-225). Here too he has something to say:

> Too many persons rather dream of a mysticism full of pleasantness and blessed quiet, without thinking that God seeks our union on the road of suffering, of scorn and of death. True mysticism leads to Calvary, finally to rest in approaching death on the bleeding Heart of Jesus in the embrace of the cross (*Introduction* to *Brieven en extasen der Dienaresse Gods Gemma Galgani*, by P. Bonifacius, C. P.)

Through all of his life, the model for Fr. Titus, Carmelite that he was, was the Blessed Virgin Mary.

> As sons of Mary with the desire to be conformed to her and in this way to become conformed to God, we are impelled towards God as she was. With her we stand at the foot of the cross to share in the sacrificial death of the Lord, and to keep living, while dead to ourselves and to the world, in the company of our Mother, led and helped by her, solely in God and for God (*Introduction* to *Carmellicht* by John of St. Samson).

In his Last Will he wrote: "In death I unite myself to the death of my Redeemer and I place myself with Mary at the foot of cross of my Lord. Forever will I sing the mercies of the Lord" (*Diocesan Process*, doc. 9).

The whole meaning of man's suffering was summarized by Fr. Titus in a simple sentence, which was part of a community Chapter talk: "We were created for Joy!"

Translated by Redemptus Maria Valabek, O. Carm.

5

MARY AND OURSELVES: GOD-BEARERS

Redemptus Maria Valabek, O. Carm.

Great people have a knack of appreciating the small, simple, beautiful things, taken for granted by others. Holy picture cards are used as book markers by even ardent students of the spiritual life. Truly holy people see them as occasions of grace. St. Therese as she lay on her deathbed, abandoned by all other consolations and even doubting of heaven's existence, had her favorite holy cards pinned to the curtain around her cot. Fr. Bartholomew Xiberta, even during the celebration of the Divine Office, which meant so much to him, would sneak in a kiss of his favorite image of Mary, which he jealously guarded in his Breviary. Fr. Titus Brandsma, Carmelite martyr in the Nazi concentration camp of Dachau, had no greater joy in prison that that of being able to gaze at an image of Our Lady. His Breviary had not been taken from him when he was interred in Scheveningen prison. "I had no stray holy picture of Our Lady in my Breviary—and surely her image ought to be in a Carmelite's cell. I managed this too. In the part of the Breviary we are now using, and which fortunately was left me, is the beautiful picture of Our Lady of Mt. Carmel. So now my Breviary is standing open on the topmost of the two corner shelves, to the left of the bed... At my table I only have to look a little to my right and I have her image before me. When I am in bed, my eye catches at once the star-bearing Madonna, Hope of all Carmelites" (*My Cell*).

This was no awkward or desperate gesture by the renowned university professor of philosophy and of the history of mysticism. It was his normal, spontaneous reaction. Titus Brandsma's Marian devotion was as unsophisticated as the rest of his life. One of the best known clerics in his native Holland, involved in a prodigious amount of religious initiatives, he never lost the simplicity of approach of his Frisian forebearers. Although he formulated a mysticism of Marian devotion, as we shall see later, far from despising the simple, Catholic forms of Marian devotion, he revelled in them. A tell-tale episode: when taken prisoner, he could not explain to himself how he could have forgotten to transfer his Rosary from his religious habit to the black suit he wore to jail. He considered it a singular grace when a Protestant minister was able to provide him with a Rosary, which witnesses report he always prayed slowly and devoutly.

Until the end, when a deadly injection was administered to him, Titus kept being friendly with his captors. Other prisoners told him to give up. He never ceased speaking kindly to the Nazi guards. On his death-bed, when his body was being used for humiliating experiments by the physicians, Titus noted that the attending nurse was from Holland and a Catholic. "How did you end up here? I shall pray for you a great deal." And he gave her his cherished Rosary. She protested that she could no longer pray. Titus' reply: "Well, if you can't say the first part of the Hail Mary, surely you can still say 'Pray for us sinners'." The nurse tried to be evasive with the comment that there were so many bad priests. Titus, not to be beaten, asked her to look at the sufferings of the imprisoned priests in Dachau. He confessed that he himself was glad to suffer for God's sake. (The nurse, subsequently, returned to the faith.)

Mary in Titus' young years

His trust in the motherly charity of Mary, Titus inherited from his pious mother. Once when he was 11 and his brother Henry 10, both fell ill. The doctor was seriously concerned. The mother invoked

Our Lady with Rosary after Rosary. A distant Carmelite cousin, Fr. Casimir De Boer, was visiting home at the time. The pious and concerned mother with a heart full of confidence in the Mother of us all asked the friar to invest the boys in the Scapular. Henry, who later became a Franciscan, notes that it is impossible to be dogmatic, but in fact the next day, Titus was cured and was able to get out of bed. Regardless of what others thought, he personally felt indebted to the Mother of God. He induced his younger brother to recite the Little Office of Our Lady for a whole month as a token of gratitude.

When it was time for Titus to decide what type of religious life he would join, there again was a Marian connection. He had been educated by the Franciscans, but health-wise he could not keep up. When his cousin, Fr. Casimir, the Carmelite, described how Carmel lived its charism, the two elements which caught Titus' attention were a life of deep prayer and a pronounced Marian devotion. As he was later to formulate, the two were not separate elements, but interpenetrating. The taking of the Carmelite habit on September 1, 1898, was the beginning of a lifelong attachment to Mary's family. For Titus, the habit was not primarily something he put on, but something that Mary in her goodness clothed him with. "We consider the Scapular no longer as a badge which we have put on on our own, but as a royal sign of honor of the Queen of Heaven, as a uniform, a livery with which her chosen servants are clothed" (Leaflet, *Maria*).

The distinctive white cloak of Carmel, which Titus unfailingly wore on the most solemn occasions, made an impression. It was all the more noticed during the year he served as Rector Magnificus of the Catholic University of Nijmegen (1932). Someone noted to Titus that he had believed Carmelites to be humble religious, yet their white cloaks made them stand out at any gathering. Titus had no apology, but only an explanation: "My friend, don't be amazed that I am so happy to wear this cloak. It is a sign of Mary's protection. I have so much trust, actually, certainty in her help!"

For this esteemed professor and organizer, Carmel cannot be imagined without Mary.

> Both superiors and members should help to promote the double spirit of the Order with the cooperation and help of the Order's Patroness, Mary, under whose patronage they should place every work and in whose honor they should sanctify all their labors. The Order is totally Marian not only in name but also in its works; for if it were not Marian it would not be Carmelite.

Philosopher that he was, Titus intuited that what a person does follows on what a person is. So an Order like Carmel, which from its beginning committed itself to the Marian ideal, must also show this inner involvement in its apostolate.

> The contemplation and meditation of the apostolic life of the Redeemer and that of the Co-redemptrix, Our Bl. Virgin Mary, should inflame each one's heart to divine works in the divine task of saving souls.

Although not given to exuberance of rhetoric, Titus could hardly be clearer as to his conviction: the Carmelite vocation is intrinsically bound up with imitation of Mary. In his mature years, while lecturing on the Carmelite charism in the U.S.A, Fr. Brandsma revealed the kernel of his thought. He refers to a "constant" in the medieval Carmelite Credo: the foreshadowing of the Virgin Mary in the cloud which the prophet Elijah spied over the Mediterranean from his Carmel retreat.

> It was on Carmel's summit that the Prophet after sevenfold prayer saw the little cloud—bearer of the rain which would deliver the parched earth. It is not necessary to give an authentic explanation of this vision. Still I may say that many commentators of the Holy Scriptures have seen in this cloud a prototype of the Holy Virgin, who bore in her womb the Redeemer of the world.

The professor then notes that in the Old Testament a cloud was often a symbol of God's descent among men.

186

In the Order this vision of Elijah has always been seen as a prototype of the mystery of the Incarnation and a distant veneration of the Mother of God. And it was because of this belief, according to the tradition of Carmel, that the old sanctuary dedicated to the Holy Maid was built on the mountain and in the midst of the hermits' caves (*The Beauty of Carmel*, p. 32-33).

Fr. Brandsma, then, gives a spiritual meaning to this episode:

In our barrenness and dryness, Mary is the providential cloud which draws redemption to us. Let us greet her. Let us trust in her. With her intercession we are sure of the grace of God. The cloud that she is, she overflows on us with the copious rain. Immeasurably great is the grace of God, much greater than we deserve. We are like the people of Israel. Mary is the Mother of Mercy. 'Hail, holy Queen, and after this our exile show us Jesus.' Banishment, exile are our life without God, or in any case, without intimate union with God... May she always make our eyes be fixed on Jesus (*Ejercicios bíblicos con María para llegar a Jesús*, ed. Cesca, 1978, p. 26).

Professor of the History of Mysticism, Fr. Titus could not be faulted for taking an historical stance towards Carmel's Marian roots. In fact, he makes much of the title Carmelites have had since their origins: "Brothers of the Virgin Mary of Carmel." "Devotion to Mary was intimately allied to their institution, and the name which the neighboring population called them after this sanctuary, stamped the former Crusaders, who laid down their swords on the altar of Mary, as Knights of Our Lady" (*Beauty of Carmel*, p. 59).

Called to be other Marys

But history is only an aid to better understanding Carmel's perennial commitment to Mary. Titus Brandsma categorizes this commitment under three headings: imitation, union, similarity.

We should not think of imitation without thinking of the union, nor of the union without the thought of the imitation. Both flow into each other, but in one period the former is more prominent, in another more attention is paid to the latter. We should rather see both trends blended together into one harmonious whole (*Beauty of Carmel*, p. 63).

In teaching which foreshadows that of Vatican II, Fr. Titus sees Mary to be all that the Church aspires and desires to be. "The *imitation* of Mary, the most elevated of all creatures, set as an example before us by God himself, shows Mary the pattern of all virtues. She is the mirror in which we should ever watch ourselves, the Mother whom her children ought to resemble ever more" (*Ibid.*) This imitation of Mary can be found at the origins of the Order, as attested by the first commentary on the Carmelite Rule, which John Baconthorpe compares to the life of Our Lady (cf. *Carmel in the World* 17 [1978], p. 151-159).

But there is more. Imitation leads to similarity and even to *union*.

If we wish to conform ourselves to Mary in order to enjoy fully the intercourse with God by following her example, we should obviously be other Marys. We ought to let Mary live in us. Mary should not stand outside the Carmelite, but he should live a life so similar to Mary's that he should live with, in, through and for Mary (*Beauty of Carmel*, p. 64-65).

For historical precedents for this Marian vision, Professor Brandsma has recourse to Ven. Michael of St. Augustine in the Carmelite School and St. Grignon de Montfort.

The Dutch Carmelite sees his Order's mission without any identity crisis: it is to produce other Marys. He says this in no sentimental, vague or pietistic sense, but bases himself on the solid theology of the Incarnation itself. Anyone who takes the enfleshing of God in Christ Jesus seriously, sees human dignity reach an unsurpassed apogee in that gesture of God. Mary provided everything human to Christ; if Christ is to be conceived in and for our society there is constant need for "Marys" to give flesh to Christ Jesus. This is the Carmelite vocation.

We should attain *similarity* to Mary, especially in that we recognize her as the highest perfection which human power by the grace of God has attained. This perfection can also be developed in us to a considerable extent, if we reflect ourselves on Mary and unite ourselves to her. This ought to be the aim of our devotion to Mary, that we be another Mother of God, that God should be conceived in us also, and brought forth by us. The mystery of the Incarnation has revealed to us how valuable man is to God, how intimately God wants to be united to man. This mystery draws the attention of our minds to the eternal birth of the Son from the Father as the deepest reason for this mystery of Love (*Beauty of Carmel*, p. 66).

The Liturgy spoke of these profound truths to Fr. Brandsma. Obviously when he left important university meetings, in order to be with his community for the praying of the Divine Office and Rosary—to the point that some colleagues criticized him—this son of Mary opened his heart to the riches which the Liturgy not only represented symbolically, but also perpetuated in a real, mystical manner.

In the celebration of the three Holy Masses on Christmas, the birth from the Father is first celebrated, secondly from the Holy Virgin Mary, thirdly God's birth in ourselves. This is not done without significance, and this threefold birth must be understood to be a revelation of one eternal Love. It should ever be Christmas to us and we should remember that threefold birth as phases of one great process of love. Mary is the daughter of God the Father, Mother of God the Son and Spouse of God the Holy Ghost. In her that threefold birth has been realized. We should learn from her how to realize it in ourselves. We also have been chosen by the Holy Trinity for a dwelling, to share the privileges which we admire in Mary, but which God is willing to bestow on us also (*Beauty of Carmel*, p. 66-67).

Marian and mystical dimensions

Carmelites, then, are to prolong in the Church what God had so admirably worked in Our Lady. As members of her family, as bearers of her distinctive

189

garb, they have no higher calling than to provide a fresh possibility for Christ Jesus to enter the world again. This is the reason why Titus Brandsma envisioned the Marian dimension of Carmel so intimately bound up with the spiritual and even mystical dimension. All Christian spiritual striving aims to put on Christ; it first happened in Mary's case. Following her lead, Carmel is meant to stress in season and out of season the fact that spiritual values, while they do not crush out material values, still have priority over them. For Titus no factor was more important in Mary's case than the fact that she was God's Mother (*Theotokos*—bearer of God). As God-bearer she remains inseparably united to God as only a mother can remain united with her Son. "However, it is the characteristic of the Carmelite vocation—and in a broad sense the vocation of all Christians—to be other God-bearers."

In a famous conference delivered at the first Congress on Mysticism, held in Nijmegen in 1920, Titus made this one of the three major dimensions of Carmelite mysticism. For him this was the summit of Carmel's rationale. Someone who wishes to follow the Prophet and live in closest possible union with God can find no richer nor more convincing likeness than that of Mary. In his openness to the contemplative life, the Carmelite seeks to live with Mary so that like her, he too may, by a free and unmerited gift of God, give birth to God and live on in Him. Grounded in this union, the Carmelite brings God to the world through his apostolic works, just as Mary gave her divine Son to the world (cf. Brocard Meijer, O. Carm., *Titus Brandsma*, Italian trans., p. 281).

This was not an ideal attainable only by a few elite. In Titus' mind it was the characteristic element of the Carmelite mystique. It would be difficult to find an article he wrote, a sermon he delivered, advice he offered, conference he held, in which Mary was not mentioned. A typical example is the widely discussed conference he delivered in 1932, the year he was Rector Magnificus of the Catholic University, which dealt with modern man's notion of

God. He discussed the approaches of many contemporaries. When, in the epilogue, he wished to present an ideal illustration to his listeners, he asked them to fix their gaze on the living image of the Mother of Jesus. A surprised murmur rippled through the crowd, yet Fr. Brandsma was undeterred. "We live and willingly speak in images and similitudes, willingly we make use of examples. For the development of our representation of God, we are not lacking images."

There was once a Virgin who became the Mother of God-made-man; she presented us with God as Emmanuel. The latter died on the cross to allow us to live in union with God and to fill us with his grace. Thus he was also born in us in the order of grace. It was in order to rectify union with God even in the order of nature and to make that union even more intimate and overflowing. Thus the Mother of God made us a gift of this intimate union with God, while she presented herself as a model for the most intimate communion. May this example be ever before our eyes. But here we have more than an example. She is called to direct our gaze towards God, just as led by revelation we recognize God in the Child in her arms, so may she lead us through our intellect to the vision of God in all that he has created in order that just as he lived in her, he may live in us and out of our activity he may be revealed to the world (*Notion of God*).

There were critical voices raised to this ending; a well-known Dominican concluded that what had begun as a serious dissertation ended up as a Marian sermonette. Few understood that Fr. Titus meant every word of what he said, no more, no less. Far from apologizing or excusing himself, in his humility Fr. Brandsma lay the blame on his inability to express himself better. "This ending about Mary has not been well received! I had a feeling that it would be misunderstood. Perhaps, in order to open the minds of all, I should have given a more elaborate explanation of how Mary in relation to our notion of God really does have something to say. Oh well, next time I'll know better." This was his conclusion to what was one of the most significant contributions he made to scientific theological thought: not that Mary is a pious afterthought that could be left out, but that

191

he must explain himself better in order to share this precious insight with his audience.

In a Marian retreat that he preached he explained himself further:

> The true concept of the Incarnation entails the notion of the divine Maternity. There are various ideas of this Maternity. For some it is only apparent, merely exterior respect. They will not be convinced of the 'born of the Virgin Mary.' They interpret it in an eminently spiritual, symbolic manner, without penetrating the reality... Mary is the Mother of God in a real, true and complete sense. We must admire this wonderful mystery with respectful love. It represents the extraordinary sanctification of human nature. No falling before the grandeur of this mystery—rather admiring the divine omnipotence which here seems to exhaust itself. Let us consider that the same God lowers himself towards us to unite himself to us. Let us never cease gazing on Mary to see and admire how God transformed her, to what glory he raised her.

Practical as usual, Fr. Titus wishes that this dogmatic truth be lived incarnationally.

> Desire to belong to the number of those who consider the glorification of Mary as the principal task of their lives. Enjoy the beautiful representations of the Bl. Virgin, enjoy hearing chants in her honor, in praise of her. Participate in activities dedicated to her. Tell her all these things (*Ejercicios*, p. 83-85).

Mary, living and caring

For Fr. Titus, Mary was not simply a woman filled with grace who lived on Planet Earth 2,000 years ago, not only she who was assumed body and soul into the glory of heaven; more importantly she was a living, dynamic, concerned person who stands as the model human being, accessible to all men. Just as God made her necessary for his coming among men, so she was necessary for our vital intimacy with God. Titus Brandsma was one who would subscribe to St. Bernard's famous dictum,

"You can never say enough about the Blessed Virgin." In fact, the Dutch Carmelite used every occasion—from the Sunday sermon to the learned conference—to implement his conviction: Mary's role can and should be understood by her Son's people.

Typical was his intervention during the Marian Days held in Zenderen in August, 1931.

Sublime creature that she is, Mary is after all what she is—like us she is in debt to grace and to divine goodness. It is true that his grace was reserved for her by an extra special divine disposition, to which, however, she corresponded without the slightest reservation. On her part, she allowed herself to be totally dominated by it. Mary opened her heart to God. He admired her in her total commitment and gave himself completely to her.

We want to be one with Christ. We want to receive Christ in our hearts, which too often, however, open themselves to his visit very badly. Instead, Mary was dedicated completely to God from her very first years. From her going up to the Temple, her whole life was nothing other than continued service, a constant offering to him, and so her heart always remained open to him. From Mary we must learn how to banish from our hearts everything that does not belong to God and how to open our hearts to him in such a way that we are filled with divine grace. Then will Jesus descend into our womb, he will grow in us, he will be born again from us, he will become visible in our deeds and live in our life. Much too little are we filled with God; much too much we live our own lives. With Mary, filled with God's grace as she was, we must lead the life of God and seek our glory and our salvation in our union with God.

The place of Mary in men's lives was Titus' favorite Marian theme. He naturally appreciated Mary's privileges and graces, but his personal preference in his prayer life and in his priestly work, in his capacities as preacher and teacher, fell on Mary's role in men's lives, and how she shows us in the flesh what it means to be united with God. A catholic spirit, Fr. Titus would enjoy a vacation in some European country if it were made possible for him. So he got to visit many parts of the world. Invariably when he visited famous museums he would search out the Christian art section, and give first priority to paintings of Our Lady and Child. Those who frequented him remember a constant bit of advice he gave: "Particularly, think of Mary. That is our vocation. Like her we are to became *theotokoi*, God-bearers and God's heralds."

St. John of the Cross, Marian mystic

In an unpublished article on the devotion that St. John the Cross had for Our Lady, Fr. Brandsma delights to point out that the Spanish mystic revealed himself as an authentic Carmelite through his esteem for the Mother of God.

> Clearly St. John acknowledges the necessity and usefulness of devotion to the saints and in the first place to the Bl. Virgin Mary. But he wishes this devotion to be healthy... The mystic doctor certainly does not condemn the honor and prayers due Mary and the saints, but he wants to see them used as a means of reaching God. Here again it is not union with the saints that should be the goal, but it should always be a lifting up of the heart to God, a new step towards union with him.

Dr. Brandsma reiterated this view on his lecture tour in the U.S.A. (1935), which was published as *The Beauty of Carmel*. "For St. John of the Cross, Our Lady is the ideal of the soul that strains upwards towards God, and is drawn by God towards himself." To summarize his thought he appeals to the conclusion of a contemporary scholar, Fr. Gabriel of St. Mary Magdalen, O.C.D.:

> Indeed, she is for him, as is truly reasonable, the ideal of a soul aspiring to the summit of Mount Carmel. He has not dedicated many words to her, but the few which he has written about her show that he regarded her as the archetype of a soul aspiring to the enjoyment of that unity, to the teaching of which he seems to have dedicated his life as an author. Other souls approach this ideal only in a lesser degree (*The Beauty of Carmel*, p. 92).

In St. John of the Cross, Titus Brandsma finds the pinnacle of Marian devotion in Carmel. The images used by the mystic doctor provide insight into his obvious love for Mary. She is like a *window through which the sunlight passes.*

If the pane of glass be clean and spotless, the sunbeam will lighten it up and change it in such a way that it seems to be the light itself and gives out light itself. That is the reason why Our Lady deserved to become the Mother of God—because she offered not the slightest hindrance to the divine indwelling. Like Our Lady we must absorb the divine light.

Another image used by the Saint is that of *overshadowing.*

To overshadow means to cover with a shadow, to protect, favor, pour full of grace... The shadow thrown by the lamp of God's beauty will be another beauty according to the kind and quality of God's beauty;... We may say the soul equals Our Lady upon whom the Holy Ghost descended in all his fullness and whom the strength of the All-high overshadowed in the most perfect way.

After expounding other images of the mystical life, Titus recommends that St. John's poetry be studied: there one will find

confirmation of the Marian character of the mysticism of St. John of the Cross... Let us, especially the Carmelites, not underrate this. Mary, our Mother, our glory, is our example, our prototype, when God selects us also for his divine favors... Illumined by him she shines for us as the mystical rose, whose sweet odors waft through the garden of the Church, so that we can repeat what we so often chant in our Office — that we draw near her by the odor of her sweetness. Like bees, we fly towards this mystical flower to behold in it the fairness of the mystical life in its highest bloom, namely God become man in her, so that he can also be born in us who belong to her (*Beauty of Carmel*, p. 98).

With perspicacity, Fr. Brandsma forestalls objections that Our Lady in the thought of St. John of the Cross is just too far removed from us and our real condition; the theme, a favorite of our times, of Mary on her pilgrimage of faith and suffering, hardly appears. "I think it extraordinarily remarkable that St. John of the Cross who evidently always saw Our Lady on the loftiest heights never reveals her on the way to mystical union, but only in the glory of her love." From incidents in Mary's life that recur in St. John's writings—the Visitation, Cana, Mary under the cross, Mary with the apostles awaiting the descent of the Holy Spirit—the underlying theme is "a revelation of love, a radiation of love, a radiation of her union with him (God)." This is how Titus summarizes Mary's role on the heights of Carmelite mysticism:

> She is for us, even in the most close union with God, an example and a Mediatrix who can procure for us the grace of having God become man in our souls also, one with us, the eternal Son of the Father, through the wonderful indwelling of the Holy Trinity, a source of vision and love (*Beauty of Carmel*, p. 101).

Mary present at the heights

Fr. Titus was convinced that Carmel's contribution in the history of mysticism was in the specific role of Mary, through whom Jesus could be reached. He could understand the nuptial imagery of St. Bernard better in the light of Mary's complete commitment to the Lord. He could appreciate better the centrality of the Trinity in the mystic vision of Eckhart and Ruysbroeck because Mary was the visible masterpiece produced by the three Persons of the Trinity. In the person of Mary we can avoid an overly abstract and nebulous notion of the heights of the spiritual life. She shows us how this sublime state makes a person human *par excellence*.

During a Conference that Fr. Titus held at the Marian Congress in Tongerloo (August, 1936), he tried to make this insight accessible to the diversified audience before him. Though he seemed to have lost them in the body of his talk, his ending caught their attention once again:

In the Communion of Saints, which is an article of faith, Mary is seated on the most sublime and unique throne. It is impossible to reach those heights, but this does not mean that we have no part in her glory, that we are not one with her... From all eternity God has also chosen us, and in creation from all eternity he loved us and predestined us to live in intimate union with him, who wishes to inhabit us by his grace. And if this union is not as sublime as that of the divine maternity of Our Lady, still we too with full rights can be called God-bearers and to us too the Lord sends his angel to ask us ever so often to open our hearts to the light of the world in order to carry it about like a lantern, as Ruysbroeck says. We also must receive God in our hearts, carry him under our hearts, feed him, and make him grow in us in order that he might be born of us and live with us as God-with-us.

Evidently, there were few themes dearer to Fr. Titus than this one: like Our Lady, we must conceive the Word, allow him to grow within us and then give him birth in favor of the world around us. Bl. Elizabeth of the Trinity had a similar intuition with her well-known "humanité en surcroît—an additional humanity." With his resolutely optimistic view of reality, Fr. Brandsma saw God's touch in all of creation. If he saw all the earth shot through with God's goodness and glory—he even considered being in jail a great grace, because then finally he could have the recollection of a cell so much part of the Carmelite way of life—it was a spontaneous reaction to find God revealed most surely and clearly in the finest creature issued from his hands: the Bl. Virgin Mary, Mother of his Son.

In fact, he found that nature leaves traces of Mary: much as does the Chruch's Liturgy, he too wished "to see frequently in the clouds, in the dawn, in the morning star, so many other symbols or images of Mary, in order to be more aware and appreciate our supernatural election" (*Ejercicios*, p. 30). It was the natural thing for him to do, then, when in prison, his very first prayer after the Sign of the Cross was a greeting to Our Lady of Mt. Carmel, followed by three Hail Marys. Though he lived in a predominantly Protestant country, and he had to lament the fact that many of his countrymen looked on devotion to Mary as an aberration from the purity of the faith of the Scriptures, Titus could never say enough about Mary's mediating role in uniting men with God. He regretted not being able to convince the world of this fact, which was so important to him, because in his life it had turned into an on-going experience. His love for God's Mother and ours could not be contained in his heart. He witnessed to it humbly, constantly, warmly.

Devotion through preaching

One method he employed was preaching retreats in a Marian perspective. Fortunately we have the text of one such retreat recently made available in a Spanish translation, edited by Fr. Melus (*Ejercicios bíblicos con María para llegar a Jesús*, CESCA, 1978).

> In my status as a Brother of the Bl. Virgin of Mt. Carmel, I wish to lead into the land of Carmel those who with me love and venerate Mary as their cherished mother, so that at the hands of the Mother and Splendor of Carmel, they can achieve the most intimate union with God, given that this union is the scope of contemplative life in Carmel. 'I have led you to the land of Carmel that you might eat its fruits, and its very best' (Jer 2:7). Just as Mary meditated on all she heard her Son do and say; just as she gave an example of a retreat in waiting for the coming of the Holy Spirit with the Apostles, so she is the surest guide for men.

> Because we are sons of Mary, we know very well that she—called the Mirror of Justice—is the most perfect model of union and intimacy with God. No one was more like God than she whom he chose as his Mother. Our union with her, the imitation of her life, are the surest guarantee of our union with Jesus, of our imitation of Christ her Son.

> If Jesus came to us by means of Mary, we can be sure that we will find Jesus in going to her (*Ejercicios*, p. 23).

But scholar that he was, Fr. Brandsma immediately adds, in a filial prayer, his faith that Mary's greatness comes not from herself or from her personal merit, but from her Son.

198

O Mary, your image presents itself to us haloed in splendor and majesty. That splendor, in turn, flows from the Child Jesus you hold in your arms, the blessed fruit of your womb (cf. Lc 1:42). Give us your divine Child. Look, we extend our arms to receive him and press him to our hearts (*Ejercicios*, p. 24).

Mary's life like ours

In various episodes of Mary's life, Fr. Brandsma is not content to contemplate Mary until he sees how she relates to ourselves, how her religious experience was on the same plane as ours. Mary's Presentation in the Temple by Sts. Joachim and Anne, for instance, should be seen as the need for on-going consecration to the Lord's service.

A vocation is not something instantaneous, nor is our creation. God continues our creation, preserving us in being. Likewise, he continues our vocation, calling us constantly. 'I stand at the door and knock' (Apoc 3:20)... We must often make ourselves aware that God called us and continues to call us, so that we might always serve him with our whole hearts and that we might live consecrated to him... We must begin anew each day. Always begin the day with Mary. Imitate her way of seeing God (*Ejercicios*, p. 33).

The Annunciation scene is applied to our own preparation for the coming of God into our lives.

Light passes through a crystal without breaking or tarnishing it. However, there is need for the crystal to be clean. Frequently our crystal is so clouded, so tarnished, with so little transparency! Where is our purity in the positive sense of consecration to God, of belonging uniquely and exclusively to him, preoccupied only about loving him? Is it not surprising that there is not more clear light in us? May holy Mary purify us ever more, disposing us more and more and better to receive divine grace... 'Behold the handmaid of the Lord.' Let us frequently repeat these words with her.

Practical as he was and unwilling to leave attitudes on a theoretical level, Fr. Titus mentions a practical means that obviously meant much to him: "To recite the *Angelus* three times a day with greater devotion. Never to omit it, so that we might always live with the memory of this great mystery" (*Ejercicios*, p. 39).

The Visitation, Fr. Titus intuits, is linked with the Annunciation, with broad ramifications for every Christian's life. "As soon as Jesus took flesh in the womb of the Bl. Virgin, he urges her on to a work of charity... The difficulties of the trip do not cause her to back away even for an instant... The mystery of the dwelling of God in us must urge us on to practise acts of positive charity, of operative love." Again Fr. Brandsma links this mystery with an everyday possibility on part of all who celebrate the Liturgy. The inner dispositions of Our Lady, so necessary for the true apostle, are vitally necessary for every follower of Christ. Thus the need to assimilate the values contained in the *Magnificat*. "Repeat the *Magnificat*, making our own the sentiments expressed in it. Always recite this canticle with special attention and meditate on it. The Church prescribes it for us every day in the Liturgy of the Hours, at Vespers. Since we recite it all too routinely, we know it only superficially" (*Ejercicios*, p. 41-42).

Mary's suffering and ours

Because he had much to suffer throughout his life, Fr. Brandsma could identify with the place of suffering on Our Lady's earthly piligrimage. He had to leave the Franciscan minor seminary because of bad health—which hardly improved as he grew older. On account of his precarious health and his overextending himself, he failed his doctoral examination the first time he took it. He was held up in studies because one professor considered him too much of a rebel. His final, terrible ordeal in concentration camps would hardly have been supported had he not learned all through his life how to see God's hand in trial and suffering. And he saw that this, and no other path, was followed by Mary. "We must be prepared to suffer with Jesus and Mary" (*Ejercicios*, p. 55).

(Mary) obeys the orders of St. Joseph, she takes the divine Child in her arms, and with him goes to meet privations and sacrifices... She goes out towards an uncertain future, without knowing how long it will last. She first goes with him to Egypt, later to Nazareth, resigned and full of trust, to give us an example of resignation and obedience. Jesus is her strength. In our difficult hours, may she remind us of Jesus, guide us and protect us... In our bitter hours let us recall the flight of Jesus into Egypt. Let us picture Mary and Joseph who suffer because they were specially beloved of Jesus (*Ejercicios*, p. 5).

In all our needs and suffering, Scripture teaches us to have recourse to Mary. The episode of Cana shows us her maternal charity in action.

We must be convinced that we lack many things. We must acknowledge that we need the intercession of Mary to attain what we lack. We must beg Mary to obtain from Jesus what is most necessary for us... We have here clearly depicted the care Mary has for us... In all trials and tribulations let us take refuge in Mary. Let us become devoted to Mary Mediatrix of graces, and deepen the true meaning of this devotion. See Mary as Mother and Queen of the Apostles, and place our apostolate under her protection (*Ejercicios*, p. 63-64).

An integral part of Fr. Titus' vision of suffering was the joy that must accompany a life spent in the company of Jesus and Mary. As so many of his contemporaries, Fr. Titus stressed the grateful happiness that should mark the true son of Mary. "At feasts, we must maintain our joy so high and so noble that Jesus and Mary enjoy staying with us until the end of the feast. Our feasts should be a confirmation of our faith and of our love for God" (*Ibid*). Fr. Xiberta has many similar reflections.

We must travel the Way of the Cross with the Bl. Virgin in our everyday life, however, not with complaints and laments, rather joyous and enthusiastic to prove the truth of the statement, 'My yoke is easy, my burden light' (Mt 11:30). The cross is a blessing from which we should not flee. 'In the cross, strength; in the cross, salvation; in the cross, light.' In a religious community, we should find only happy faces, radiant with a happiness of a superior and intense order, and such a disposition should not be disturbed. The Bl. Virgin, our Mother, is the Queen not only of heaven, but also of earth. And we are the sons of this Queen (*Ejercicios*, p. 78).

Obviously, it cost Titus Brandsma to remain happy in the face of adversity. His arrival at a monastery was a distinct joy for his confreres; he had the gift of lightening many an evening recreation. In this too he was following a Marian trait: "Look on Mary as the 'strong woman' (Prov 31:10), prepared for suffering by long years of meditation on all that Jesus had preached. Consider that Mary is not surprised at what St. John tells her, rather she immediately gets up and runs to share in his suffering" (*Ejercicios*, p. 65). His own long years of meditation on the value of suffering convinced him that it was the deepest proof of love. "With Mary and with John, let us kneel beneath the cross, in order to understand true love. Place ourselves in the hands of God in life and in death. With Mary contemplate the wounds of Jesus, especially that in his side, and hide ourselves in it. Renew our heart, making it a glorious tomb for Jesus" (*Ejercicios*, p. 69). Titus could not have had a presentiment of how realistically he would be called on to imitate the Passion of the Lord in the atrocities of Dachau, but his convictions were strong:

'And I, when I will be raised up from the earth, will attract all to myself' (Jn 12:32). Let us stay beneath the Cross, so that the Blood of Jesus falls on us and purifies us. Yet again let us listen to those words on his lips: 'Behold your mother' (Jn 19:27). This is the final proof of his love. With Mary let us approach Jesus and from his side drink of his pure Blood, which will transform us into new men (*Ejercicios*, p. 89).

One of the resolutions he proposed for the retreatants is significant: "Flee from melancholy regardless of how difficult is the trial which we are suffering. Precisely on these occasions, make the Way of the Cross with Mary, with the scope of preserving joyous features and judge the sorrows of the world under a higher light—that in which they will appear to us as a sign of predestination and a motive of comfort" (*Ejercicios*, p. 79). He would have us fix our gaze on Mary:

> Our Lady made the Way of the Cross with vigor and with love. 'Was it not necessary?' (Lc 24:26): Our Queen and Mother knew that a sword of sorrow had to pierce her heart: that was her glory. She could not escape it. And we? Do we follow her? Our Lady points out the path of suffering for us. Later will come the resurrection and ascension. But first we have to merit our glory. This is what God wants. He has reserved a place and throne for us. We must work so as not to lose it. Let us say to Mary: 'Save our place; we are on our way' (*Ejercicios*, p. 86).

But already in our present situation, Mary is working to transform us into worthy candidates for the Kingdom.

> Let us stay in the midst of the apostles. We are sons of God and of Mary. She is our refuge and our hope. We wish to pray with her to receive, at her intercession, the Holy Spirit, who transforms us into new and different men. We have continued to be the same in spite of the awful times in which we live. Would that finally we would be transformed into other persons! Our Lady brought to earth the Fire which must inflame it. May it be enkindled and burn in us too, not beneath the embers, nor in the ashes. May the blaze of fire rise high! (*Ejercicios*, p. 76).

Mary the sunflower

Like so many other writers, Fr. Brandsma had recourse to imagery to describe Mary's role vis-à-vis the Carmelite and the Christian. Often Mary has been compared to various types of flowers. For Fr. Titus, she can be compared to the sunflower. In what is a good recapitulation of his thought on Mary, he writes (*The Beauty of Carmel*, p. 67):

> The devotion to Mary is one of the most delightful flowers in Carmel's garden. I should like to call it a sunflower. This flower rises up high above the other flowers. Born aloft on a tall stem, rich in green leaves, the flower is raised yet higher from among the green foliage.

It is characteristic of this flower to turn itself towards the sun and moreover it is an image of the sun. It is a simple flower: it can grow in all gardens and it is an ornament to all. It is tall and firm and has deep roots like a tree. In the same way, no devotion is firmer than that to Mary. The fresh foliage, the green leaves point to the abundance of virtues, with which the devotion to Mary is surrounded. The flower itself represents the soul created after God's image in order to absorb the sunlight of God's bounty. Two suns shining into each other, one radiant with an unfathomable light, the other absorbing that light, basking in that light and glowing like another sun, but so enraptured by beams of the Sun which shines on it, that it cannot turn itself away from him, but can only live for him and through him. Such a flower was Mary. Like her, so may we, flowers from her seed, raise our flower buds to the Sun, who infused himself into her, and will transmit to us also the beams of his light and warmth.

6

FR. TITUS BRANDSMA
AND ST. TERESA OF AVILA

Adrianus Staring, O. Carm.

A well known Dutch litterateur, Godfried Bomans, who as a student was following Fr. Titus Brandsma's lectures on mysticism, asked him one day: "Professor, you are talking with so much enthusiasm about Teresa of Avila and John of the Cross. I hope you don't think me impertinent, but may I ask you, are you yourself calced or discalced?" And Fr. Titus answered jokingly: "I try to combine the two of them; during the day I am calced and at night discalced." Perhaps this anecdote best characterizes Titus' undivided admiration for the persons and the work of the two saints, whereas he always considered their particularities tied to place and time, as non-essential.

His first book

As a boy he had been educated in a Franciscan environment both in the parish of Bolsward and in the school at Megen. Yet Teresa's profound saying, "I live, but not in me... I die because I do not yet die," which he found in a prayer book, already made a deep impression on him, as he himself later confesses (cf. *De H. Teresia en de H. Eucharistie* in *Eucharistia* 19 [1923] 13). In his grandfather's prayer book he also read Teresa's well-known prayer in Dutch translation: "Let nothing disturb thee, nothing afright thee, all things are passing, patience gains all. He who serves God wants for nothing. He alone is sufficient."

The fact that he considered St. Teresa the patron saint of his mother Tsitsje, perhaps was not extraneous to his interest in the saint. His first letter from the novitiate is a congratulatory message to his mother on her name day, the 15th of October. During the two years of novitiate, 1898—1900, he got to know the works of St. Teresa. The novices customarily translated parts of spiritual works and this perhaps gave rise to his first publication. He was only a cleric in his first year of philosophy when in 1901 his *Anthology of the Works of St. Teresa*, translated from the French, was published. It was of prayer book size, made up of 272 pages with excerpts from *The Book of her Life*, the *Foundations, Spiritual Relations, The Way of Perfection, Meditations on the Song of Songs, The Interior Castle*, and from her *Letters*.

St. Teresa's complete works are thus represented and the selections were such as to illustrate her personality and her spiritual doctrine in particular. In Boxmeer there was a French translation of the saint's complete words by Arnauld d'Andilly and Marcel Bouix, S. J. If the choice of the excerpts is by the young Titus himself, as is likely, it shows that he was very much at home with the works of the great saint. The little book, written in an oratorical style, as was then taught to the young clerics, appeared at a time when mysticism was considered by the majority of confessors in Holland as "something dangerous," certainly a sign of a progressive spirit.

The edition of her works

During the years of the First World War, when Fr. Hubert Driessen and Titus Brandsma both were professors in Oss, there matured the plan to translate the complete works of Teresa into Dutch. The critical edition by Fr. Silverio, O.C.D. had begun to appear in Spain in 1914. It was at that time a daring plan for the publisher Paul Brand as well, with whom Titus communicated at the beginning of February, 1917. Fr. Titus describes the course of events in the *Album amicorum* of Hubert Driessen in 1937:

Each afternoon on our walk on the way to Heesch up to the pollard willow, we discussed what could and should be done... During those same years we began our fine grand edition of Teresa's writings, which has become the source of much blessing, and has given again to the name of Carmel in Holland a good reputation as an Order of prayer and mysticism. Very often we discussed how the Saint of Avila would have understood her elliptic sentences, what she wanted to say by her words which were sometimes obscure because of their brevity. The *Works* of St. Teresa did more than keep us at work; they deepened our spirit, they put us in a more interior and devout mood, they revived our love for the primitive spirit of the Order.

Early in 1918 the first part, *The Book of her Life*, translated and introduced by Titus himself, appeared in print. It has been remarked that in the saints Titus unconsciously puts to the forefront those qualities that characterize his own person, or should we rather say that he had assimilated those qualities by conscious imitation, because he admired them so much? In the Introduction he writes:

No saint perhaps was as faithful as she in the little things of daily life. Nor did any saint perhaps live like she, in an almost constantly perceived and seen presence of God. As simply as possible, as if sitting and talking to you, she speaks to you in her writings. But it is precisely that artless, true, sincere, warm and alive quality that makes her works so beautiful. All artificiality is foreign to her. Full of admiration and respect, we look up to this woman, who on a physical level was weak and ailing, and yet she inflamed and moved a great number of souls, both men and women, through the strength of her spirit to aim at the same perfection.

Fr. Titus also speaks of her reform with great admiration. It was "inspired more because of her love and desire of perfection than because of an excessive relaxation and degeneration of the Order in which she lived." Several parts of this Introduction, he repeated in an article: *De H. Teresia* in *Carmelrozen* 7 (1918) 129-134. He describes St. Teresa as mother of the spiritual life:

Certainly, now Mary stands foremost in the veneration of her brethren, but they don't deem it is derogating from that beloved mother, when they honor the most graced of her children as another mother, a mother who gave them not existence, it is true, but who regenerated them to a new life.

The second part of her *Works*, the *Book of Foundations*, appeared in 1919, translated by Fr. Athanasius van Rijswijck, who together with Titus also looked after the third volume, *The Way of Perfection* and *The Interior Castle*, which appeared in 1926. The fourth part, translated by Hubert Driessen, contained the first part of the *Letters*, and had appeared already in 1924. However, after 1926 no more volumes appeared, although there were second editions of some volumes. Titus, who in the meantime had become professor in Nijmegen, had to read up first for philosophy and then for the totally new field of medieval Dutch literature and mysticism. Neither did his many additional apostolic activities afford him the leisure and free time required for this work. Dr. Eugenius Driessen, who according to plan should have translated one or more volumes, never achieved his aim. In 1937 Titus wrote to Hubert Driessen:

> Nothing hurts me more than that, because I am so easily carried away by enthusiasm, all kinds of other work have left this project unfinished, even though it is beautiful, great and so important for the Order. You yourself handed over two additional completed parts of the *Letters*, the result of regular, imperturbably regular work each day, week after week, month after month, nay, year after year, for it has been a work of years. Naturally, there are many things in my life that I regret. There are many things that I could and should have done better, but I regret nothing more, especially on an anniversary day such as this, than that the edition of Teresa's writings, into which, for my sake as well, you put so much effort, lies unfinished. On this day I will speak about it to tell you that I regret it and cherish the hope that I will finish this edition in the near future.

His illness and the subsequent war prevented this intention's realization as well. Still, in one of his last letters, that from the prison in Kleve, dated May 28, 1942, Titus wrote: "Tell Hubert that in this seclusion

I have firmly determined first of all to finish the edition of Teresa's works." Fr. Thomas Keulemans, O. Carm., completed the edition after the war.

Inspired by her

In his lectures on philosophy, especially those dealing with the idea of God, Titus spoke with preference about God's "inhabitation" of man. He did not confine himself to the purely philosophical, but his life in God's presence expressed itself spontaneously and almost unconsciously in all kinds of remarks that gave a close-up view of his spiritual life, and especially his views on St. Teresa. In his lecture on the anniversary day of the University in 1932 on "The Concept of God," he raised the question of the most fitting image of God for contemporary man, also alluding to mysticism. "Although only a few chosen persons may arrive at the heights of contemplation, all of us should tend towards a contemplation that grows ever clearer. People have to see God again and live in contemplation of Him. One calls this mysticism. Be it so" (*Godsbegrip*, Nijmegen-Utrecht [1932], 28, 32).

Habitually, he stressed more the harmony than the differences between things, more what unites than what separates. And so, between the great Spanish mystics of his Order and the Dutch mystics of the Middle Ages, he especially saw what united them. This finds striking expression in his article, "The Growth and Flowering of the Mystical Life according to St. Teresa and Blessed John Ruusbroec" (*Ons geestelijk erf* 6 [1932], 347-370). Titus does not blur the differences, but he does not see them in opposition. He points out the differences of nationality and time, of speculative and psychological descriptions, but in both he sees an agreement on the most essential points, namely, the description of the various degrees of prayer.

Titus was not inspired only by St. Teresa of Avila. Other saints too, and not least those of his own country, were a model for him. As in philosophy he did not confine himself to the strictly Thomistic school, but sought and found the good in other scholastics and philosophers as well, so also he tried to see Teresa in the broader context of the Carmelite tradition, always looking for convergence, but with an eye open for each individual's character and the relative differences of nationality and time. To get to know the background and local color of Teresa's mysticism, he made a trip to Spain in 1929. In 1935 he travelled to the United States, this time to give lectures about Carmelite mysticism, which were published in book form as *Carmelite Mysticism* (Chicago, 1936; *The Beauty of Carmel*, Dublin, 1955). Though now we see some historical details in another way, this slender volume, in our opinion, remains the best synthesis of Carmelite mysticism in its totality written up to this time. Titus deals with Elijah as the model of Carmelites, with the origins and expansion of the Order, with its veneration of Mary, with John Soreth and the spiritual life of the nuns, with Teresa and her spiritual doctrine, with John of the Cross as a Marian teacher, with John of St. Samson and the Reform of Touraine and finally with Therese of Lisieux and Carmel's apostolate.

He speaks of Discalced Carmel with admiration; here too he considers more what unites than what separates. "Not the letter, but the spirit gives life." "We, even more than the reformed branch, need to study and absorb their works, and let them blossom forth in life and deeds" (*Carmelite Mysticism*, 79). The ideas of this book he summarized a year later in his article *Carmes* in the *Dictionnaire de Spiritualité* (I, col. 157): "St. Teresa and St. John of the Cross are not the creators of the Carmelite school of spirituality, but the restorers as well as its most splendid lights." In 1938 he wrote in an article:

> The great influence of St. Teresa's reform also brought about the renovation and revival of the old branch, so that between the two there exists only a small difference of life style. So she has become a blessing for the whole Order, while her heroic life of love has attracted many from outside the Order as well, and she is venerated, especially for her spiritual writings, as a mother of all who lead a spiritual life (*De H. Teresia* in *Carmelrozen* 27 [1938], 132).

Especially after 1930 Titus occupied himself considerably with the mysticism of suffering. The love of suffering, which he admired so much in the great saints of his Order, he also found in the Dutch *devoti* of the Middle Ages: St. Lidwina, and in the devotion to the Passion of Christ by John Brugman. Suffering had not passed him by: three times he himself had had stomach hemorrhages, and in prison and in the concentration camp he would show that what he wrote about the love of suffering was not mere theory, but a practice deeply experienced. He tested the phenomena of Theresa Neumann by the doctrine of the great St. Teresa. After a visit to Konnersreuth he declared that the external phenomena had made little impression on him. He found them "not so important, but the fact that man can live so totally with God, yes indeed." Most important for him was "the inner union of imagination and spirit in the Lord's Passion."

When Titus was arrested on January 19, 1942, with all his exterior optimism he did take a long detention into account. He took with him Cyriel Verschave's book on *Jesus* and a new edition of Fr. Kwakman's biography of St. Teresa. Some days later he was in the prison of Scheveningen, "already quite at home in my little cell." "The little poem that St. Teresa always had with her in her breviary and that I sent to my colleague Brom when he was in prison, is an encouragement for me too. 'Let nothing disturb thee, nothing afright thee, all things are passing, patience gains all. He who serves God wants for nothing. He alone is sufficient.'"

This poem of St. Teresa had already been known in Nijmegen as Fr. Titus' motto, and Prof. Gerard Brom had written it in Titus' *album amicorum* of 1939. Characteristic of both St. Teresa and Fr. Titus is unlimited trust in God and a marvellous balance under stress. In his cell, Titus made a kind of altar out of a small folding table. In the centre, he placed a small image of the Sacred Heart, "next to it I put on one side St. Teresa with her motto 'To suffer or to die,' on the other side St. John of the Cross with his 'To suffer and be despised for you'" (*Mijn cel*, Tilburg, 1944, 8, 15). His time was divided according to a monastic timetable; from half past three until four o'clock in the afternoon he read Kwakman's biography of Teresa (H. Aukes, *Het leven van Titus Brandsma*, p. 311).

His last book

In 1941 he had agreed with the publishing firm Het Spectrum to write a biography of St. Teresa. Finally, having time at his disposal, he threw himself into this labor of love. In the morning and sometimes in the afternoon he worked a few hours on the biography. In his letter of February 12, 1942 he asks for the book *Saint Thérèse écrivaine* by R. Hoornaert. Though sent, it was never given to Fr. Titus. On March 12th he writes: "From ten to half past eleven, reading and, if I have paper, also writing. I am busy with the life of St. Teresa for Spectrum. As a first draft, I have finished six of the twelve chapters. At two o'clock Vespers and Compline. After that reading or writing." "If I have paper..." this posed a real difficulty. He used prison stationery, toilet paper and later he took apart the book by Verschaeve and wrote on the empty pages and between the lines of the text. He filled 325 pages with his clear, regular handwriting. This was about half of the projected book; he provided a table of contents of the remaining chapters.

His only source was his memory and Kwakman's book, which did not particularly satisfy him. He did not have access to St. Teresa's works. After the war the book was completed by Fr. Brocard Meijer, O. Carm. The text and style of what according to Fr. Titus was only a first draft have been corrected here and there and published in this way as *De groote heilige Teresia van Jezus* (Utrecht-Brussels, 1946). Understandably, this biography, written in such difficult circumstances and practically without sources, and moreover not completed by the author, was, in many respects, inferior to the excellent books about St. Teresa which were translated into Dutch after the war. But the admiration and love with which it had been written, and not least the serene spirit of Titus which speaks through the pages, make the book a precious memorial. One reviewer wrote: "the book of a saint about a saint."

It seems that even in the camp of Amersfoort Titus wanted to work on the book. For that purpose he managed to obtain a copybook, but he was not able to do much writing in it. Back in Scheveningen he shared his cell with two Protestant young men. To them, too, he recounted how his heart was full of St. Teresa "and other great figures."

Four weeks before his death Titus reached other churchmen in Block 28 at Dachau. Full of courage and trust in God, at first he wanted to give spiritual conferences, but he found little interest: the prisoners were over tired and worn out. So, each morning he gave to a small group of interested prisoners a brief point for reflection, normally a thought of St. Teresa. After three weeks he was not able to do even this. He went to the sick bay and within a week he was dead.

"Only from afar are we able to follow those sublime examples, and God grant that we follow them, rather than relax in the zeal with which we once decided to serve God," he wrote in 1918 about Teresa and John of the Cross (*Werken der H. Teresia*, I, *Het boek van haar leven*, 27). He hardly suspected that someone would apply those words to himself as well. In his own personal way Titus imitated these saints. His first and his last book were dedicated to St. Teresa. He lived in her spirit and that of her reform, though striving to belong heart and soul to the ancient branch of Carmel. And what Teresa had longed for even as a child, but never realized, God gave to him: martyrdom.

IV

SELECTION FROM HIS WRITINGS

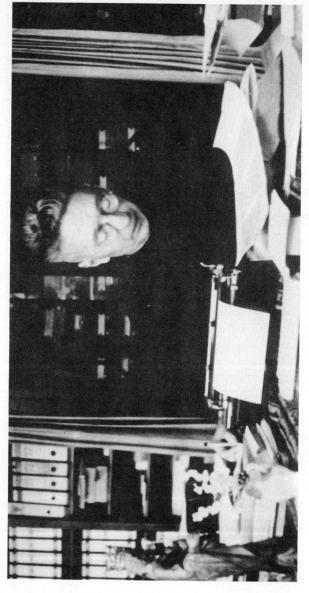

Father Titus at work in his room in the Carmelite Monastery, Nijmegen

Fr. Titus had an easy pen and made full use of his Underwood typewriter. When collected for the beatification process, his writings filled 136 volumes. He had recourse to every literary genre from poetry to position papers to a vast repertoire of letters. Much of his writing was topical and occasional: because addressed to very specific themes, such as preservation of Frisian culture, or an introduction to a colleague's book, or a series of articles on sociological themes for a national magazine, these writings are of limited interest.

Still, much of this mine of material remains a closed book to the majority of readers because it was written largely in Dutch. The one volume which has been available in English from the beginning is *Carmelite Mysticism* (another title: *The Beauty of Carmel*), the result of his lectures on Carmelite spirituality in the U.S.A. Other writings have sporadically been translated into various, more accessible languages.

In the following eighteen items, the editor aims at a panoramic view of Fr. Titus' writings. Not only is it a sampling of his literary output, but, since he put his heart and soul into his every endeavor, much of this diminutive friar's "spirit" can be discovered in these writings. People have often asked for more information about the "spirituality" of Fr. Titus. Actually, he rarely wrote about himself; spiritual journals were definitely not a part of his "spirit." However, a committed writer such as he could not but betray his inner life of the Spirit in what he wrote under varying titles.

For the first time we print an English translation of his well-known entry in the *Dictionnaire de Spiri-*

tualité, "Carmelites" (n. 1). The two following entries are outlines of retreats, which he preached so frequently. A lengthy introduction to an anthology of writings on the blind brother, John of St. Samson, soul of the Touraine Reform, follows (n. 4). Fr. Titus collaborated in many joint ventures, such as a series of leaflets on Marian themes; he dealt with the scapular devotion on four brief pages (n. 5). Because of his position as "the Professor," his confreres often called on his expertise for position papers on various questions, such as what should be the apostolic work of Carmel (n. 6). The final section (nn. 7-18) contains samplings of his vast correspondence, ranging from a letter written from Rome as a student to his friend Aloysius van der Staiij, O. Carm., to the last letter from Dachau, sent to his family in obviously excruciating circumstances only two weeks before his martyr death. Most of these latter documents are from his days of imprisonment, when the mettle of this authentic son of Elijah and Mary was tried to the extreme degree; he was not found wanting.

1

THE SPIRITUALITY OF THE CARMELITES OF THE ANCIENT OBSERVANCE

Translation of the article "Carmes" *in the* Dictionnaire de Spiritualité, *fasc. VII, col. 156-171.*

1) Antiquity of the Carmelite School.

St. Theresa of Avila and St. John of the Cross had no other goal than to restore to the Order of Carmel its ancient spirit; they are not the founders of the Carmelite school of spirituality but are nevertheless its restorers and most brilliant lights. Their glory will not be diminished if the radiance which this school produced before their reform is shown. Far from being opposed to the first centuries of the Order, they often went there to seek examples. St. Theresa recommends the poverty of the early fathers to her daughters; the memory of the hardships they endured in solitude should encourage Carmelites to bear theirs patiently—"the little illnesses of mischievous women." Still more explicitly the Saint writes: "... All of us who wear this holy habit of Carmel are called to prayer and contemplation; this was our original institution, we belong to the race of those holy Fathers of Mount Carmel, who in such deep solitude and complete renunciation of the world, sought the treasure, the precious pearl of which we speak."

M. L. Van den Bossche has written correctly that St. Theresa added a psychological finesse to the primitive foundation of Carmel.

2) Primitive and Fundamental Elements.

From its beginning, the Order of Carmel has the remarkable privilege of having drawn its spirituality from two sources—the imitation of Elijah and the veneration of the Blessed Virgin.

A. Imitation of Elijah. *—As its name indicates, the Order of Carmelites took its origin in Palestine on the mountain famous from the Old Testament for the sacrifice of Elijah and for the grotto where the Prophet retired when he had accomplished his missions near Israel: "From there he went to Mount Carmel" (2 Kgs 2: 25).*

Ancient inscriptions, from long before the Crusades, bear witness that Byzantine Christians venerated the Prophet in the very place where, according to legend, the School of the Prophets had been located—El Chader, at the foot of the mountain on the side by the sea.

The rule states explicitly that the hermits were assembled near the fountain of Elijah higher up on the mountain.

An itinerary from the beginning of the 13th century makes a distinction between "the Latin hermits who are called Brothers of Carmel" living near the "wadi ain es-Siah," the fountain of Elijah; and "the hermits of Carmel" who live near El-Chader, the School of the Prophets. Many others itineraries confirm this testimony and bear witness to the veneration given the Prophet Elijah on Carmel. Benjamin de Tudela, who visited the Holy Places in 1163, relates that two sons of Edom (thus he designates Aymeric and Berthold) built a chapel in honor of the Prophet near the Grotto of Elijah.

The monk John Phocas, who journeyed to Palestine about 1177, says that some years previously a monk, originally from Calabria, had raised the monastery of Carmel on its ruins and that he lived there with

ten companions; as a result of a revelation, he established himself and built a chapel there.

Further confirmation of these facts is given by
Jacques de Vitry who relates that several Crusaders led
a solitary life "in narrow cells after the example and in
imitation of the saintly solitary who was the Prophet
Elijah, like bees of the Lord gathering into their hive
the honey of spiritual sweetness." The authenticity of
some documents pertaining to the early history of the
Carmelites can be debated, but from clearly authentic
works, it appears even to those who reject many other
traditions of the Order, that the spiritual life of Carmel
is completely impregnated with the spirit of Elijah and
that imitation of the Prophet has given the Carmelite
school its special stamp. The Abbot Trithemius (1516)
was correct therefore in writing: "Although it was not
he who gave them a rule in writing, Elijah was nevertheless the example and model for the holy life of the
Carmelites." To prove this, it is not necessary to dem-
onstrate historically an uninterrupted succession of
hermits on Carmel imitating Elijah up to the time of
the Crusades. It is sufficient that the hermits of 1155
chose the Prophet as their model and that contemporary evidence makes the fact of this imitation certain.

B. Veneration of the Virgin. —We must note as a
very remarkable circumstance of the foundation of the
Order that the first hermits assembled around a chapel
dedicated to the Virgin, "Saint Mary of Mt. Carmel." This is the origin of their name; at once they
were called "Brothers of Our Lady of Mt. Carmel." Nomen fuit omen. From the very beginning,
by a particular design of Providence, the new Order
received its other character, a very special devotion to
the Blessed Virgin. The legend in the breviary relates
that Saint Brocard, second Prior General, when dying
said to his brethren: "We are called the Brothers of
Our Lady. Take care to make yourselves worthy of
this beautiful name." Les Pelerinages por aler en
Jherosalem (1220) and also Les Chemins et les Pelerinages de la Terre Saint (before 1265) mention this
"little church of Our Lady." The Descriptio Terrae
Sanctae by a certain Philippin (1263-1291), edited by

W. A. Neumann, expressly designates it "Monasterium S. Mariae Carmeli." It is with good reason also that in 1282 Peter Emilien, the Prior General, wrote to Edward I of England that he would pray for him "to the Savior and to the aforesaid glorious Virgin for whose honor and glory the Order was specially instituted beyond the seas." The General Chapter of Montpellier (1287) expressed the same thing. In 1311 King Edward II of England wrote to Pope Clement V that he was particularly attached to the Carmelites because they were founded in honor of Mary; Clement V's opinion was the same. One of the most celebrated writers of the Order, John Baconthorpe, wrote of the Virgin at this time, commenting on "Your head is like Carmel:" "And since she is honored, and appreciated by Carmel, it is fitting, that on Carmel which was given to her, she should have Carmelites to venerate her in a special way. This is how it was from of old." The same author in his Expositio analogica Regulae Carmelitanae describes the Carmelite life as an imitation of Mary. It would be easy to multiply the evidence. But it is sufficient to add that the Carmelites, called by the people "Brothers of Our Lady," received as their official designation the title "Brothers of the Bl. V. Mary of Mt. Carmel," to which Popes and Bishops attached indulgences. The Devotion of the Scapular, Mary's habit, contributed partially to the Carmelites' becoming known as the Brothers of the Virgin.

This double ideal forms the first article of the oldest constitutions preserved for us, those of the General Chapter of Barcelona (1324). Here we read that from the times of the holy Prophets, Elijah and Elisha, devout hermits lived continuously on Mt. Carmel, sought this holy mountain and loved its solitude in order to give their minds over to the contemplation of heavenly things; they built a chapel here in honor of the Virgin and thus deserved to be called the Brothers of Our Lady of Mount Carmel, a name recognized by Popes. St. Albert gave them a rule which was approved. The Carmelites are imitators and successors of these hermits. Thus from its origin, the two specific elements of Carmel's spirituality have been imitation of Elijah and veneration of the Blessed Virgin. The

Carmelites have always been mindful that they should imitate these two models, Elijah and Mary. They are the Sons of Elijah and the Brothers of Mary. From here also Carmel's mystical orientation proceeds.

3) Special vocation to the mystical life.

In 1370 the Spanish Carmelite, Philip Riboti, assembled some documents on the origins of the Order, in which the mystical vocation of its members is particularly affirmed. The authenticity of these documents has given place to very serious debate, but also to important defence. The collection contains the Institutio primorum monachorum, *attributed to John XLIV, Patriarch of Jerusalem; a letter from about 1235 by Saint Cyril of Constantinople, third Prior General; and finally, the Chronicle of William of Sanvico, the author of which was one of the last to flee from Mount Carmel in 1291 at the time of the general massacre by the Turks and who assisted at the General Chapter of Montpellier (1287) in the capacity of definitor of the Holy Land.*

Should they be of the 14th century only—which is by no means proved—these documents would still furnish us with very precious information about Carmelite Spirituality and what was regarded in the middle of the 14th century as the mystical tradition of Carmel and its ideal. According to the testimony of the Dominican, Stephen of Salagnac, in the second half of the 13th century, the Institutio, *even as apocryphal, remains a traditional paraphrase of the rule of life created by the Patriarch Aymeric of Malafay in 1156 to which allusion is made in the prologue of the Rule of 1205. The* Institution *describes the spiritual life of the hermits of Carmel and indicates clearly the double goal of the Order, and affirms consequently from the beginning its members' arrival at mystical graces if they are faithful to their rule and if God judges it opportune. "This life," says the* Institutio *(Ch. 2), "has a double goal; we acquire the first by our virtuous labor and effort with the help of divine grace. It consists in offering to God a holy heart, free of all stain of sin. We attain this end when we are perfect and in*

*Carith, which is to say, hidden in charity... The oth-
er goal of this life is communicated to us by a pure gift
of God; I mean not only after death, but even in this
mortal life, to taste in some way in one's heart and to
experience in one's spirit the power of the divine presence and the sweetness of glory from on high. This is
called drinking from the torrent of God's pleas-
ures." Not only the purgative way and the illumina-
tive way, but even the unitive way and infused contemplation are clearly proposed as the end to be attained, the goal to be pursued, the ideal to be realized;
but still this union and participation in the heavenly
life are declared at the same time to be a "pure gift of
God." Never in any Order, to my knowledge, has a
book furnishing a norm of life and declaring the end
toward which its members should strive, enunciated
the vocation to the mystical life in so formal a manner.*

*This double end is the "double spirit" asked by
Elisha for his disciples and the imitators of Elijah. Occasionally this double spirit is interpreted as
the double portion of the firstborn or as the union of
the active and contemplative life. But more generally
it is admitted that it pertains to active contemplation
which the divine Goodness crowns with passive contemplation.*

4) Proper ideas on the mixed life.

*The rule, which places the summit of the spiritual
life in active and passive contemplation, has a concept
of the mixed life which differs from that of the Thomistic School. The latter sums up its ideal in this formula—contemplata aliis tradere; to crown the contemplative life with the active life is the highest perfection for St. Thomas and the Dominicans. For Carmel,
it would be rather complete dedication to contemplation; it should be interrupted only because of necessity
—when there is need to go to men and speak to them
of God. Only charity toward one's neighbor or obedience can be reasons for leaving God for the sake of
God. "Deum propter Deum relinquere." As the rule
prescribes: "To meditate on the law of the Lord day*

and night, watching in prayer, unless occupied with other justified tasks." The words of Our Lord about Mary Magdalen, which the Church applies to the Blessed Virgin on the feast of the Assumption, have been applied to Order of Carmel: "Mary has chosen the better part and it shall not be taken from her." For the Carmelite, contemplation is "the better part." This difference in concept is felt very little in practice; the Carmelites took into account the necessity of interrupting their contemplation for the care of souls, and the Popes have called upon them for preaching, missions, and numerous apostolic works. Love of neighbor and submission to the head of the Church have constrained them to undertake the mixed life; also to give to others the fruit of their contemplation, but this ideal has been imposed upon them by circumstances. The Order has always sought to preserve its proper ideal for as many of its sons as possible; it asks them to return with the greatest haste as soon as their exterior duties are accomplished to what is the direct and primary object of their calling. Nicholas the Frenchman, seventh Prior General (1265-1271), who relinquished his office for solitude, characterises this primitive orientation well: "Conscious of their imperfection, the hermits of Carmel persevered in solitude for a long time. But since they aspired to be of use to their neighbor so as not to be culpable in their regard, they sometimes, although rarely, descended from their hermitage. They went to tread on the threshing floor of preaching and to sow with generous hand what they had reaped with delight in the desert with the sickle of contemplation."

5) Contemplation remains "the better part."

This orientation has not changed. In the middle of the 13th century when the Carmelites passed over into Europe and took their place among the Mendicant Orders, they received from the Popes a more marked tendency toward the active life. St. Simon Stock, Prior General, then did his utmost to protect the contemplative ideal as well as he could. On this point the rule underwent no modification, when at the request of the Saint, Innocent IV adapted it to the new living conditions of the Carmelites. These, it must be recognized, were a serious danger to the contemplative life, and many religious no doubt were given over to the active life very much. Two successors of St. Simon Stock regretted that the Friars could no longer enjoy the delights of contemplation. The first, Nicholas the Frenchman, in a severe letter recalls the traditions and vocation of the Order in emphatic terms; this letter, destined to kindle in the hearts of Carmelites the living flame of love for the heavenly things promised and given in contemplation, is entitled Ignea sagitta, the Flaming Arrow. Adding example to his words, the Prior General after ruling for six years resigned and retired to a hermitage. Ralph the German, his successor, was in office no more than three years when he too went to seek solitude in the English hermitage at Hulne, near Alnwick. If this sublime ideal was not followed in the whole Order with the same ardor, this double withdrawal clearly show that the tradition had not been forgotten by the highest authority. That there were others to follow the example of the Priors General is testified to by the Acts of the General Chapter of Montpellier (1287) where different measures were taken to maintain "the citadel of contemplation" in the Order.

6) Special love of solitude.

Although the necessities of the apostolate had turned the Order to an ever more active life, the custom of establishing new convents in solitude was maintained during the first centuries according to the rule, until it was permitted to choose other sites when there was need. In 1254 the Friars refused the house which St. Louis offered them in the center of Paris and preferred the one which the King gave them outside the city. A decree of John XXII ordained that ten convents be transferred to cities so that the Carmelites might occupy themselves with the care of souls the more easily. In the beginning of the 14th century, John Baconthorpe, the greatest scientific authority in the Order at that time, vindicated foundations in solitude; he exalted meditation in the cell with the example of the Virgin, who by her prayers in the seclusion of Nazareth deserved to conceive the Son of God.

We have proof that these solitary convents, asylums of contemplation, continued; in the life of St. Andrew Corsini, bishop of Fiesole (+ 1366), for example, it was to a house of this kind that he retired for his First Mass and obtained his first mystical grace, a vision of the Blessed Virgin. Blessed Angelus Augustine Mazzinghi (+ 1438) founded hermitages in the following century and the reform which he inaugurated had no other purpose than to remind the Order of its mystical glory.

Not only the rule, but all the constitutions recommend solitude; the cell is a sanctuary where each one lives with God and ascends to him. No province is complete or prosperous without "deserts," even under the mitigated rule. That is why solitude for the Carmelite is the expression of detachment from the world and nearness to God. Poverty moreover has a significance which differs from the meaning that the Franciscans, for example, attach to it; while the Friars Minor regard it especially as an imitation of Christ and opposition to the world, the Carmelites view it principally as a consequence of their adherence to God in contemplation of heavenly things. To neglect it is a sign that one is less united to God and prefers inferior occupations. In the pursuit of contemplation, poverty is intimately joined to solitude; "How sordid the world becomes for me when I gaze at the heavens."

7) Practice of the Presence of God.

Inspired by the words of the Prophet Elijah, "The Lord lives, in whose sight I stand," the Institutio attaches special importance to the practice of the presence of God.

This practice is a very efficacious means of living with God and meditating on his law "day and night," as the rule prescribes. Devotion to the Holy Face of Our Lord is one of the original forms of the prayers and daily occupations of the monks being performed in his sight. Among other evidence of this practice, let us point out the images of the Holy Face in the churches of Mayence and Frankfort-on-the-Main painted on the

227

arches of the presbytery and surrounded by texts which recall the presence of God.

Brother Laurence of the Resurrection (+ 1691) was therefore well within the framework of Carmelite tradition when he wrote Le Practique de la Presence de Dieu, translated into several languages and famous throughout the whole world. St. Therese of the Child Jesus revived this devotion. Paintings of the Holy Face are found in many Carmels.

8) Adoration and devotion to the Blessed Sacrament.

In speaking of the Carmelites' tender devotion to the Sacrament of the Altar, it goes without saying that we do not wish to imply that it is peculiar to them, but only to point out some of the remarkable aspects of it. They have always seen a symbol of the Sacred Host in the wonderful food which the angel pointed out to Elijah and which strengthened the Prophet in such a way that he was able to cross the desert and reach Mount Horeb. The Eucharist is the power which permits them to arrive at contemplation. The rule already prescribed daily assistance at Mass and the construction of an Oratory in the middle of the cells. The history of the Order furnishes admirable models of this devotion. St. Peter Thomas (d. 1365)—Procurator General at the time of the Avignon Popes, Patriarch of Constantinople, Apostolic Delegate of Pope Clement VI for the East at the time of the crusade against Alexandria—was not hindered by the many occupations of a busy life from spending several hours each night before the Blessed Sacrament; oftentimes he was found there lost in adoration. Blessed John Soreth, Prior General (d. 1471) and great reformer of the Carmelites of the 15th century, his life imperiled, grasped the Blessed Sacrament from the hands of sacrilegious men and rescued it from a burning church. At the end of the same century, Blessed Bartholomew Fanti, the Master of Novices at Mantua who counted Blessed Baptist Spagnoli among his disciples, taught his novices that one cannot be a good Carmelite without special devotion to the Blessed Sacrament: he cured the sick with the oil from the sanctury lamp. What determined St. Mary Mag-

dalen de' Pazzi to enter the Carmel of Florence was the practice of daily communion observed in this convent—a thing rare for the times. The Carmelites are rightly numbered among the mendicant orders, for their constitutions demand the greatest simplicity in their monasteries; but for their churches and the cult of the Eucharist grandeur was always permitted. The documents establishing several houses give as the reason for foundation the desire of assuring splendor for the liturgical ceremonies. In Carmelite Churches, the scene of Elijah in the desert represented in painting or sculpture is traditional.

9) Chivalric ideal echoed.

By the formulas in which it is expressed in the rule, Carmelite spirituality preserves the echo of the chivalric ideal of the crusaders who established it, almost in the same way in which the Exercises of St. Ignatius retain in their wording something of the military ideal of the Knights of Pamplona. Elijah was venerated as the daring champion of God's cause: "I am burnt up with zeal for the Lord God of Hosts." Six pieces of spiritual armor are described there; the cincture is the symbol of purity, indispensable for one who desires to reach the holy mountain of the vision of God: "Blessed are the pure of heart, for they shall see God." The corselet which protects the vital parts of the body represents good thoughts: "Holy thoughts will protect you." The breastplate which covers the whole body represents justice, a well regulated life, the observance of the commandments and duties of daily life. The shield is faith; for a living faith is the best safeguard for the spiritual life. The helmet symbolizes hope, confidence in God, which gives us the right to walk with freedom and confidence. Finally, the sword indicates conversation with God which as a double edge blade comes to our aid and defends us in all our difficulties.

10) Harmonius middle course between infused and acquired contemplation.

According to the ancient tradition expressed in the Institutio, *the Carmelites admitted that man can strive* for mystical graces and arrive at the presence of God; the religious of the Order are called to this height by special vocation. Elijah, strengthened by heavenly food, arrived at the vision of God during this life. Strengthened by the Eucharist, the Carmelite crossing the desert of this life does his utmost to attain the Horeb of contemplation. Although the task is arduous, their ambition is to follow their father. To realize this ideal is impossible without a free gift of God. But that is nothing else than a reason for esteeming their vocation and that of the entire Order; an exhortation to turn every obstacle aside which would make them unworthy of God's designs for them.

The ancient constitutions, as also the most esteemed writers of the Order, such as John Baconthorpe and John of Hildesheim, are in perfect agreement with the Institutio on this point. The great diffusion of the Institutio, which was regarded as the manual of Carmelite spiritual life, proves that at the outset of the 14th century at least, the Carmelites considered their religious life as a constant practice of virtue and a preparation for the mystical graces which are its crown. But far from becoming proud because of this sublime vocation, they built their spiritual edifice upon a solid foundation of humility, being filled with admiration for the overflowing Divine Goodness which rewards its chosen ones during life.

11) Intimate relationship between the sensible, intellectual, and affective elements of contemplation.

The Dominicans have considered the intellectual as the most important element in contemplation while the Franciscans generally have placed greater importance on the affective and sensible elements. The first insist on vision; the second, especially on seraphic love of which their father was so eloquent a singer. Carmel takes the middle course between the two schools: this includes several disciples and admirers of St. Bernard, but for them the affections of the heart and the sensible representation of God's mysteries are perfectly united to the consideration of the mind and are intimately joined with intellectual .contemplation. Here also are found disciples and admirers of Eckhart, but more ponderous than their master and very ready to combine the most elevated intellectual abstractions with sensible images and very tender love. We have an example of this in the sermons of Henry Hane, who is none other than the Henry de Hanna (d. 1299), who was the faithful helper of St. Simon Stock in spreading the Order in England, the Netherlands, Germany and France. They are preserved in an Oxford manuscript which bears the title Paradisus animae intelligentis, the text of which P. Strauch edited. They contain more than one image found in the works of St. Teresa; the Saint certainly did not know the sermons of Henry Hane, but both of them drew from the same tradition. Hane was influenced by Eckhart but he was on his guard against the too daring expressions of the great Dominican mystic. Sometimes the Carmelite school is called the eclectic school; it would be more correct to say that it takes the middle course between the intellectual and affective schools; this is the reason why it exercised so important an influence on popular devotion, especially in the 15th century. Great St. Teresa and St. John of the Cross were faithful to this tradition of avoiding extremes and harmonizing spiritual life, although St. Teresa leans toward the affective school and St. John of Cross toward the intellectual; the synthesis of their mysticism, which will remain the glory of Carmel, is a harmonious connecting of the different elements of contemplation we find sketched in the medieval Carmelite school.

Another authoritative witness of the school at the beginning of the 14th century is Sibert de Beka, founder of the convent at Gelderen, later provincial of Germany and doctor of Paris, who is famous for his Ordinale Ordinis and for a commentary on the rule. He sees the consummation of the contemplative life in perfect love as long as it is joined to a sweet and savorous knowledge of the Goodness of God, a knowledge, moreover, which can only be habitual or implicit. He is therefore also a witness to the harmonious combination of the intellect's action and the will's.

12) Decline and Reforms.

The expansion of the Order, the increasing necessities of the apostolate and consequently the prolonged stay of many religious outside the convent contributed to the multiplication of foundations in the center of cities, and caused worldly principles to penetrate into the monastic life. Solitude was practiced less, poverty was weakened; studies themselves were a cause of decadence unfortunately by creating privileges from the regular observance and by exempting the most distinguished members of the Order from the common life. The Western Schism opened the door for mitigations. Yet there remained those who observed the rule, faithful even to sanctity: St. Peter Thomas, of whom we have already spoken, and who was one of the founders of the faculty of theology at Bologna, was a Frenchman from Perigard; St. Andrew Corsini in Italy; in Germany, John of Hildesheim (d. 1375), who in his Historia trium Regum *retains the traditions of the Order in such remarkable fashion, and with him, representing the Carmelites of the school of Eckhart, Henry of Hanna; in England, the Carmelite translators of the works of Richard Rolle, the hermit of Hampole. Hermitages were established at this time in England as well as in Italy, which proves that the ancient tradition was not completely forgotten.*

What is remarkable is that the Order had so much vitality to restore the primitive ideal after a period of decline. Decadence, moreover, is never such that there are not some convents where the primitive rule is kept intact. The reforms which operated for the great benefit of souls here and there in one or another province prevented the Order from losing its initial orientation. At the beginning of the 15th century when the Popes mitigated the rule, a group of Italian convents in the region of Mantua remained faithful to the primitive spirit, and approved moreover by Papal authority, were organized into a congregation which would flourish greatly. Along with Bl. Angelus Augustine Mazzinghi, a very renowned preacher who devoted all his free time to solitude and contemplation, we cite among its most illustrious members Bl. Baptist Spagnoli (d. 1517), the great humanist, six times Vicar-General of the Mantuan Congregation who became Prior General of the entire Order; his neo-classical poems sing the praises of the Virgin and of the saints of the Order, and also of the contemplative life which he tried to maintain with all his strength.

Other reforms of the same type were established at Albi (1499) and at Mt. Olivet (1516). But the most important reformer of all was Bl. John Soreth who was Prior General for twenty years (1451—1471).

13) Mitigation of the rule. Appeal for methodical prayer. Blessed John Soreth.

The mitigation of the rule pertained to two points especially. The first was the restriction of solitude. A less hermitical life was granted to the Carmelites, a life which brought them more into the life of the people. But despite this, the primitive end of the Order was not abandoned; on the contrary, as though the dangers which threatened the spirit of prayer had rendered more lively the consciousness of the Order's destiny and inspired it to take the necessary measures to assure its realization, the new constitutions explicitly recommended contemplation and insisted that a place be made for prayer and contemplation.

It is perpetually repeated, "Prayer is the best part for Carmelites;" the Carmelite should guard the contemplative life as a treasure, and the active life should not be an obstacle to it. There is a direct relationship between the reform of Bl. John Soreth who lived ordinarily at Liege and who was an intimate friend of the Duke of Burgundy, and of the propagators of the Devotio Moderna in the Lowlands. This latter did much to popularize methodical prayer, regular meditation, and a mental prayer more accessible to the greatest number because it utilized the imagination and the sensible memory more. The great Carmelite devotion to Mary was in perfect harmony with the chief spiritual themes of the Devotio Moderna, namely, the Imitation of Christ, and meditation on the life and passion of our Savior. The Carmelites were apostles of the devotion to St. Joseph, St. Anne, St. Joachim, and the Infancy of

Jesus and the Holy Face. To facilitate meditation on the mysteries of Christ, several of them wrote itineraries of the Holy Land, in which imagination plays a greater part than reality, but which exercised a considerable influence on piety. It is in one of these itineraries—that of John Pascha (d. 1530), Prior of Malines, Een devote maniere om een gheestelijke Pelgrimage te trecken tot den heylighen Lande, *Louvain, 1563*—that we find the most ancient formulas of our present-day Way of the Cross with its fourteen stations. Carmelite poets relate pious legends about the sojourn of the Virgin and the Infant Jesus on Carmel on their return from Egypt. Several saints of the Order are represented with the Infant Jesus in their arms—St. Albert of Sicily (d. 1306), Blessed Joan Scopelli (d. 1491). The Historia trium regum, *so widely circulated in the 15th century, contributed to the propagation of devotion to the Infant Jesus. John Soreth was a providential man. His* Expositio paranetica in Regulam Carmelitarum, *written in 1455 and entirely animated with the ancient spirit, adapts the life of the Order to the new circumstances. A Frenchman, he underwent the influence of the Victorines and St. Bernard; but, from all evidence, he was won over to the* Devotio Moderna *and to systematic meditation. For him meditation has a three-fold object: 1) the book of nature in which God teaches us so many mysteries and which we should admire because it reveals God's law to us, the ordinary subject of the Carmelite's consideration according to the rule; 2) the book of Holy Scripture which must be constantly read because it was written for us and contains the law of God; 3) the book of life which God writes for each of us and which will teach us how we should observe God's law. Thus there are three distinct forms of meditation which can, however, be combined. In the exposition of the rule, the insistence on the practice of virtue and the exercise of meditation is remarkable. But what is perhaps more astonishing is the fact that this follower of the* Devotio Moderna *spoke so remarkably of the vision of God and of mystical graces about which the authors of this school are in general very reserved. Particularly the reading of Holy Scripture, which is the law of God, should fill us with great joy from the fact that God lives in us by his grace, and we are able to progress like* giants, carried away beyond our strict obligations by the pure love and joy which is the cause of our election. Prayer is not an oasis in the desert of life: it is our life. During the hours of meditation we prepare the food which maintains it throughout the day's work and renders our prayer continuous. It is to be noted that these developments of methodical meditation serve to explain the following passages of the rule: "To meditate day and night on the law of the Lord and to watch in prayer;" for thus apostolic activity is subordinated to the primary end of the Order which is conversation with God. And so providentially exterior activity proceeds from union with God but should not interrupt it.

14) Abstinence and the mitigation of the rule.

The second point which the mitigation affected was abstinence. The mitigated rule permits the use of meat three or four times a week. This was not such an important deviation from the primitive rule as is sometimes stated. One of the most authoritative commentaries on the rule—that of Sibert de Beka (d. 1333) —relates that when the Carmelites were transplanted to Europe and sought to adapt the rule to their new needs, before presenting it for the approbation of Pope Innocent IV (1247), and influenced perhaps by the Rule of St. Benedict which promises blessings for those who abstain from wine, they asked if they might not rather abstain from wine. On this they were in agreement with the writers of the primitive rule who, according to Sibert, always followed the example of the Rechabites and the Essenes, whom they venerated as predecessors and models. The latter did not abstain from meat because they had to partake of the sacrifices in the temple. By virtue of an analogous principle St. Albert, the author of the rule of 1205, prescribed abstinence from meat and not from wine, matter of sacrifices in the New Testament. In 1247 two Dominicans were appointed by Innocent IV to revise the rule, Cardinal Hugh of St. Cher and William, Bishop of Tortose, who decided on abstinence from meat. They likewise admitted the possibility of dispensation.

A significant episode! Carmelite spirituality will always insist rather on abstinence in general as a fundamental of the spiritual life than on the particular form of practicing it.

15) Establishment of the Carmelite nuns under the mitigated rule.

   Although in preceeding centuries devout women had sought to enter into intimate contact with this or that house of the Order as recluses who situated their cells near the Carmelite churches, such as Bl. Joan of Toulouse (13th century), it is only in 1453 that the Carmelite nuns were officially founded by Bl. John Soreth with Nicholas V's approbation. The Prior General did not intend to create a new Order, but to confirm the Order's vocation by joining to it a group of members who would be entirely dedicated to its primary end, the contemplative life. The mitigated rule under which he established them was not an obstacle to regular observance, to a poor, solitary life of continuous prayer and union with God. The convent of Couets near Nantes was particularly famous for its good example. Directed in its beginnings by Bl. Frances of Amboise, Duchess of Brittany, whom John Soreth himself admitted to Carmel, it was lived in so fervently after one hundred years of existence that its reputation had reached as far as Spain. No doubt St. Teresa was thinking of Couets when she proposed to leave for a convent in the north in order to live more faithfully according to the traditions of the Order.

   The new institution soon spread from the Lowlands and the Rhineland to France, Spain and Italy; at Florence, St. Mary Magdalen of Pazzi obtained permission to observe the primitive rigor. The foundations of Bl. Soreth are distinguished by a very special love of simplicity, poverty, solitude and prayer. The cloister was less severe than it would be after the Council of Trent; in the Lowlands and in the Rhineland it was stricter; but in Spain, much more relaxed.

16) Affinity of the Carmelite School to Ruysbroeck and the *Devotio Moderna*.

   A circumstance which favored the establishment of the Carmelite nuns was the legation and canonical visitation of Cardinal Nicholas of Cusa in Germany and the Lowlands (1451) in which he decreed that the devout women living in common in several cities but without a definite rule, e.g., the Sisters of the Common Life, should choose an approved rule and unite themselves to an existing Order. A group of women who were under the direction of the Carmelites of Gelderen and living near their church, asked for affiliation to the Order of Our Lady of Mt. Carmel. This was the occasion for the Prior General to ask Nicholas V for permission to establish a second order of women with the first order of Friars. It is known that the companion of Cardinal Cusa, Denis the Carthusian of Ruremonde, Capitular of Gelderen, was the author of several treatises on the life of the sisters and on the reform of their convents. These details explain a little the close relationship of the Institute of Carmelite Nuns with the Devotio Moderna. *The Charterhouse was a spiritual master for Carmel also. History tells us how much the Carthusians favored Ruysbroeck's mysticism and the spirituality of the* Devotio Moderna *in general; because of their love for solitude and the contemplative life, they served as an example and a stimulus for the Carmelites who aspired to a more strict observance. The contact between the Carmelite nuns, their spiritual Fathers and the masters of the* Devotio Moderna *was not merely occasional; it was a matter more of a common spirit. In a very striking way Father Martin, S. J., has demonstrated that the terminology and images of Ruysbroeck and St. Teresa are closely related and sometimes even identified. Above we established some analogous relationships between Bl. John Soreth and the writers of the* Devotio Moderna. *This is, it seems, an additional and very significant indication of the middle and conciliatory position which the Carmelite school has taken between the different schools.*

17) Strict observance under the mitigated rule. Reform of Touraine and John of St. Samson. Aspiration.

The reform of St. Teresa, undertaken with the permission of the Prior General and of the Provincial of the Order, after divers and sudden changes, resulted in the separation of the reformed branch. But this result must be attributed to fortuitous circumstances and not to any formal opposition. What proves that the Old and New Observances did not live in a spirit of opposition is the fact that shortly after the Teresian reform a very austere reform was introduced in France under the jurisdiction of the General. In the early years of the 17th century Fathers John Behourt and Philippe Thibault (d. 1638) started a "stricter observance" at Rennes in the Carmelite Province of Touraine, of which a blind lay brother, John of St. Samson (d. 1636) was the soul and greatest mystical writer; H. Bremond rightly calls him the St. John of the Cross of the Calced Carmelites. It is remarkable that this reform, inspired by that of St. Teresa no doubt, reclaimed the ancient traditions. In the treatises which the blind mystic dictated, an appeal for the primitive customs of the Order is made, and in a much more explicit way than in the works of the two Spanish mystics. Besides the great historical and spiritual works published during the same century by the Carmelites of the Ancient Observance especially in Belgium—the Speculum Carmelitanum and the Vinea Carmeli of Fr. Daniel of the Virgin Mary, veritable arsenals of ancient documents, and the Introductio in terram Carmeli by Fr. Michael of St. Augustine (d. 1684)—we could consult the spiritual works of the mystics of Touraine to instruct ourselves in the spirit and traditions of the Carmelite school.

John of St. Samson insists very strongly on the mystical vocation of Carmelites. The active life should not have first place. Recalling that the rule demands a life of prayer, he chooses this prayer—"to be lost in the object of contemplation, God and the things of God." No doubt it is necessary to preach, study and work, but because of the dangers which exterior activity brings, it is necessary for young scholastics to exercise themselves intensely in the principal object of their vocation and establish themselves solidly in the practice of meditation and contemplation. Contemplation is still a pure gift of God; but it is important that we for our part remove all the obstacles and practice the virtues so that we may be found

238

disposed in the way which God demands before giving his mystical favors. In this doctrine, human activity enjoys a considerable part; in its higher degrees, contemplation remains an absolutely gratuitous gift. Thus equilibrium is maintained between the school of acquired contemplation and that of infused contemplation. John is careful to note that perfection does not consist in ecstatic phenomena but in union with God who lives in us. This fire, which burns in us, sets us aflame, and the flame of our love is united to Divine Love which enflames our heart.

It is necessary that Carmelites understand this vocation and prepare for it. As a means of arriving at the dispositions required by God, John counsels a form of prayer which the Franciscan Henry Herp especially honored, namely, aspiration. It has four degrees: inhaling God, exhaling God, living in God, living by God. Entirely filled with God, we must hunger and thirst for God without ceasing and open our mouth to breathe God. We should start by offering ourselves and every creature to God. As Bl. John Soreth already showed, contemplation by its nature should elevate us to God. But we must not delay in the admiration of the marvels of nature; this is only a step by which we must mount. In view of God's riches, let us ask him to enrich us, for in the measure that he gives himself to us, he renders us unceasingly more like to himself. We should collaborate in his action by uniting ourselves ever more intimately to him; and we should forever rejoice over this union with God. The kingdom of God which is within us—the old comparison of the "the soul's spark"—must be extended without interruption or end by occupying us completely.

18) Two branches of the same trunk.

Looking at Carmel from above, its two branches are united at their summits. Despite the separation which exists on the trunk, the two branches intermingle their foliage and blossoms without our being able to distinguish those which belong to the one from those which belong to the other. The blind singer of Rennes, Ven. John of St. Samson, does not have a dif-

ferent melody from that of the inspired singer impri-soned in the Carmel of Toledo, because both repeat what the Institutio primorum monachorum *had in-culcated in the Carmelites of the first centuries, name-ly, that all Carmelites, Brothers and Sisters of the Order of Our Lady of Mt. Carmel, in order to be faithful to their vocation should do their very utmost to go, under the guidance of the saintly hermit and prophet Elijah, across the desert of this life up to the Mt. Horeb of the vision of God, strengthened by the heavenly nourish-ment which is shown on the altar.*

2

THE SAINTS OF CARMEL:
POINTERS FOR A RETREAT

1. The holy Prophet Elijah: *to live in the presence of God.* "*The Lord God of Israel is living; in his sight I stand!*" *(1 Kgs 17:1). Aware of his calling and of his sublime mission. Faith in God. On Carmel he waits for God's reply by means of fire. "If I am a man of God. . ." (2 Kgs 1:10). Fearlessly he presents himself before Ahaziah the King.*

He is guided by God. He places all his trust in him and totally committed himself to him. A man of prayer and meditation, he sought the glory of God in everything.

To live in the expectancy of God requires a spirit of faith. God revealed himself to him in a light breeze. To see God in everything: in all created things. To seek him and to love him with one's will.

Joy in the presence of God. St. Teresa: sheep together with their Shepherd. Ask for God's help and trust in him.

Acknowledge his constant benefits.

Holy Communion, pledge of our eternal union with God.

2. St. Berthold and the saintly hermits on Mt. Carmel: *love of solitude.*

Crusaders who left for the Holy Land, spurred by sublime ideals. Soldiers of God and propagators of his Kingdom.

They felt an attraction for the Holy Places, so that they might enjoy a greater intimacy with God.

They became hermits in the caves of Carmel and spent their time in prayer and penance. Many of them chose to die in the sacred places rather than leave them.

In 1291 all those who still lived on Mt. Carmel were massacred.

In spirit let us go to the holy mountain. Let us clothe ourselves once again with their spirit.

St. Mary Magdalen de' Pazzi used to kiss the walls of her monastery. St. Bernard said: "O blessed solitude, O only happiness!"

"Elijah climbed to the summit of Carmel" (1 Kgs 18:42). After having lost sight of God in the hustle and bustle of the world, there is need to seek him in the solitude of the cell, of the cloister. Mary and Joseph met Jesus in the Temple.

Recollection is necessary outside the cloister as well.

We should build a cell for ourselves inside our hearts. And there converse with Our Lord.

Lead an authentically interior life. "Alone with God alone."

3. St. Simon Stock: *Devotion to the Bl. Virgin.*

A great General of the Order, elected to transplant it to Europe, to the West. He can be considered our third founder.

According to the traditions of the Order, he was especially devoted to the Bl. Virgin Mary. "Brothers of the Virgin Mary."

He had recourse to Mary in particularly difficult circumstances. Apparition of the Virgin.

The holy Scapular, emblem and pledge of brotherhood or confraternity with the Bl. Virgin Mary. The spread and propagation of the Order flows from this. "Hail, Star of Morning." "Flower of Carmel."

Gratitude to Our Lady for all her benefits. Gratitude shown through our works. Honor Our Lady and imitate her. Live her life. She is the glory of Carmel. The venerable tradition of our Order is that it has always been known as an eminently Marian Order.

Re-read the Constitutions where they speak of Our Lady.

4. St. Peter Thomas: *Zeal for the service of God.*

One of the glories of the Order, whose canonization and veneration the Order ardently desired.

A great mind. One of the founders of the Theological Faculty of the University of Bologna. Esteemed for his knowledge, virtue and eloquence at the Papal Court in Avignon, charged with important missions by the Pope. Bishop, Patriarch of Constantinople, Papal Legate to the East.

Always in the vanguard, fearless in dangers and always a religious.

Man of prayer, devoted to the Bl. Virgin Mary. The name of Mary was imprinted on his heart. In difficulties he trusted in the protection of Mary.

Apparition of Our Lady as recounted by John of Hildesheim.

Learn from him how to work and pray. Work assiduously, but above all be a man of prayer, an essential condition for fruitful work.

Another example of work and prayer: St. Andrew Corsini.

Words of Bl. Mary of the Angels: "We have all eternity to rest."

5. Bl. John Soreth: *Poverty and simplicity.*

Great reformer of the Order, founder of the Carmelite nuns in France.

Extremely simple, despite the great esteem in which he was held. He did not want to be made a Cardinal, and he knew how to make the Pope agree with him.

He strenuously condemned luxury and riches in our houses.

He saved the Bl. Sacrament from the hands of profaners.

Fearless defender of the Bishop of Liége.   Energetic visitator.

Listen to his exhortations to religious on simplicity and attempt to imitate his example of love for poverty and simplicity.

6. St. Teresa of Jesus: *Love for religious observance.*

Called by God to restore regular discipline.   Extremely careful to observe all the prescriptions.

Reformer of discipline not only among the nuns but also among the friars.   God grant that she also restore the love for regular observance among us!

The Reform of Rennes: the stricter observance.   John of St. Samson and Michael of St. Augustine.

Perseverance of Teresa in her zeal for the restoration of discipline.   She was the first to give the example.   Guarantee the flowering of the Order by the diligence of each member in the observance of the rule.   Prefer death to the voluntary transgression of a prescription.

St. Teresa made the vow of always doing the more perfect thing.   Her source of energy was Holy Communion and the life of intimacy with God.

She left the keys of the monastery in the hands of Mary, whom she considered to be the effective Prioress.   She placed an image of Our Lady in the Prioress' place.   St. Joseph was her patron.

Her faithfulness and punctuality were the proximate preparation for the great mystical graces which she received.

Faithfulness in small things.

Compare St. Teresa with the little St. Thérèse.   The way of spiritual childhood.

7. St. John of the Cross: *Love of sacrifice.*

"To suffer and to be despised for your sake." To live solely for God, without being preoccupied with the judgements of men.

St. John of the Cross was despised by his own brothers.

The Calced Carmelites considered him as an innovator and one who disturbed the Order; they imprisoned him in a cell in order to neutralize his activity.

The Discalced accused him of immoderate and hasty zeal; they resolved to send him to some mission, with the intention of depriving him of participation in the running of the reform.

As he desired, he died in a convent where he was unknown and whose Prior was not very happy with him as a sick guest, who was thus a burden on the community and meant added expenses.

They kept him far removed from the nuns, who greatly desired to have him as their confessor. All of this was a path for him by which he was ever more united to God and achieved greater perfection.

There is a radical opposition between God and the world: this contradiction appears in religious life as well, and in our convents. The person who loves justice must prepare himself for persecution and for being despised.

We must struggle for the ideal of not just putting up with things patiently, but also of desiring persecution and being despised. However, many times the opposite occurs.

St. John of the Cross is a unique example for us. His life is a clear and eloquent lesson.

8. St. Mary Magdalen de' Pazzi: *Love of God.*

Infused, theological virtue, which however can always be developed in us.

Already as a child this saint had and expressed an intense love for God, which led her to speak of him constantly. She taught other youngsters to love God.

She entered Carmel in order to be able to receive Communion frequently. Her ecstasies were a continuous contemplation of God, especially of the Bl. Trinity, of the divine Essence.

This is precisely what will be the object of our happiness in heaven, of which we should experience an anticipation here on earth. We should enjoy reading much about God, and also hearing much about him. God should be the frequent object of our meditations and contemplations. Speak of God frequently. That our lips speak out of the abundance of our heart (cf. Mt 12:34). Our conversations should be proof that we greatly love God, that our love for God is authentic.

Rouse this love in others. Faith, hope and charity; however, charity is the greatest of the three (cf. 1 Cor 13:13). Charity remains. St. Mary Magdalen de' Pazzi was ardent with love. She rang the convent bells, inviting her fellow sisters to love God, lamenting that God is not loved enough.

We too should be sad that God is so forgotten. Kindle within ourselves love for the Sacred Heart of Jesus and for his Sacred Face; for the Blessed Trinity and for the Holy Spirit.

The Saints, together with Our Lady, should be intermediaries for us, who raise us to God and to divine contemplation.

Translated from Spanish by Redemptus Valabek, O. Carm.

3

TEN-DAY SPIRITUAL RETREAT WITH MEDITATIONS ON THE BL. VIRGIN MARY LEADING TO INTIMACY WITH JESUS

Introduction

As a Brother of the Blessed Virgin Mary of Mt. Carmel, I wish to lead into the land of Carmel all those who with me love and venerate Mary as their beloved mother. The scope is to reach the deepest union with God at the hands of the Mother and Beauty of Carmel, given that this union is the goal of contemplative life in Carmel. "I have brought you into the land of Carmel that you might eat its fruits and the best it has to offer" (Jer 2:7).

At another time—almost a thousand years ago—the crusaders left their lands in the direction of the Holy Land, intent on reconquering it for Jesus Christ, to restore worship, to recover the Holy Places for the Church and to restore them to their original luster and splendor.

We too are crusaders!

We too are anxious to re-conquer for Jesus Christ the Holy Land which once was his. Not exactly that land beyond the seas, but the holy land of our souls, the garden of our heart which at another time was consecrated to Jesus and which belongs to him. However, because of our lukewarmness and weakness, it has been invaded by an innumerable host of enemies of the Cross of Christ. It has been overgrown by weeds to the degree that it has ceased being the beautiful garden in which the Lord was well pleased. Would that the same enthusiasm that impelled the crusaders animated us so that we were entirely at the service of his ideal after having completely abandoned it!

For a few days let us forget everything else, committing ourselves to a holy crusade that would recuperate for Jesus the blessed land of our soul for God, to whom it belongs by full right and who wishes to be served within it. For a few days let us leave aside our usual concerns in order to undertake this spiritual crusade. Let us repeat with crusaders of former days: God wills it!

In his history of the crusades, James de Vitry tells us that some of the crusaders retired to Mount Carmel, where they hid in caves and grottoes. Like industrious bees they produced the honey of meditation on former mysteries realized in the Holy Land of our redemption. They gathered about the Chapel of Our Lady in silent contemplation of the sublime truths that were revealed to us there.

Following their example, let us also retire to the solitude of Carmel to meditate on the eternal truths of our faith and to reflect for a few days on their value and meaning for our practical life. Let us also gather about the shrine of Mary, the Mother and Beauty of Carmel, so that we in turn might taste the honey of meditation on what has been prepared for us at the summit of this sacred mountain. From there we see Nazareth, Jerusalem and Bethlehem at our feet. We see the road from Egypt which Jesus had to take to return to Nazareth. Before our eyes rises the sacred mount Horeb, Calvary and the Mount of Olives. Wherever our eyes turn, we see represented before us scenes of the life of Jesus and Mary. On entering the Holy Land we could not find a more suitable place to take in all that land sanctified by God. We can rest a bit on Mount Carmel with Mary, under the watchful eye of St. Joseph. By way of Carmel she brought back Jesus from Egypt to Nazareth where she had received him. The Scriptures tell us that Mary pondered in her heart everything she heard about her Jesus, as well as all that she heard from his lips. "Mary, on her part, preserved all these things and pondered them in her heart" (Lk 2:19, 51).

248

We wish to come close to Mary and to weigh everything she has in her heart. Like her we wish to ponder the life of Jesus, at the same time contemplating hers, which was so closely and intimately united with the life of her Son.

In the primitive Church—at its very foundations —we have an interesting example of a retreat of ten days in close union with Mary. The climax of the retreat was the coming of the Holy Spirit on the Apostles; by that very fact they were transformed into new men.

Uniting our prayer to Mary's, let us call down the Holy Spirit:

> Come, Holy Ghost, Creator blest,
> And in our hearts take up thy rest;
> Come with thy power and heavenly aid,
> To fill the hearts which thou hast made.

Like the Apostles, we wish to persevere with one mind in prayer with Mary the Mother of Jesus, shielded by trust that, by her intercession, the Spirit of renewal will come down on us, rekindling our cold hearts.

Mary be our Guide!

Since we are sons of Mary we know very well that she—entitled Mirror of Justice—is the most perfect exemplar of union and intimacy with God. No one ever ressembled God more than she whom he chose to be his mother. Our union with her, our imitation of her life is the safest guarantee of our union with Jesus, of our imitation of Christ her Son.

Through Mary, by remaining joined to her, we realize we are being led to Jesus. Her arms offer him to us that we love him as she did. Jesus came to us through her. Let us, then, go to Mary, assured that we shall reach Jesus!

We wish to dedicate these ten days to meditation on the life of Mary, because in this way we shall be in union with God, and at every moment our gaze shall be rivetted on Jesus her Son.

Purpose of this retreat: to reach a deeper union with God. Let us make every effort to make it guided by the hand of Mary. We shall let her lift us up.

249

*O Mary, your image is before us haloed with splen-
dor and majesty. Those splendors, in turn, flow from
the Child Jesus whom you hold in your arms and who
is the blessed Fruit of your womb (cfr. Lk 1:42). Give
us your divine Child. Look at how we extend our
arms to receive him and press him to our heart.*

*We place this retreat under your protection, so that
we go to Jesus guided by you. We unite our heart to
you once more, as we did during the most beautiful
days of our life, when we consecrated ourselves to you
by means of our profession.*

Preparatory Prayer

*We place ourselves in the holy and adorable pres-
ence of God. He is with us in the Blessed Sacrament
of the Altar. "Because where there are two or three
gathered in my name, I am there in the midst of them"
(Mt 18:20). He is always with us. He fills the heavens and earth with his presence. He created all
things. He preserves everything that exists. In everything, he is acting. In everything, he dwells. His
power extends to all things. He also abides in my
heart: he acts in it, he speaks in it. He asks me to listen.*

*O Jesus, we greet you, we adore you. Speak, Lord,
your servant is listening.*

*We also greet your Blessed Mother. The Magi
from the East found the Child with his Mother. When
we seek, when we find, when we greet Jesus, we also
gaze at his mother. We find her at his side. We find
Jesus in the arms of Mary. Let us greet Mary with that
most pleasing of greetings, which the Archangel Gabriel
used when he announced to her the Good News in her
home at Nazareth, "Hail Mary."*

DAY II

Meditation 1

Resolutions: *Conversion. Keep our eyes fixed on
God. We cannot serve two lords. Far from us all*

double-dealing, all hypocrisy. *We commit ourselves to God joyously and gratefully. Do all that is to be done in his service, to fulfill his will in everything. We shall often think of Mary as the little cloud that brought deliverance to Israel, and will also pour an abundance of God's grace on us.*

Meditation 2

Resolutions: *In our weakness, we shall seek our help from God, preferably through the Bl. Sacrament. Here strengthen ourselves every day anew for that* one *day. "Give us this day our daily bread."*

Consider our life as a march through the desert towards Horeb to see God there. The future possession and contemplation of God can give our life a new and more pleasing aspect.

Meditation 3

Resolutions: *Often remember that God has loved us from all eternity,* ab aeterno, *and has willed to create us. To assure our salvation, he has also willed Mary's Immaculate Conception* ab aeterno. *We should see ourselves united to Mary in the eternal plan of God.*

Frequently humiliate ourselves before God for having despised his love. Invoke and praise the divine mercy.

Rejoice in the Immaculate Conception and for the Nativity of Our Lady, as a foreshadowing of our redemption and eternal salvation.

DAY III

Meditation 1

Resolutions: *Prostrate before the altar and re-consecrate ourselves to God with all our heart and with that same fervor and with an even more ardent love, since now we understand better what it means to commit ourselves generously to God in union with Mary.*

Meditation 2

Resolutions*: To be satisfied with the situation in which God has placed us. Not to strive after human respect by reason of our talents or of our call. When we are contemned and judged unfairly: suffer, remain silent, trust in God.*

Meditation 3

Resolutions*: Always think of the Annunciation of the angel to Mary as the actualization of the greatest mystery of God's revelation, the mystery of hope and of promise.*

Recite the Angelus *more devoutly three times a day. Never omit it, so as always to live with the remembrance of this great mystery.*

We shall dispose ourselves to receive God's grace.

DAY IV

Meditation 1

Resolutions*: The constant thought that God's abiding in us should press us to acts of charity. These latter are the dynamic expression of God alive in us and of our own life in God.*

Remember Mary our mother and our model. Let us never think that we are too important or dignified to be of humble service, to do small favors. Rejoice that God has committed to us an activity that irradiates love. Consider it a privilege, a token of blessing, an honorable choice...

Meditation 2

Resolutions*: We must be more aware of our duty to prepare for the coming of Jesus. We do not want to* be like the inhabitants of Bethlehem, as if we have no time or room for Jesus. Give all the time necessary for what is holiest in our life, the most important moment of our day... We must be deeply convinced of this.

Meditation 3

Resolutions: *Frequently think of our heart as a manger in the stable at Bethlehem. We must be convinced that we do not receive Jesus in a worthy way, even when at times we think we are doing him great favors, even when we receive him daily in Holy Communion. We are poor, unfortunate people. What is there to boast about? (Ps 51:3; Jer 49:4). We should be ashamed of ourselves. Let us put the manger in order and prepare it as best as possible. Let us beg Mary and Joseph to aid us in this task.*

DAY V

Meditation 1

Resolutions: *Make a definitive break with our routine and drowsiness. Get up and go to Jesus in his humiliation. Endure it when someone laughs at our faith or makes it out to be something of little importance—the same with our acts of piety and reverence.*

"The Master is here and is calling you" (Jn 11:28). Jesus is above everything. What he asks for we have to do diligently without the least human respect.

Meditation 2

Resolutions: *We must seek out Jesus. We are so surrounded by darkness that we need the light of his star.*

Withdraw from all that is not united with Jesus in love, from all that would kill Jesus within us.

Meditation 3

Resolutions: *Filled with trust wait for the Messiah, certain that we shall see him when he comes in due time. Esteem union with Jesus as the highest good. If we achieved that, it would be enough. Be aware that this union demands suffering...*

Meditation 1

Resolutions: *In our bitter moments recall the flight of Jesus into Egypt. Call to mind Mary and Joseph who suffer, insofar as they are well beloved by Jesus.*

Like him, obey the dispositions of divine Providence, filled with enthusiasm and trust.

Look at Jesus as the treasurer who repays all our grief, all our sufferings.

To foster the desire of the need to flee one day with Jesus, to see what this really means and implies. Beg for the strength needed for this...

Meditation 2

Resolutions: *Strive to live pervaded by the presence of God. Always call to mind the basics of this practice, which is not only of faith, but also of reason.*

Seek Jesus in those good works done out of love for him, in prayer... "Where there are two or three gathered together in my name, I am there in the midst of them" (Mt 18:20). Place our faith beyond sentiment...

Meditation 3

Resolutions: *See God in superiors. Not to reason about what we are obliged to do, rather to do what we are told. We must often propose Jesus as our model of obedience.*

Meditation 4

Resolutions*: "In every trial and grief" we should take refuge in Mary. We must become clients of Mary Mediatrix of Graces, and deepen the real meaning of this devotion. See Mary as the Mother and Queen of the Apostles, and place our apostolate under her protection.*

DAY VII

Meditation 1

Resolutions*: Do not run away from suffering; put up with scorn. These unite us to Jesus and make us understand the meaning of sorrow. With Mary go to encounter Jesus on the Way of the Cross. In suffering, be united to Mary, model our life on hers, in order to share in her generosity.*

Take advantage of the opportunities we find to meditate on the Passion of the Lord. In order to make the Way of the Cross, pay special attention· to the crucifix in our rooms and where we work.

Meditation 2: Episode—The Bl. Virgin under the cross. Taking down from the cross. Burial.

For the space of three hours, beneath the cross on which Jesus is agonizing in undescribable pain. Go and see Jesus with Mary. "Learn from me, for I am meek and humble of heart" (Mt 11:29).

The seven words: how Jesus forgives us! He thirsts for our love. He speaks to Mary and John. Mary is our mother, we are her children. A confirmation of what took place when, in Mary, Jesus took on human flesh. Now he states it clearly. The testament of Jesus: sublime heritage. Love Mary so as to show our love for Jesus. With Mary, offer Jesus to his heavenly Father. Repeat with Jesus: "Father, into your hands I commend my spirit" (Lk 23:46). To die with Jesus. We should offer ourselves with him. Renewal of the sacrifice of the cross during Mass.

Jesus is taken down from the cross and embraced by the arms of his mother. Mary cleanses his wounds, she removes the crown of thorns from his head and contemplates how much her Son had to suffer. Let us contemplate him with her, the Mother of Sorrows and of Compassion. Etch deeply in our memory the living image of the sacred passion.

Burial of Jesus. In silence Mary accompanies the crowd. We remain with her. Finally Jesus is buried; he disappears. What profound humiliation! The opinion of the Jewish world: his mission is a fiasco. The apostles are filled with fear and doubts. Mary, untroubled. Her confidence. She says he will rise again: Mary believes. Jesus is in the tabernacle as in the tomb. Believe and trust with Mary.

Teachings contained in this episode

1 — The death of Jesus: final, supreme manifestation of his love. Often take our place with Mary and John beneath the cross to meditate on the sacred passion. Jesus tells us: "When I shall be raised up from the earth, I shall draw all towards me" (Jn 12:32).

2 — Unite ourselves to Jesus in his death. Unite our death to his, unite our sacrifice to his. "Into your hands I commend my spirit" (Lk 23:46).

3 — Listen to the seven words with Mary and deepen their meaning. Put ourselves under Mary's protection.

4 — With Mary contemplate Jesus' wounds and rouse compassion within us.

5 — Consider the tabernacle as a symbol of the burial of Jesus, and of his deep humiliation. Make frequent visits. Faith and trust.

Conversation with Mary

Mother of sorrows. In her, suffering with her Son is made fruitful. Be united with her in the contemplation of the passion and with her offer it to God. See the wounds of our Savior as so many roses blooming on the rose-bush of love. Especially see the wound in his side, in order to hide there and find the way to his heart. What a place Mary had in it! What a place she leaves there for us!

With Mary bury Jesus in a newly-hewn tomb, the renewed tomb of our heart. Hide him there until he asks us to act in order to reveal his life in us.

Conversation with Jesus

Crucified: he extends his arms to embrace us. May he attract us to himself so that finally we might understand his love, as we see him die for us. Choose our place beneath the cross with Mary and with St. John.

Take him down from the cross of shame, of human respect, to press him to our heart, express our love for him and give him honor and glory. Ask him to show us the wound of his side, in order to set on the path to his divine heart. Hide there and warm ourselves with the fire of his love that never died. Bury him in our heart, entirely renewed by the contemplation of his passion and death. We wish to bury him in this new tomb; "And his tomb shall be glorious" (cf. Is 11:10).

Resolutions

With Mary and with John, to prostrate beneath the cross, in order to understand authentic love. Place ourselves in God's hands in life and in death. With Mary contemplate the wounds of Jesus, especially the wound in his side, and hide ourselves in it. Renew our heart, making it a glorious tomb for Jesus.

Two thoughts to aid us to remember this meditation

1 — Jesus dies in order to open his side to us.

2 — Jesus is buried in our renewed heart.

Meditation 3

Resolutions: *Trust in the promise of Jesus to raise us up with himself. "I believe in the resurrection of the body." Often recall how suffering leads to victory, death to life, humiliation to exaltation in the eyes of God.*

Then begin a new life with Jesus. Not to allow him to abandon us as he abandoned Jerusalem. Acknowledge how good God has been to us, and how he will continue to be such always.

DAY VIII

Meditation 1

Resolutions: *We must often remember that we have a Father in heaven who helps us here to find and to follow the way towards our paternal home.*

Think of how much others have done before us in order to gain heaven. We can do what they did. Help us, God. We must always be available for everything, to undertake everything.

Meditation 2

Resolutions: *Often reflect on the fact that on our own we are capable of nothing, that our zeal and our will to work are minuscule. Often beg through the intercession of Mary that he send us his Spirit to transform us. Commit ourselves to God and trust in him.*

Meditation 3

Resolutions: *Consider life as a Way of the Cross, but take the cross on our shoulders joyously and coura-*

geously, because by his example and by his grace, Jesus has made it light.

Avoid sadness regardless of how difficult the trial we are suffering. Then more than ever make the Way of the Cross with Mary, in order to keep a happy face, and to see the sufferings of this life in a higher light, where they become a sign of election and reason for comfort.

DAY IX

Meditation 1

Resolutions: *Learn to die. Help others to die. Teach them to see death in this way. Often picture the deathbed of Mary and ask her to make our death like hers.*

Live a life of love.

Consider life a slow death. "I die each day" (1 Cor 15:31).

Live in a way so that we deserve to die of love.

Meditation 2

Resolutions: *Honor our mother, especially as Mother of God, through whom Jesus came down to us. Be glad to be able to contribute to the perennial honor paid her.*

Closing: Consecration to Our Queen and Mother

Filled with trust we present ourselves before the throne of grace. "In spirit we go to heaven, where we contemplate our Lady in glory. We place ourselves by her throne to praise and glorify the Trinity with her. All around the Queen of Heaven there stand all the angels and saints in numberless hosts. Among them there is a place reserved for each of us. "Filled with confidence, then, let us present ourselves."

Renewed in spirit by this retreat, we fix our eyes on things above: "our homeland is in the heavens" (Phil 3:20). Let us rejoice by reason of our future glory and imprint it vividly in our spirit. The thought of heaven should be an important stimulus during life.

This is our destiny: our retreat has confirmed it once more. There remains for us a brief struggle, a few years of renunciation and strife: these will not be overly difficult if we are on the alert. "Have confidence, my sons, I have overcome the world" (Jn 16:33).

Our Lady made the Way of the Cross lovingly, with commitment. "Was it not necessary?" (Lk 24:26). Our Queen and Mother knew that a sword of sorrow was to pierce her heart: this was her glory. There was no escape. And we? Do we follow her? Our Lady shows us the way of sacrifice. Later will come resurrection and ascension. But first we have to merit this glory: that's how God wills it. Our place, our throne is reserved for us; let it not slip from our grasp. We should say to Mary: "keep our place for us; we are coming!"

We must be resolved not to lose any of the glory that the Lord has reserved for us. Our Lady must keep our place for us and remind us when we tend to leave the path that leads there.

What happiness, that during this retreat we have found again our place in the convent, in life, a place that we never wish to abandon.

Let us place everything in the hands of Our Lady.

May she lead us as a mother does her children. Everything we do, everything we have, let us place it all in the hands of Our Lady. Let her keep and preserve it for us, showing us the finality of everything in our life. The Star of the Sea, the fixed Star, she shows us the path to take in life. An ever shining exemplar.

The Gate of Heaven! Guided by her hand, our entry is guaranteed and sure. A filial dialogue with our mother: "Show yourself to be our mother" (Hymn Ave maris Stella). We wish to be your sons in the strictest sense.

Renewal of vows

We should see the Mass as the expression of our sacrifice to God and Holy Communion as its complement. "Do this in memory of me" (Lk 22:19; 1 Cor 11:24).

At the Last Supper he gave himself to us as food. On the cross he finalized his sacrifice, which is renewed in the Mass.

At the offertory, when the matter of sacrifice is on the paten and in the chalice, let us offer ourselves to God as well, so that he who transforms and changes the bread and wine into the flesh and blood of Jesus, also change us to the degree that we may say with St. Paul, "I live, no, not I, but Christ lives in me" (Gal 2:20).

During Mass, we call down the blessing of God on our offerings. "Let my prayer rise as incense in your sight" (Ps 140:2). The priest incenses the offerings, the matter of sacrifice, saying these sublime words: "May this incense, blessed by you, O Lord, rise before you, and may your mercy come down on us."

"Raise up your hearts," open for the Lord so that he may enter with his mercy and grace.

"And I, when I am raised up from earth, will draw all things to myself" (Jn 12:32). We are beneath the cross so that the blood of Christ may fall on us and purify us. Once more we hear these words on his lips: "Behold your mother" (Jn 19:27). This is the final proof of love. With Mary let us press close to Jesus and drink the pure blood from his side, which will transform us into new men.

Holy Communion is the seal on our vows.

"The Body of Our Lord Jesus Christ keep your soul for eternal life. Amen."

4

LIGHT ON CARMEL

*An anthology from the Works of
Brother John of Saint Samson, O. Carm.*

INTRODUCTION

*In the last half of the sixteenth century Saint Tere-
sa of Avila and Saint John of the Cross attempted to
lead the Carmelites back to the closest possible approxi-
mation of their pristine or mystical spirit and, with the
special grace given them by God, set out to bring about
in that Order a reform which produced much noble
fruit in the mystical life. These facts we may take as
common knowledge. The movement has led to a division of the Order into two main branches, that of the
Ancient Observance, sometimes called the Calced, and
that of the Reform, frequently referred to as the Discalced. There is, of course, some difference between
the two observances.*

*With regard to the practice of solitude and contem-
plative prayer, as well as in abstinence from meat, the
Ancient Observance follows certain mitigations granted
by the Popes of the fourteenth century. The Discalced
have abandoned these mitigations and, in a certain
sense, lead a more retired life, devote themselves to
mental prayer one hour more a day, and abstain altogether from meat. Since they wear no shoes they have
been given the name "Discalced." This more severe
manner of living actually constitutes no substantial
difference from the Ancient Observance, who, though
they have accepted a few mitigations, still follow a rule
which—considering the many saints and* beati *it has*

produced in the course of the centuries—not only does not hinder the full flowering of the mystical spirit of the Order but also, in a high measure, furthers and supports it. They are bound by the precept of fasting more than half the year. At least four hours of the day are consecrated to prayer. Mental prayer is the first exercise of the morning, and in the evening another half hour is devoted to it. The use of meat is tolerated, but confined to four days of the week, when it is allowed not more than twice a day, and on one of these days, as a rule, only once. The difference, not very extensive in theory, is often, in the actual commerce of life, even less pronounced. What is true of the Carmelite Fathers is true to an even greater degree of the Carmelite Sisters. The life of both Orders of the Carmelite Sisters is so nearly akin, that were not the separation a matter of historical development, and had not the respective Observances become dear to each for various intangible reasons, there would scarcely seem sufficient reason for distinction and separation. Indeed, shortly after the separation, a reform also occurred in the Old Observance, which was, in a certain sense, less radical, but which led to no less exalted mystical paths and was blessed by God and rendered fruitful. Thus the previously established difference was reduced to the smallest compass by a renewal of the Ancient Observance, and a new proof was given for the fact that the accepted mitigations not only did not deprive the Order of her exalted calling, but were in every respect reconcilable with the highest mystical gifts. Of the Carmelite Sisters this is even more true. They had come into being and first springtide fervor when the mitigations were already generally accepted.

It is therefore really regrettable that in lay circles, where distinctions are often made on the grounds of a few insignificant and subordinate appearances, more thought has not been given to the fact that the spirit of Carmel is one and the same. One spirit equally animates both Observances; one ideal is before the eyes of each. One calling unites those who have devoted their lives to it, an exalted mystical calling, already set down in the ancient Institutio Primorum Monachorum which, whether of eleventh or thirteenth century origin, is the expression of the two-fold purpose placed by divine Providence before the Brothers of Saint Mary on Mount Carmel.

A double goal is set before the Order of Carmel. First, the Carmelite must strive, by his own effort and constant practice, to attain, with the help of God's grace, personal sanctification. In other words, he should perform his duties, striving to avoid all sin, apply himself to the practice of virtue, while at the same time feeling sure of the help of divine grace. But besides this there is a second and a more exalted goal— the result of the sheer goodness of God. This is that even while living upon earth, he taste in his heart and to some degree experience in his soul the inner working of the divine presence and the sweetness of heavenly bliss. Here the Order's mystical vocation, her mystical institution, is defined in unmistakable terms. The call to Carmel contains the vocation to the mystical state, a pure and simple gift of God—a gift which he desires to give to those called to Carmel, if only they will open their hearts to him and dispose themselves to receive this extraordinary divine grace.

It is not surprising that, in view of such a high and exalted calling, the number of mystical gifts is unusually great in Carmel. The Order of Carmel, under this aspect, appears to take a special place in the Church.

In every order a definite feature of the spiritual life is outstanding. If the sons and daughters of Saint Francis excel—and are obliged to excel—in the love of poverty, the bride of their founder; if the sons of Saint Ignatius practice exemplary obedience; if we observe in every order and congregation certain outstanding virtues by reason of which God seems to grant more than ordinary graces to that order, to cause its special virtue to shine forth with the greatest lustre possible; we may say that, considering her institution and history, God has bestowed on the Order of Carmel the special grace to love prayer and to seek the most intimate union with God, even in the highest degrees of the mystical life.

Prayer, interior prayer, the contemplation of God, assume a prominent place among the virtues and graces we see shining in the lives of the saints and bea-

ti *of the Carmelite Order—her greatest crown and glory.*

*In the history of prayer and of mystical gifts, Car-
mel's sons and doughters take the most prominent
places. "The Mystical Doctor," Saint John of the
Cross, "the Mother of the Spiritual Life," Saint Teresa
of Avila, whose lives were the most intimate possible
realization of the spirit of Carmel, and who have given
the Order her greatest glory, are the most authoritative
and leading figures in the Church on the question of
prayer and the spiritual life in its more exalted gifts.*

*Of the many spiritual writers of the Carmelite Or-
der, a blind brother of the seventeenth century, Brother
John of Saint Samson, of the convent of Rennes, in
France, occupies a prominent position. Belonging to
the Ancient Observance, and living under the mitigations of the rule granted by the Popes, he proved by his
life and writings that the spirit of the Order could be
renewed without abandoning the mitigations. For
that matter, Saint Teresa admitted as much in the
clearest possible terms when she would not allow her
own convent of the Incarnation to renounce these mitigations—the spirit of observance was entirely to her
satisfaction. Our Lord himself warned her, when he
inspired her to reform the Order, that she should abandon the idea that whoever did not follow her upon this
way did not possess the true spirit. In fact, these
might well be loved and inspired by him in the same
degree. He merely desired that she lead a group of
generous souls to an even stricter solicitude and segre-
gation; to a stricter abstinence and penance—their example and enthusiasm to renew and deepen the spirit
of the Order. The work of her reform took place under the guidance of, and with the complete concur-
rence of, the General of the Order. At the outset there
was no question of a break or division. Just as Saint
Mary Magdalen de' Pazzi, while remaining within the
fold of the Ancient Observance and with the permission of her superiors, did not avail herself of the mitigations that had been conceded, so did Saint Teresa, in
returning to the Rule of 1246, desire least of all to tran-
gress the then existing boundaries of the Order. Only
many years after her death did opposition spring up
through the attitude of a few, and lead to a division*

which originally was by no means the intention of the holy reformers.

In the light of all this we can now understand the situation in France at the beginning of the seventeenth century, where the liaison with the Ancient Observance, following the example and inspiration of reformers like Teresa and John of the Cross, a not less illustrious reform of Carmel occurred which adhered to the mitigations granted by the Popes. It is the "strictior observantia," or stricter observance propagated by a group of convents in the province of Tours, in La Touraine, with the convent of Rennes at its head.

It was indeed a remarkable triumvirate that divine Providence brought together in that convent. The Prior, Peter Behourt, gave the movement its first impetus in 1604. In his subprior, Philip Thibault, he directly had at hand an enthusiastic adherent, who, after Peter's death, became the great motive force behind the reform, and also succeeded him as Prior of Rennes. But the soul of the movement soon became the blind brother, John of Saint Samson, who entered the convent of Dol in 1606. He was summoned to Rennes by Father Thibault in 1612 and died there in 1636.

Because of his mystical life and profound writings he is often referred to as the John of the Cross of the Ancient Observance. One of the finest pieces of literature ever produced by the Carmelite School, treating of its spirit, came from his hand: Le Vray Esprit du Carmel.

Historians of the spiritual life of the Order—members of the Reformed Order least of all excepted—regard him as one of the most authoritative writers of Carmel. Father Jerome of the Mother of God, a member of the Discalced Carmelites of Belgium, who himself has written exceedingly deserving works on the spiritual life and has also published a very valuable study on the essence of the spiritual life of Carmel, recently called Brother John of Saint Samson "un témoin autorisé", a weighty exponent of the mystical life. The well-known Henri Bremond devotes ample space to him in his telling work, Histoire Littéraire du

Sentiment Religieux en France, *and does not hesitate to call nim* "un de nos mystiques les plus sublimes."

John of Saint Samson—or rather Jean du Moulin —had not been blind from birth, but became so as a result of a bungling treatment for an illness while he was yet a very small child. He grew up in the greatest of poverty, and after many wanderings at length found asylum in the Carmel of Paris. In return for the care bestowed upon him, he often played the organ in church, and in a short while became so skilled in this art that many were attracted to the Parisian Carmel by his playing. In the convent he was secretly revered because of his deep-seated piety which, without being in any way affected, attracted attention by its very warmth and profundity.

He was already thirty-five years old when, becoming gradually more and more penetrated by the spirit of the Carmelite Order, he made known to Father Matthew Pinault, a young priest who had just finished his studies at Paris and was returning to his convent in Dol, his desire to accompany him to Brittany and to be received into the Order at Dol. Upon the representations of Father Matthew, those at Dol made no objections to his reception. Soon it became known throughout the Province how fortunate Dol had been. The fame of his holy life caused Prior Thibault of Rennes to resolve to take him into the nucleus of the new movement for stricter observance, to strengthen its spirit. Here life was led on a higher level.

This was a joy and a great satisfaction for Brother John—who had received the name of Saint Samson as a second name. Still the unlettered blind Brother was no little embarrassed by the great number of persons who came to him to speak of spiritual matters and to receive enlightenment from him on the paths of the spiritual life. Even priests of other orders, ecclesiastics in high places in the world, came to Rennes to see him—a rather unprecedented procedure which led the prior to insist upon the Brother's writing a precise delineation of his method of prayer and intercourse with God.

Saint Therese of the Child Jesus once received a like command. Her answer was the admirable His-

toire d'une Ame. *The answer of Brother John of Saint Samson was a treatise entitled,* On the Loss of the Subject in its Object. *The Prior submitted it for approbation to persons well versed in mystical science and to several Discalced Carmelites with whom he lived on terms of the greatest friendship. Their unanimous response was one of sincere approval and admiration and an assurance that he could with safety permit persons to ask the unlettered Brother for advice and enlightenment concerning questions of the spiritual life. "He has the true spirit," sums up briefly the answer of the scholars. Thus he gathered about him a ring of spiritual friends. The convent of Rennes became known far and wide as a house of admirable observance and of the most profound spiritual activity. He had the special gift of inciting young novices to enthusiasm and complete self-sacrifice and of strengthening the spirit of the Order for posterity.*

From France, the Stricter Observance spread to Belgium and the Netherlands, to Germany and Austria, to Poland and Russia and to Ireland, causing in all these countries a new blossoming forth of the Order. Particularly in Belgium and the Netherlands did this spiritual revival bear rich fruit. From the middle of the seventeenth century there flourished here a little known renascence which signalized itself not only by the great number of persons renowned for virtue and holiness who died in the odor of sanctity, but also for the number of spiritual works which even today bear testimony to the movement. With the renewal of the spiritual life a revival of study and practice went hand in hand—particularly of the philosophical and theological sciences.

A natural consequence of that revival was the founding of still more convents. The founding, in the Northern Netherlands, of the convent of Boxmeer in 1653, was speedily followed by the establishment of a convent of Carmelite nuns in the same place in 1672. These convents became the respective motherhouses of the Netherland Province of the Carmelite Fathers of the Ancient Observance, and of the four Carmelite convents for women of the same observance.

As members of this school we may mention Father Daniel of the Blessed Virgin Mary (van Audenaerde),

268

popularly known as "the holy father," who died at Antwerp in 1678. He wrote some fifteen spiritual and historical works, the most striking and distinguished of which are the exhaustive history of the Order in four parts, entitled Speculum Carmelitanum, a briefer work, Vinea Carmeli, and a delightful little book in Flemish, an Instruction for a Devout Life. Besides him, there is Father Michael of Saint Augustine (van Ballaert), the most authoritative writer of this school, who died at Brussels in 1684. In nine works he has pictured the whole richness of the spiritual life of Carmel. Of these a Latin Introduction to the Interior Life, in which he ascends to the contemplation of the most sublime mystical life; a Flemish Introduction to the Land of Carmel; and a small work on the "Mariform" life; are perhaps the most significant. It is not surprising that the first and last were reprinted in 1926 by Father Gabriel Wessels and have again found a wide distribution. In the ascetical and mystical works of these two friars of the Low Countries we may perceive the spirit that animated the stricter observance of Touraine, of which the blind Brother John of Saint Samson has already been called the soul.

Turning to this source of Carmel's spiritual life, we uncover the consoling thought that all who are called to the Carmelite Order may see in that call a vocation to the highest spiritual life, mystical experience not excepted. There are many upon whom God wishes to bestow this interior intercourse with himself, this enjoyment of himself. The vocation to the Carmelite Order is an indication that he selects these chosen ones to this end in a special manner, provided they place no obstacles to his grace, and remain firm in the realization that communication of it always remains, in the words of the well-known Institutio Primorum Monachorum, a free gift of God.

John of Saint Samson lays great stress upon this vocation and selection. The first concern of all who are called to the Order must be to place no obstacle in the way of the grace of God—destined for them in such overflowing measure. It is necessary for them to labor and to study, to preach and to perform other works in the care of souls, but these activities must never hinder them from living with God and speaking with God in the most intimate intercourse. This is their primary and most sublime vocation. It must not be jeopardized. Therefore that foundation must be laid first, and upon that foundation further construction may proceed. From this it follows that Brother John desires the novices, from the moment they are in the Order, to strive to attain an interior and deep spiritual life; to open themselves to the grace of God, in order that God may unite himself to them and lead them to the most intimate union with himself. This first foundation is laid, so that, resting thereon and being truly and deeply united to God, they are able to withstand the distractions of work.

He clearly indicates that the mystical life does not consist in visions and apparitions, in stigmata or levitations from the ground, but only in the perception of God for us, with us and in us, and in the resultant deep love of God. The latter burns like a flame within us, and we desire nothing else than that God consume us with his fire and cause us to ascend into himself. He rejects with the utmost emphasis the thought that this mystical life is not for us, is not something for each of us. Naturally he does not neglect to point out that the disposition thereto and the steps in that ascent to God, are gifts and graces of God, that we cannot attain to it by ourselves. He no less emphatically points out that God has disposed us to it and that we must develop that receptiveness granted us, free from all hindrances. Then he notes that a negative avoidance of all that might place a hindrance in the way of our ascent to God is not sufficient, but that we also can and must cooperate positively in that ascent by the continuous practice of virtue.

A second consoling thought of John of Saint Samson is his representation of the Order as a school or a family where, with mutual fellowship and assistance, we strive after the same goal. We can, he says, no more dispense with the element of education in the spiritual than in the natural life. We need teachers and leaders. It is exceptional for God not to require the cooperation of a religious Order in order to lead his chosen ones to the higher levels of the spiritual life. And that is why, he says, it is of such great worth and significance that there should be in the Church so many schools of the spiritual and mystical life, each with its own traditions and ideals. Thus, by different means, they lead variously disposed persons along the way to God best adapted to them. It makes no difference if the paths diverge somewhat from each other. They all end in God and find their common goal in the same justification. God has given a rich variety to nature. In the spiritual life he likewise wills an adjustment to the diversity of aptitudes and educations and demonstrates that he knows how to share his gifts and graces under a multitude of forms. His wise and loving Providence has, besides many others, also planned that the Carmelite Order lead many to the most sublime heights of the mystical life. He has stamped that Order as an entirely distinct school of mysticism by the doctrines it holds in reverence and by the members who have attained great sanctity. When he sets out new slips in that garden, he desires to see them develop and bloom as flowers, receiving the full sunlight and the full ardor of his warmth, the sun of that garden. When he calls so many young souls to the Order, the Order is obliged to devote to them the care proportionate to their calling.

A third consoling thought of Brother John of Saint Samson is that God would like to operate in us much more efficiently than he actually does, and that he pursues us with his love. Nothing is more imperative than entire surrender to God, the complete placing of oneself in his hands. By his infinite and hence incomprehensible love—his infinite and hence inexhaustible wealth—he overwhelms us with his gifts and benefits. He would fill us with himself, if we do not shut our hearts from him by filling them with much that is not himself. If we only knew how to empty our hearts and detach ourselves from all that is not God, we would be astonished at his work in us. Were one thoroughly penetrated by that truth, he would be entirely wrapped up in God. And the body would follow the behest of the soul instead of weighing it down, and subjugating it to itself.

It goes without saying that Brother John stresses attention to oral prayer as well as to contemplation. This is a result of the very nature of life in Carmel. Besides this, he asks that particular attention be

271

paid to a form of prayer which he calls at once the continuation and the abiding fruit of contemplation: manifold, repeated, love-inspired ejaculatory prayer. It has always been known in the Church, and we find it mentioned or designated by the oldest writers, because it is natural for a man who seeks God, and is united to him, to be continually preoccupied with the thought of him and to speak to him according to the circumstances of the moment. Yet even here there is not lacking a certain development, and the ejaculation, from being a spontaneous utterance, has become a systematized exercise.

A particular service of the Devotio Moderna in the Netherlands of the fifteenth and sixteenth centuries, is that it insisted strongly on this exercise and pointed out the way to it. Everyone had his mine of nuggets of sifted gold in the form of pithy sayings and ejaculations culled with love and care from spiritual writers. Although this devotion was at first an exercise entirely left to individual impulse and piety, in time method entered. Above all it was the Friar Minor, Henry Herp, who systematized this manner of praying and uniting one's self to God. He calls it aspiratio, aspiration, or the lifting of the spirit to God. He treats of it in Chapter XLVI of the third part of his Spiehel der Velcomenheit, known and edited under its Latin title, Directorium Contemplativorum. Father Lucidius Vershueren, O.F.M., prepared a splendid edition of it in 1931, in which the chapter in question is found in the Latin and Flemish on pages 266 to 285. Herp is not a pioneer in this field, but builds on the Theologia Mystica of Hugo van Balma, a Carthusian of the latter half of the thirteenth century, a little work that had a wide circulation throughout Western Europe. It often appears as a treatise of Saint Bonaventure, among whose works it was repeatedly published. But Herp more narrowly circumscribed his doctrine of aspiratio and above all was responsible for its wide dissemination. It is apparent that John of Saint Samson took his description of this mode of prayer, not from Hugo van Balma, but from Henry Herp. And for him, as well as for Herp, aspiratio is the most potent and ardent way of ascending to God, for remaining united to him and for becoming yet more intimately united to him. Both urge us as earnestly as possible to exercise ourselves continually in "offering," "supplicating," "resembling" and "uniting," as Herp expresses it.

It would lead us too far afield to set forth in greater detail how John of Saint Samson still further develops this method of prayer—describing and perfecting this wonderful devotion. We will confine ourselves to describing the four steps in a few words: to offer oneself entirely to and for God; to continually petition his grace and assistance; to make ourselves ever more conformable to God; and to make ourselves more and more one with God.

The Brother grants that this is far from easy, and that it is only with continual practice that a reluctant progress is achieved. But his way leads us to the unbroken vision of God and to continual conversation with him. It becomes second nature to us to have God ever present before our eyes and within our hearts, and to go through life united to him. All that pleases the senses cannot bind us, for we transcend them. Still, Brother John warns us after the manner of Saint Teresa, we must not carry this to the point where we no longer have an eye for the physical imagining of the life and passion of Jesus, our God who became man for us.

He goes on to say more about this vision of God. It transcends all things. The subject loses itself entirely in the Object. A marvelous interaction arises between God and the soul. But the soul loses itself in God, realizing that it desires to comprehend the Incomprehensible, to express the Inexpressible in words and concepts. It is at one and the same time surrounded by light and darkness. It can find no words to describe what it sees and comprehends, and is drawn to enjoy this in the depths of its being, and there to commune with God. There glows that spark implanted by God as a marvelous capacity for knowing and understanding him and of directing one's life toward him. That knowledge of God and striving after him becomes all-absorbing in the soul, and that "spark" becomes a light and a fire which causes true wisdom and the most upright and pure love to become in the soul the beginning of the "life with God."

Finally, Brother John of Saint Samson would not be a leading figure of Carmelite mysticism did he not regard Mary in a special manner as our Mother and guide in the spiritual life. She is the Queen of Love who is to lead us into the kingdom of love at the head of a galaxy of saints; she is the Queen of the World— the Kingdom of God. She is full of grace and must share this fulness. She is the Almoner of God, our continual Advocate. Through her we participate in the most intimate union with God, for through her God has seen fit to unite himself to us and become man. That is why we must always remain at her side, under her maternal protection, and consider it a privilege to receive her guidance and assistance, her example and aid.

In an effusion to God he cries out that no creature better or more clearly represents him to us, and possesses more conformity to him than Mary—interiorly in her heart as well as exteriorly in her life. If we penetrate her perfection, we penetrate God himself, for she is most like him, a second self. We must contemplate her just as we are bound to contemplate God. In quiet admiration we should look up at her exalted qualities, realizing that they transcend anything God has given to man. In her we acquaint ourselves with the most glorious expression of God's love, and by contemplating her we see how much God loves man after all. The sight should transport us into ecstasy.

Truly it is good to be a child of Mary. As children of Mary, desirous of being comformable to her, we are drawn to God. We stand with her at the foot of the cross, sharing in the sacrificial death of the Lord; dying to ourselves and the whole world; living only in and for God—in union with our Mother, guided and assisted by her.

Father John Brenninger, O. Carm., closes an article on Brother John of Saint Samson in Volume III of the Analecta Ordinis Carmelitarum with the following beautiful words, taken from the ninth of his spiritual letters: "All our lives we must seek only to die to self. This should be our only satisfaction. To this our effort should, according to the highest wisdom, be directed, that we behold God in solitude of soul and

*body, as the spirit of the Order recommends. That sol-
itude, that lonely intercourse with God, we should never leave, except it be that God plainly calls us elsewhere, in order there to do other deeds. That is the
best part, may we abide in it."* Father Brenninger
calls this a brief summary of the spirit and meaning of
life in the Carmelite Order.

Nijmegen, March 1, 1939

Dr. Titus Brandsma, O. Carm.

5

THE SCAPULAR

BADGE of Honor. *One in the service of a person of great distinction likes to declare himself as such. There is personal pride in representing a highly placed person.*

Among those who receive a distinction from her Majesty the Queen there are few who do not wear the sign of it in their buttonhole.

One who has the right to wear a uniform wears it with a certain pride, at least if he values the position or situation which requires him to wear that uniform or livery.

But people go further still. They also wear distinctive signs to show that they are members of a society or association. By wearing the insignia they want to witness publicly that they are members of this or that association, that they are striving after the ideal of that association.

For Catholics the Scapular is also such a distinctive sign. *They wear it as a sign of royal favor, as a livery which identifies a group of servants, as a uniform which indicates an office or situation, as an insignia that points to membership in an association.*

Put yourself first of all in the attitude of Catholics toward devotion to Mary. *As you have been able to read in previous pamphlets we honor Mary highly, very highly. Let it be again repeated, Mary remains for us a human being: we pay her no honor due to God. Let it also be again repeated, all that excellence for which we honor Mary we regard as grace which* she has received from her Son, Jesus Christ. Thus we honor in Mary's gifts the grace of Christ.

We not only honor Mary, we also ask her intercession with God, and it is because she is the Mother of Our Lord Jesus Christ that we believe her intercession to be so powerful.

In that sense we honor her as the mighty Queen of Heaven.

After reflecting on all this you will understand how in the course of time groups of persons arose who considered it an important part of their task to honor Mary, to promote her honor.

Thus the Franciscans specially defend her Immaculate Conception, the Dominicans promote devotion to her through the prayer of the rosary, etc.

The Brothers of Our Lady of Mount Carmel—this is the official name of the Carmelites—also chose as their special vocation the honor of Mary. The characteristic part of their clothing, of their livery as Brothers of Our Lady, is the Scapular, a long, wide strip of brown woolen cloth, half of which hangs down the chest, the other half down the back.

Not everyone can become a religious, but the ideal that inspires many to enter an Order, that ideal by no means leaves others cold. What happens as a result? Men and women living in the world, inspired by the desire to honor Mary, join the Brothers of Our Lady, join the guard of honor of Mary. Likewise many who have no connection with the cloister have themselves enrolled in the Third Order of St. Francis, because the ideal of the Poor Man of Assisi attracts them also. They receive as a mark of distinction "the habit of the Order." In like manner those who join the Brothers of Mary, the Carmelites, receive as a distinguishing sign the characteristic part of the habit of their Order, the Scapular.

What does wearing the Scapular mean? By joining the guard of honor of Mary the Catholic accepts the obligation to live as the child, the servant, the devotee of Mary; that is, exactly and faithfully to fulfill the commandments of God and the duties of religion in honor of and in imitation of the Virgin Mary.

277

The Scapular is sometimes called a "pledge of salvation," a "shield from danger," a "guarantee that the wearer will not stray from the path of good." This should not be taken to mean that one who wears the Scapular can sin all he wants and still attain heaven. Far from it! Only if one lives as becomes a servant of Mary, observes all the commandments, and avoids sin, will one attain heaven. But through the intercession of Mary he hopes to receive special help from God.

A royal livery. We Catholics however regard the Scapular as something more than the insignia of a group of Marian devotees.

According to trustworthy witnesses—and their testimony may be investigated with the strictest methods of historical criticism—the sixth prior general of the Carmelites, St. Simon Stock, had a vision in which the Blessed Virgin assured him that for those who wore it, the habit of the Order would be a pledge of her particular protection. On these grounds we regard the Scapular not as a badge we ourselves have assumed but as a royal sign of honor of the Queen of Heaven; as a uniform, a livery with which she clothes her preferred servants.

The present form of the Scapular. The Scapular, as it is worn today, is made of brown woolen cloth. It consists of two halves, of which one falls down in front over the chest, the other behind over the back. The two halves are connected over the shoulders by woolen ribbons or strings.

The Scapular medal. Just as the elegant costumes of the former Orders of Knights have been replaced by a ribbon or a button as a symbol of the clothing indicative of the wearer's high station, so the popes have permitted a medal to be worn in place of the two-piece woolen Scapular.

No talisman, no amulet. Perhaps the thought has occurred to you that the Scapular is like a talisman, an amulet, a motorist's charm, something to which a mysterious, often supernatural power is attributed?

As you will have already understood, the Scapular is something quite different. If you want to compare

278

our Scapular with anything, you should think of an Order of Knights.

We attribute to the thing itself not the least power, but we expect that for those who wear her badge of honor and wish to go through life as her children adorned with it, Mary will obtain God's help in danger, particularly in the hour of death.

Conclusion. *If the Mother of Jesus with God in heaven receives special honor from her Son, if we may honor the great men and women of history, if not only the living but also those standing in glory before the throne of God can intercede for us with him, if the Mother of the Savior has more power with God than any other creature, then you will understand why we Catholics wear with pride the Scapular, the insignia of Mary.*

No. 9 in a series of ten pamphlets by various authors, published in a folder with the title Maria, 'sHertogenbosch, 1925.

6

WHY WE ARE CALLED CARMELITES: A POSITION PAPER

The Order should always and in all events strive to maintain the distinctive qualities which throughout the past centuries, as history attests, were proper to it by the disposition of divine providence. There are two things, then, that the Order should strive to attain with special zeal: prayer and dedication to learning. By Pontifical command we have been called from the eremitical to the active life. As such, we are not only to dedicate ourselves to prayer and learning for ourselves in our cells, but to direct both of them to the salvation of souls.

The spirit of mission should be fostered by prayer. By the contemplation and meditation on the apostolic life of the Redeemer and of his Co-redemptrix, the Bl. Virgin Mary, each should inflame his heart for the most sacred of all works, that of cooperation in the salvation of souls.

Let them follow the example of St. Angelus, who following the original charism of the Order gave himself over to prayer, but then, inspired by divine grace, he lept into the world with a burning zeal for the law of the Lord, even to the martyr's crown.

Let them follow the example of our holy Father Elijah. While leading an eremitical life, he was called by God to leave his country and magnify the glory of God in Zarephath of Sidon.

Those who cannot go to the missions physically should become sharers in the work of the missions spiritually by their prayers and sacrifices.

Thus we are urged that each convent be committed to the care of souls, especially those that are more closely linked to the life of prayer. Above all, therefore, they should work for the salvation of souls in retreat work, in the preaching of missions, in instruction of the people, in hearing confessions, in writing, and similar things.

Where the secular clergy is not sufficient to meet the demands of parochial service, for instance in non-Catholic areas, and where the lack of priests leaves parishes unattended, they should dedicate themselves to this apostolic service with the greatest zeal in all its aspects. Parishes which we accepted when priests were lacking, certainly need not be given up once the number of priests increases, because they provide an historical witness to our vocation to an apostolic life of mission.

Likewise, in studying they should not aim only to ferret out the secrets of learning in order to raise their spirit to higher things and to lead to the contemplation of divine wisdom; each should subordinate his study to the active life. Superiors should use all their diligence in obliging, with their sage advice, younger Carmelites to study. This study should be adapted to the abilities of each, but also adapted to meet the needs which scientific Christian learning encounters within the territory of one's Province, especially on a secondary and university level, to which the Order contributed validly in times past.

Besides internal schools in which we train our clerics, each province should strive to erect schools for the laity, in which the priests of the Order, either on their own or aided by secular teachers, teach secondary school materials to young people, following the norms and demands of schools instituted or recognized by the state.

Insofar as the situation of the Province and of the place permit, we should want such schools to be attached to each of our convents, like mission territory assigned to each Province.

In this way both superiors and the individual members should strive to foster the double charism of our Order, with the cooperation and aid of Mary the unique Patroness of our Institute. Let them place all activities under her patronage, let them sanctify all their works in her honor, and so make them proper to the Order. For the whole of the Order is Marian not in name but in fact. If it is not Marian, it is not truly Carmelite.

Oss, during the Octave of the Presentation of the Bl. Virgin Mary, 1919.

P. Titus Brandsma

7

Dear Aloysius,

You ask if I shall return to Holland.   You fear that I won't.   Given that we write to one another, I wish to add, as really you should know, that I'll never be anxious to wish something special for myself, even if sometimes, according to the natural turn of events, I do expect something.   If the superiors think that I can be useful in Australia, Japan, Russia or the United States, I am ready to leave early tomorrow morning.   In this I don't change.   In this sense my bond with the Dutch Province could be called weak, but not for lack of attraction or affection.   No, on the contrary, I would be very willing to do something about this.   But, thanks be to God, I'm a member of a Catholic Order, and in Greek that means universal. . .

Yours, Titus.

Nijmegen, December 2, 1939

*To the Illustrious Professor, Canon Dr. L. Bellon
President of the Theological Faculty
of the Catholic University of Nijmegen*

Distinguished Colleague,

In reply to your appreciated letter of November 30, I will give you my opinion: the Catholic faith in our country is seriously threatened and weakened by very many doctrines which culminate in German National Socialism, in which they find their strongest expression. These doctrines are attractive. This influence can best be halted on the one hand by exposing the theory of this National Socialism and the philosophy from which it rose—above all that of Nietzsche—in its lamentable tendencies, and to confute it. On the other hand by clearly stressing, in an enthusiastic and positive way, the value of the human person in both the natural and supernatural orders.

In reply to the question what have we done in a practical way, I think it sufficient to note that during the past academic year, in my university course on the history of contemporary philosophy, I gave lessons on National Socialism from a philosophical viewpoint, and in my course on the Philosophy of History I spoke for the whole year about the growth and development of National Socialism as a typical example of a reactionary phenomenon.

I am always willing to provide further information.

*Your servant in Christ,
fr. Titus Brandsma, O. Carm.*

The letter we print here was written by Father Brandsma in the hectic days before his arrest. It was sent to us by Mrs. Daniels of Croydon, N.S.W.

Carmel,
Nijmegen,
November 18, 1941.

Dear Madam, —May I congratulate you most heartily on the happy news that your son will be released on December 20th. You will have a difficult month trying to wait patiently for his return, but at least there will be the happy anticipation of his being among you again in five weeks time.

I have thanked the Burgomaster for his co-operation. He informed me of the result by letter. I was very sorry that I was not here when you came to bring the glad tidings, but Father Prior told me as soon as I came in.

How successful all the efforts of yourself and your daughter have been! I rejoice with you that everything has gone so well.

With kind regards to yourself, Madam, your daughter and your son,
Yours faithfully in Christ,
fr. Titus Brandsma, O. Carm.

Circumstances of the Letter

Mrs. Daniels, who migrated to Australia after the war, sends these details:

". . . My mother received this letter and I am the daughter mentioned in it. She still lives in Holland

but sent this letter to me to keep as a relic. Mother knew Professor Brandsma from the time when he was a young priest.

"You may like to know about my brother's release. My brother Jan, aged 20 at the time, had served in the Dutch army in 1940. After the capitulation he went back to the Merchant Navy College. But he had a gun in his possession. Carelessness on his part and treason on the part of some collaborators resulted in a raid of the German Gestapo. My brother was taken prisoner. That was in January, 1941. After spending some weeks in a Dutch prison he was transferred to Wuppertal in Germany.

"You can understand what a heavy cross this was for my mother. In her sorrow she turned to Father Brandsma, who promised to do what was in his power. Practical as he was, he discussed with mother the best way to approach the German authorities. We knew already that mother's tears would have no effect. Father Brandsma knew that they were very sensitive to "big names," so he suggested the drawing up of a petition and having it signed by several influential people. I never read the petition, nor do I know all the signatories to it since Father Brandsma told us to leave everything to him. The result was that we were notified that Jan would be released on December 20th.

"On that day my elder brother and I went to Nijmegen to meet Jan. We had to watch the trains coming from three directions since Jan could have crossed the border at different places. It was already getting late when we met Father Brandsma at the station. He had just got off a train and was on his way home, but when we told him that we were waiting for Jan he stayed with us.

"Then three trains came almost at once to different platforms. Father Brandsma watched the passengers get off one of the trains. Jan arrived and he was the first one to welcome him home. He saw us off on the train that took us to Oss and I still remember how sincerely he rejoiced with us.

"That was the last time I ever saw him. A short time afterwards he himself was taken prisoner."

Personal Recollections

"You ask me what my personal recollections of Professor Brandsma are. Well, once when I was only a girl I went to see him at the monastery in Nijmegen. I know that I went with a feeling of awe. After all, Father Brandsma was a professor, and everybody knew that he did a great deal of other work as well and led a very busy life. I cannot recollect the purpose of the visit but I do remember how very kindly I was received, how my interests were discussed as if they were the only things that mattered and, above all, how I did not get the slightest impression that I was sitting opposite someone for whom every minute counted.

"Shortly afterwards I mentioned this visit to Father Voordermeer, O. Carm, and I remember his saying that nobody could understand how it was possible that a person with such delicate health and such a frail body could manage such an enormous amount of work.

"During the time my brother was in prison my mother frequently went to see Professor Brandsma. A talk with him always cheered her up and gave her new hope. Once when she went to see him he was just leaving for the University. He expressed his regret and then asked her to walk with him to the University so that they could still have a little talk. During this period he once happened to be in Oss and paid us an unexpected visit one Sunday afternoon.

"All this happened during the months preceding Father Brandsma's arrest. Those who have read his life will know just how full of anxiety and worry these months must have been for him. Still, he never failed to cheer mother, whenever he had the opportunity. Those who never knew could never guess the strain he must have been under. I think that the fact that mother did not hesitate to turn to him in her sorrow speaks for itself. . ."

287

10

JANUARY 19, 1941
FATHER TITUS IS ARRESTED

Having spent the night in Arnhem, I was told that I must spend another night there. With these words I was brought into cell 577 on January 20. Next morning I had to be ready at half past eight to be tried at the Hague. This would probably be finished in the afternoon, and in view of my health I would probably be allowed home. On the night of January 21, I was told that my confinement was to be prolonged in order that more evidence might be obtained. Mr. Hardegen, who tried my case in a courteous way, said that this would not be difficult for me on account of my religious life. Indeed, it was not. I remember an old stanza of Longfellow which I have retained since my college years in Megen, and it is particularly appropriate in my present situation:

> *In his chamber all alone,*
> *Kneeling on a floor of stone,*
> *Prayed a monk in deep contrition*
> *For his sins of indecision;*
> *Prayed for greater self-denial*
> *In temptation and in trial.*

As to that "trial," it was not so difficult as I had expected, though one has to get accustomed to many things in prison. Indeed, going to prison at the age of 60 is a strange experience. Jokingly I said so to Mr. Steffen who had arrested me, while entering the prison. His answer, however, comforted me: "It is your own fault, for you should not have taken the Archbishop's commission." Now I knew why I was here and I said to him fearlessly that I looked upon such a thing as an honor, and that I was not conscious of having done anything wrong by doing that. I said the same thing to Mr. Hardegen and I added: "On the contrary, it was an honest effort to relax the contrasts." On the one side this was accepted, on the other side it was looked upon as an organisation of resistance against the occupying power. I had to oppose this last opinion, and to stress the exclusive intention of communicating both to the press and to the Reichskommissariat the Catholic point of view about the propaganda of the National Socialist Movement, as it was pointed out by the Bishops. This point of view was to be communicated to the Reichskommissariat, even if the managers and editorial staffs of the Catholic dailies were not in agreement; but undoubtedly, they were.

The first day of my commission I asked Mr. Schlichting to go to the Reichskommissariat; on account of his journey to Rome this interview took place after mine with the Catholic press. Meanwhile I quite understand that the attitude of the Bishops and of the Catholic press is not considered agreeable, and that the commission of the Archbishop to me and carried out by me, is looked upon as some act of resistance. Our Catholic principles are at conflict with their principles; the contrast of principles is there. For this confession I joyfully suffer what is to be suffered.

My vocation to the Church and to the priesthood brought me so many grand and beautiful things that I willingly accept something unpleasant in return for it. I repeat in complete agreement with Job: We have received good things at the hand of God, why should we not receive the evil he sends us in his Providence? The Lord gave, the Lord hath taken away. Blessed be the name of the Lord. Apart from that, I have not had too bad a time. And although I do not know what will become of it, I know myself to be wholly in God's hands. Who will separate us from the love of God? I am thinking of my old motto:

> Prenez les jours, comme ils arrivent,
> Les beaux d'un coeur reconnaissant
> Et les mauvais pour ceux qui suivent,
> Car le malheur n'est qu'un passant.

With Gezelle, I praise "my old breviary," which was luckily left to me and which I can say now as quietly as possible. Oh! in the morning Holy Mass and Holy Communion are missing, I know full well, but nevertheless God is near me, in me and with me. It is in him that we live, and move and have our being. "God, while so near and yet so far, is always present." The well-known couplet which was always in St. Teresa's breviary—I sent it to my colleague Professor Brom when he was in prison—is also a comfort and encouragement to me; "Let nothing disturb thee, let nothing frighten thee. All things are passing. God does not change. Who possesses God wants for nothing. God alone suffices."

Scheveningen Police-prison,
January 23, 1942.

11
MY CELL

"Cella continuata dulcescit." *A cell becomes more sweet as it is more faithfully dwelt in.*

Professor van Ginneken rather strongly propagated the opinion that the Imitation *has a pessimistic outlook, but in regard to dwelling in the cell, the writer really has an optimistic view, and I myself, as an optimist by birth, have experienced here anew how gladly Thomas à Kempis, and those in whose spirit he wrote, have looked upon the solitary life in a silent cell, after having themselves lived like that.*

Well, being brought into a prison cell late at night, the door being heavily closed behind you with locks and keys, you stand and feel rather strange for a moment. The comic side of this affair, my going to jail in my old age, urged me to laugh rather than to cry, but strange it was all the same. There I stood. I arrived rather late, at least for a prison; about half past seven. By then it was time for bed, and labor was finished. I was not expected. Actually no cell had been made ready for me. But then there is not so much to prepare. I was given a jar of water, a towel and also a piece of cloth, to clean something or for serviette, I do not know. As there had been a phone call that I still had to eat, I received a small loaf, which was also meant to do for next morning, and a tin cup of skim milk; on the table was a small pewter wash-bowl with some water; on the bed—a straw mattress—two blankets; I had to manage for myself. Though lights in other cells are switched off at eight o'clock, my light was kept on about half an hour longer.

It was not an Inferno, my small cell, number 577. And while entering there I did not read over the door: "Abandon hope all ye who enter here." It did not look ominous, and when the assistant warden pointed out to the soldier that the cell was not ready, the latter said: "It is only for one night."

I did not receive a sheet. I always happen to be unbearably irritated by the tickling of woollen blankets at my head. To arrange things I turned the clean towel down over the upper end of the blankets. On the bedstead were two straw mattresses, one upon the other. In most cells there are two prisoners, in some of them even three. In those cases one of the mattresses must be put on the floor, I think. I experienced that already in my cell at Arnhem where a bedstead was missing. To be quite honest, those straw mattresses and blankets disgust me a bit when they are to be used without any sheets. So for the first night I kept my stockings on. Next morning I received a sheet and a towel. I said to the young man—he was also a prisoner but he was allowed or had to work a little—that he was late in bringing the sheet, because I would leave that day. "I would take it," he said kindly. "I was only going to be here for three days and it looks as though I'll be here three years." He foresaw things better than I did, and I am very glad to have my sheet and my second towel.

For a pillow I had nothing else but a straw bolster, which also causes some discomfort to my head. Having spent a sleepless night at Arnhem, and desiring to be as fresh as possible next day at the prolonged trial, I invented something in order to be more comfortable. I had taken a jersey undervest with me. I folded this around the pillow and put a new towel over it. It began to have the appearance of a soft pillow. It could have been worse. Every night now I make my bed in this way. Since I cannot go on wearing my socks for ever, I put my second towel over the foot of the mattress, stretch the sheet over myself, and then the two blankets and, for the first days, when it was pretty cold, my duffel greatcoat also. After all this, little fault could be found with my bed. In prison this matter is rather important, seeing that one has to go off to bed at eight o'clock and to rise about seven o'clock in the morning. It is out of the question that I could sleep all that time, but the light is switched off at eight and switched on only at seven o'clock: where can one stay if not in bed?

My little cell itself is not so bad: a tiny bit of a room with the bed occupying the whole breadth. That defines the breadth of the cell, which may be about 1 m. 80, 1 m. 90: six times the length of this piece of paper and a small piece besides (till the mark). The length is nearly double, approximately twelve times this paper, plus a small piece besides (till the mark at the foot of this page). The height is nearly the same as the length. Two thirds of the side walls are made in clean brickwork. I count sixty five bricks in the height with a rather thick seam; around the bed the wall is plastered; that is tidier. The walls are a light yellow up to the height of the door; above that they are white. They look rather neat. The door, in the middle of the front wall, is painted brown. Right in the centre is a little square iron shutter through which the food is handed.

Over that shutter is an iron peephole, but I have not seen it open yet. On the first night I thought there was no window, but the next day I perceived that this was to be found high over the door towards the ceiling, taking the whole breadth of the cell and being divided into three parts. The middle part is easily opened by means of a handle. So the light is abundant and the possibility for ventilation excellent. But the windows do not show me anything but the sky; now and then I see a sea gull skimming by. Till now the windows are full of the most beautiful frost decorations for the greater part of the day, although the sun and the central heating see to it that at least sometimes there are here and there free spots of light. Yes, there also is central heating. At some height over the bed run three heating pipes. They do not give very much warmth. On the coldest days I shiver a bit practically all day long, but they take away the worst cold, and it can very well be endured. At least I do not think it is cold enough to put on my coat, even when sitting.

There is a stone floor, made of fairly big blue tiles, but in front of the door was a good mat, which I put under the table during the day and beside my bed at night. "Table" is actually a grandiloquent name. It is a tip-up table on the wall at the left, a bit smaller than the opened newspaper which serves as a table cloth. I lay my table with the "Vaderland"; it shows its nice title ("Fatherland") on both sides. There has to be something appealing in such a bare cell! Before me I have a small altar, or whatever you may like to call it. I found a paper checkerboard in my cell with checkers. I don't think I shall start playing, but I also found a piece of packingpaper. I wrapped it around the board and, using a nail from a cigar box—one has to manage to get on, for I have been deprived of both knife and scissors—I made three nicks in the packing-paper; in these nicks I put three holy pictures from my breviary. So in front of me I have the picture of Christ on the Cross, and although it is not full length, at least it is a nice bust with the wound of the Sacred Heart, and it is Fra Angelico, too! On one side of it I put St. Teresa with her motto: "To die or to suffer," and on the other side St. John of the Cross with his: "To suffer and to be contemned." I also found two pins and I used one for putting under the three pictures a paper with St. Teresa's motto, "Nada te turbe, etc." in the middle: "Gott so nah und ferne, Gott ist immer da;" and lastly my favourite maxim: "Prenez les jours comme ils arrivent." I had no stray picture of Our Lady in my breviary—and surely her image ought to be in a Carmelite's cell. I managed this too. In the part of the breviary we are using now, and which was luckily left to me, is the beautiful picture of Our Lady of Mount Carmel. So now my breviary is standing wide open on the topmost of the two corner shelves, to the left of the bed. When sitting at my table I only have to look a bit to the right and I can see her beautiful picture; while lying in bed my eye is first-ly caught by that star-bearing Madonna, Hope of all Carmelites.

I have no chair, only a three-legged bench, which is rather comfortable. If I need a back-rest—for one gets more tired here by doing nothing than by doing hard work at home—I put my bench next to the table near the wall and then I have a most comfortable arm-chair. There is not much to be told about the rest of the furniture, and it is soon counted: a broom and dustpan for tidying up my cell, a small pail and a floor cloth, a wastepaper basket, a big pail with a useful lid which is carried away once daily, and a blue stone jar of water. Lastly, there is a tin soap dish and a row of three pegs. The lamp is put over the tip-up table on the wall. It is switched on and off from outside.

"Beata solitudo, *blessed solitude.*" I am already quite at home in this small cell. I have not yet got bored here, just the contrary. I am alone, certainly, but never was Our Lord so near to me. I could shout for joy because he made me find him again entirely, without me being able to go to see people, nor people me. Now he is my only refuge, and I feel secure and happy. I would stay here for ever, if he so disposed. Seldom have I been so happy and content.

Scheveningen, January 27, 1942

12

MY TIMETABLE

"Now read, now pray, now work with fervor; so time will pass quickly and work will be easier."

On the first days I had some difficulty in fixing up a timetable; but now that I have been here for a week and know the order of things I have tried to follow a daily rule. It is difficult to do everything to time for, firstly, the ordinary things of the prison routine do not keep exactly to the clock and, secondly, it is not easy to know what time it is.

This was especially difficult in the first days because my watch, together with most things, had been taken away from me. Fortunately, I received it back last Wednesday night. I had to give a written answer to a question. I was allowed to smoke so I asked for my pipe, tobacco, etc., and at the same time for my watch. Of course it had stopped and I chose a time at random, more or less correct. There is no clock here and in things which are timed the hour is not reliable because one does not keep to it exactly. But my watch goes and so I have my own time, independent of Greenwich, Amsterdam or Berlin.

Between 6:30 and 7:00 o'clock in the morning the first sounds are heard. Then the wardens seem to awaken the young prisoners, who perform divers current jobs. About a quarter to seven a bell is rung, but very softly. Slowly further alarm is raised. Some time later people go around, the double locks seem to be opened, and the light is switched on. That is the time, at least for me, to rise. After all, it is about time to get up, having had such a long night's sleep. I

296

make the Sign of the Cross, greet Our Lady of Mount Carmel on the shelf over my bed, and put on my stockings and slippers. Then I say three Hail Mary's and a short prayer. Then I start stripping my bed. I shake the blankets and fold them neatly and do the same with the sheet. Then I put my water jar outside the open door. Still in my pajamas, the folded blankets lying on the mat, I kneel down and in my own manner, and supplying what I do not know by heart, I say Mass, make a spiritual Communion and say the prayers of thanksgiving. It goes more quickly, in more ways than one. It is a good start to the day. At home there is meditation first and after that the Office but here I prefer to say Mass first, even though I am in night attire.

Soon the jar is brought back with fresh water. The door opens for a moment. We say good morning to each other and I begin to wash myself. I would very much like to shave but this luxury has been reduced to Wednesday and Saturday afternoons. On those days the doors open for ten minutes and we receive a safety razor, if necessary soap and shaving brush also, with which we have to manage very quickly. If the razor is not sharp we are allowed to ask for another one. When I am washing myself in the morning—about half past seven—a man comes with coffee. All of us have a nice tin cup with a handle, a plate and a spoon. At night the plate and spoon are put outside but in the morning we receive them back when the water is brought around. I crumble my bread on the plate and pour the coffee over it making quite a full plate. Then I finish dressing and leave the bread soaking. By eight o'clock I am a gentleman again—except for my beard—and dressed in black. I sit down on the stool at the table, say the Angelus, an Our Father and a Hail Mary, as in the convent, and partake of my breakfast with my spoon.

Oh, I used to do that in our Bavarian convents thirty five years ago. There, too, we crumbled the bread into the coffee and ate it with the spoon. Having cleaned the plate and spoon I commence my morning walk, enjoying my pipe as I do so, thinking of the past and the present, and repeating my Memento of Holy Mass more fully. I remember many who are remembering me and I try to live in the Communion of Saints. I do not walk far—six paces there and back, and then the same again. This walk starts at half past eight and ends by nine o'clock, by which time my pipe is empty. Then I say Matins and Lauds and Prime, often still walking. When I am tired I sit down quietly beside the table on my stool against the wall. By the time I have finished it is half past nine. Between nine o'clock and half past the light is switched off, sometimes so early that I have to stop saying my Office, although last Sunday it was kept on till ten o'clock. At half past nine I have my morning meditation, reading and meditating the life of Jesus by Cyril Verschaeve. I was able to take this book with me by permission of the officer who arrested me, and also the life of Saint Teresa in the Kwakman translation. At first they were not given to me but by later request I was permitted to have them in my cell.

At ten o'clock I start writing. During the first days I was occupied in writing an answer to the question: Why do the Dutch people, especially the Catholics, resist the National Socialist Movement? I tried to give an answer in eight pages like this one. Now I am trying, during my hours of writing, to fix my impressions of the time spent here; furthermore, I am writing the life of Saint Teresa, which I undertook for "The Spectrum." When I start writing I light a cigar. At half past eleven, walking again, I say Terce, Sext and None. My writing was interrupted on a few mornings by physical exercises. We have to do these every day, sometimes in the morning, sometimes in the afternoon. It is a comical affair. We are called for by loud shouts. The doors open and we stand erect at the other side of the corridor until all have left their cells, each one holding his numbered dust pail in his hand. We start moving, put our pails down at the end of the corridor, pass some corridors, and arrive at an open field behind the prison: a fairly long but narrow strip of ground surrounded by a high wall.

The gymnasium teacher stands in the center. We walk around him in a broad ellipse, now in ordinary step, now on the double, now taking high steps. Sometimes we have to stretch our arms for-

298

ward or to the side in a certain rhythmical movement, at others we have to keep our hands on our hips.

I continue reading until four o'clock, now and then lighting my pipe. At four o'clock I kneel down for half an hour's meditation on the life of Jesus and on mine. About half past four bread is brought for supper, which also has to serve for next morning. Until Thursday it was the ordinary bread, a lump cut into four. On Thursday morning the doctor came to see me. I told him that my stomach was fairly delicate, that on four occasions I had had a serious hemorrhage of the stomach, and that I was suffering from a rather dangerous infection by Colibacilli. I told him briefly about the treatment by several doctors and pointed out to him that my abnormally light weight, added to my chronic disease, made extra food necessary, and that this had been allowed to me by the food office in Nijmegen. He said he would have me weighed and would see what he could do. I was weighed: one hundred and twenty-six pounds, from which four pounds were subtracted for clothes. As a result I now receive milk bread instead. I have not noticed very much difference, but I think there may be some milk in it. Furthermore, the slices are buttered. At supper I receive a large sized cup half filled with whole milk instead of a full cup of skim milk.

Nothing came of the other extra food allowance. As a consequence of the concession there is a card hanging on the door of my cell now marked "Milk" and another one marked "white bread." It seems more than it is, but I can do with it. As soon as the bread is brought I let it soak in the milk and eat that. One has not much time because cup and spoon must be given back very soon. Our supper is finished by quarter past five. Then it becomes very quiet. We do not receive anything, we do not have to give anything. After supper I say the Angelus and have adoration, spiritually united with the convent. Then I light a cigar and have an evening walk up and down a stretch of twelve paces as in the morning. At six o'clock I start writing and continue until quarter to eight. Then I make my bed and say night prayers at the side of my bed. It does not matter to me much when the light is switched off. I continue praying for *some time and then I tuck myself under the blankets till next morning.*

Scheveningen, January 28, 1942
T.B.

Saturday, January 31, 1942

I have to add something. I cannot say that I do not get any meat. Last Wednesday and Thursday there was meat in the soup and in the hotch-potch. It was mixed, ground into small pieces, and though not abundant, I did see meat again.

On Thursday morning, January 29, it was the feast day of St. Francis de Sales, gentle patron saint of journalists. I had cleaned my pipe and had lighted it for my morning walk when a German soldier entered with a new order. I had to hand over tobacco and cigars, pipe and matches. I was not allowed to smoke any more. Luckily I happened to think of the mild Francis de Sales, otherwise I might have said something unkind. I emptied my pipe and gave it up. The soldier said in pity that it was not his fault. I understood. To comfort me he said that I could keep the other things—books, paper, and so on—which is very fortunate. They will profit me more, though I miss my pipe and cigar. I deleted "smoking" from the daily timetable and the day went on. Now I take these things for granted. I was very fortunate that I was permitted to smoke on the first and most difficult days.

T.B.

13

Scheveningen
German Police Prison

February 12, 1942.

Fr. Privincial, Fr. Prior, Reverendissime, Confreres, Brother, Sisters, Brother-in-law, children, friends,

Very best greetings from cell 577 Scheveningen. I am alone here. Two by four (meters) and the height is also four. A cell dwelt in becomes sweet, says Thomas à Kempis. I already feel at home here. I pray, read and write, the days are too short. From eight till seven it is night. I am quite all right in my solitude, although I miss the church, Mass, communion, and although no priest comes here. Yet God is near to me, now that I cannot go to people any more, nor people to me. I am very calm, happy and content, and I adapt myself. I will hold out very well.

My diet is looked after a bit: at night a quarter litre of whole milk and instead of the ordinary dry bread, four thick slices, buttered. In the morning, I put two of these in the coffee, at night two in the milk and I eat it with the spoon. At midday hotchpotch or soup, very well prepared, and for me abundant. Now and then there is some meat mixed with it, on Fridays some fish. Further also sugar, jam, butter and soft cheese, but in very moderate quantities. Would you be so kind as to inform Dr. de Jong that he should not worry or make himself reproaches about me. I suffer here with joy and I am quite all right. Say the same to Dr. Woltring. Send me, please, an Imitatio in Latin, a

Missal of the Order, and rosary beads, the next part of the Breviary with the Kalendarium. *Then, A. Hoornaert,* Sainte Thérèse écrivain, *Brugge, Desclée. It is on the table. Shallow, light blue cover, three fingers thick. If you can't go in maybe you can get it elsewhere, or order a new one. Further three writing pads, good ruled paper. Fortunately I am allowed to write. The first days I was also allowed to smoke. Further, pajamas, preferably the blue ones. Two shirts and two pairs of pants, stockings and handkerchiefs and a double sack with name, for the laundry, and finally somebody who every ten days exchanges the soiled laundry for the clean. Dr. Onings will be willing to find someone to do this. If you can get into my cell, send also the short jacket which is hanging behind the door or maybe better still the entire suit. If you wish to send some dessert with it, all right, but we have no knives and no tins, and are not allowed to have them either.*

If Vos de Waeel has not received the doctorate yet, don't let him wait for me. Perhaps Professor Kors will want to take my place—or Professor Post. Thanks in advance. Congratulate his mother and himself on my behalf. Let Stappers (Oldenzaal) find a solution to the situation of Michel Polatian with the expert accountant Winters of Venlo, as we agreed. Ask Father Van Keulen and Wijnhoven, Boxtel, to look after Sister Feugen according to her need; tell him that she has put everything in my name. The will is in Wolters' hands, so don't be worried about the situation of the Apostolate. During April of last year Miss P. Verstraaten and someone else of the Social Theology Department did their preliminary exam with me. I forgot to give them a document of proof.

Get in contact with her; ask her for the name of the other person and let Professor Hoogveld know that they did the preliminary exam successfully.

A copy of the translation of the Dark Night *of P. Mauritius, Geleen, is on the table in my cell. I will no longer be able to go over it. Tell Father Wijnhoven that the copy of Sloots'* Eastern Heresies *was also confiscated. Sloots will have a copy. I would be very pleased to see it divided into chapters and at the beginning and end of every chapter throw some light, in each heresy, on the need for a correct description of the faith, the readiness to sacrifice, etc. It's all too much in a minor key. Let Rector Canisius know that the circular letter of the Willibrord Union for the election of members of the Council of Appeal was also confiscated, and so was not continued. And pray for me in the Communion of Saints.*

Your Fr. Titus, Carmelite

Scheveningen, March 5, 1942.

Very Reverend Fr. Prov., Fr. Prior, Rev.me, Confreres, Brother, Sisters, Brother-in-law, Children, Friends,

Once again, greetings from cell 577. Now I am here already over six weeks. But I hold out quite well. My health is all right. February 21, I had a little warning, a bit of fever and pains that made me fear that the kidney inflammation of December, 1939, would re-appear. Also I asked for the doctor. But while I was afraid that it would turn worse, when the doctor arrived the next day, it had improved a lot so that the doctor saw no necessity for doing anything. For a couple of days some after-pains, less appetite, and it was over again. At the moment I am very well. Psychically I am not troubled in the least. I need neither to cry nor to sigh, sometimes I even sing a tune in my own way, not too loudly of course. I cannot manage the nights here. I cannot sleep from 8 till 7. So I am much awake at night, more than the nights exceed their normal length (sic).

I shall tell you my timetable, but you must not take it too punctually. That does not exist here. I rise at about 7 o'clock. Bell is rung, light is switched on. A short morning prayer. I strip my bed, fold blankets and sheets, receive water. Then I kneel down and say the prayers of Holy Mass, spiritual communion. Then the coffee is about to arrive, a tin half litre cup. I soak the bread in it. Angelus. Breakfast. After that, a few times weekly, cleaning up the cell. Sometimes we are given a newspaper in the morning, which I read after breakfast. Then wash and dress. Until then I live in pajamas, quite practical. Then it is about half past eight, nine. I say Matins, Lauds and Prime, and after that half an hour of meditation. They are different hours from the convent, but one has to adapt oneself. From ten to half past eleven I read, and when I have paper I also write. I am working on the Life of St. Teresa, for Spectrum. I have finished the first draft of six of the twelve chapters. After half past eleven I say the little hours. Then lunch. Angelus. Adoration in the spirit. I sing an Adoro Te. Then a walk in my room, three meters forward three meters back, and then the same again. Sometimes I have to laugh about it. At two o'clock Vespers and Compline. Then read or write. At four o'clock half an hour of meditation. At about 5 o'clock evening bread with milk. Angelus. Adoration. From six to half past seven read or write. 7.30 evening prayer. Rosary. At night, the light is not switched on any more. The timetable is sometimes interrupted by exercises on command, each day, except on Sundays, sport: we are about 70 from the same corridor in a small court, to walk around, to trot, to throw out arms and legs, it is fun. Ten minutes, a quarter of an hour. On our way out we take our dustbin with us and take it back, emptied, on our way back. Usually twice weekly we may shave and razors are distributed, sometimes after 2 days, sometimes after 4, and once even after 8 days. I started looking patriarchal. Sometimes there is an order to scrub the woodwork or to swab the cell, etc. I just take part in everything. Twice I have been taken to a bathing cell for a shower.

The day before yesterday I received from the laundry two sacks of underwear, and I gave along the soiled linen. Splendid. There was only one pair of socks, that is a bit little. I was very happy to receive Fr. Prior's letter of February 21, in reply to mine of 12. I received the letter on February 26. That was a joy. Mary thanks for letter, Holy Mass and prayers, and for carrying out all the instructions. It is the first and until now the only one I received. It will be best if Fr. Prior writes for all, as the Provincial does for Amandus. Much news in few words. He would also be the indicated person to apply for a visit. How is the family doing? Gatsche, best wishes on March

13. *How are Hubert, Cyprian, the Pastor, P. Thomas, Ewald? How are my colleagues? Did Vos de Wael get the doctorate? Has the Rochus home been furnished already?*

Until now I haven't received any parcel. Maybe I'm not allowed to. I have started again at Septuagesima. Remember me, you all, I will remember you, reciprocally.

In Christ your p. Titus Brandsma, O. Carm.

15

Amersfoort, April 1st, 1942

Prisoner
Prof. Dr. Titus Brandsma
Block: 2 A N. 58

Dear Father Prior, etc.

At the beginning of each month we are allowed to write one letter and so today I can tell you again that I have been able to adapt myself very well, although the change from Scheveningen to here was a big one.

The many acquaintances to talk to, and the many new ones are a big contrast with the Scheveningen solitude. My state of health and age are taken in consideration here also fairly well, so that you need not worry about that. There are more possibilities for medical care here than in Scheveningen.

Here as well I will hold out as long as it is judged necessary to keep me. About the duration, nothing can be said. I was very happy to receive your letter of March 21. Just as well that you wrote again, because no letters have been forwarded to me from Scheveningen.

Thanks to Father Provincial for the greetings and the prayers on behalf of all. On my part, I am with all of you in spiritual communion. I am saying Breviary now in the same way as the brothers. I would like to ask whether the 15 Our Fathers for Laudes Vespertinae cover Vespers and Compline, or whether 7 Our Fathers are to be said for Compline also? What is usual? I hope and pray that Cyprian, Pacificus, Ewald, Vitalis and the others who are sick get better soon. Special greetings to Hubert. Don't be worried about me.

Gatsche's letter did me a lot of good. I understand very well that they are praying for me, and speak of me a lot. I thank every one, Henry and Barbara too.

I would like to know something more about my substitute at the University courses. I wish George every success. Also best wishes to Fra. Simon and Fra. Franco on their new appointments.

The news about Utilitas I read with divided heart. It was something to be feared. Greetings to Bodewes. I don't know why the doctorate of Vos de Wael has been delayed. But today there's a lot of things that we don't understand.

There's a reason for this too.

An Easter full of blessing to all. I jubilantly intone the Alleluja with you, you know. We remember each other.

In Christ yours, f. Titus Brandsma

16

(Original text in German)

The Hague, May 6, 1942

Dear Brother-in-law and Sister, etc.,

Now I am in Scheveningen again, but only for a short time, because it has been decided that I shall go to the concentration camp at Dachau near Munich, probably next Saturday. There also I will find acquaintances, and Our Dear Lord is everywhere. I am in good health. You need not worry about that, and fortunately I am able to let things come calmly. Kind regards to the children, Barbara and Henry, all the members of the family, the parish priest and curate. I understand that you are worried about me. You and the little ones pray for me and I am grateful to you for your love. In God Our Lord we remain united until we see each other again. From Dachau I will write again to Father Prior in Nijmegen and you can send him again an answer. I congratulate Helen on her birthday on April 25, Teresa on May 18, and am always with you.

Your brother in Christ

f. Titus Brandsma

17

Kleve, May 28, 1942

Dear Father Prior, etc.,

At the beginning of May you will have been expecting a letter from Amersfoort, because there I would have been allowed to write again on May 1st, but a few days before, on April 28, I was suddenly taken back to Scheveningen. There one writes every three weeks, but one has to be there at least three weeks before one is allowed to write. Before that term had passed, on May 16th, I was put on the way towards Dachau. Fortunately the voyage did not continue uninterruptedly, and for the time being we are in the prison of Kleve, to be transported from there in groups to different destinations in Germany. One always stays here one or two weeks. Each week about forty leave. Although usually one is allowed to write only from the place of destination, I got permission to write from here, because it is so long ago, and also because it is not yet determined when I am to go on.

In The Hague I have been tried more in detail about some letters. On my departure from Amersfoort I have also been informed that I will he kept prisoner because I am inimically disposed towards Germany and because it is to be feared that I will abuse my liberty against Germany.

Being sent to Dachau does mean that I'll be detained until the end of the war. Dachau near Munich is a camp with various branches. You will hear later on in which section I'll be, if anyhow they stick to this sentence. The Provincial could attempt to have it commuted to a transfer to a German monastery (Mainz, Vienna, Bamberg, Straubing), with eventual extensive restriction of freedom and of permission to work, with the obligation of remaining in that city or perhaps in the convent and of reporting in on a regular basis, of having no correspondence with Holland, etc. Pastor Bulters of The Hague was duly freed on condition that he transfer to Venray. In my opinion, the better thing would be to speak of this matter at The Hague with Mr. Hardegen, Provincial Dept. of the German Security Police, Binenhof 7, Room 137. It was he who always interrogated me and who also told me that Brandsma the lawyer from Zwolle had been there for me and that he gave him my large suitcase. He would not obtain anything else for me, but I feel I should be very grateful to him for his interest.

He could go for a talk even now, alone or with Fr. Provincial or someone named by him. This doesn't seem bad to me, but I leave the decision to you.

Of the more than six weeks in Amersfoort, I have been ill more or less for five. Providential. A rather light dysentery. Yet, this continual diarrhea weakened me. When it had gone, I got into trouble with my stomach, and these spasms rather bothered me. Little by little it has passed. Now I am all right again. My complaint, the kidney inflammation, although completely uncared for, bothers me next to nothing. In all those four months, it has caused me trouble and pain only three times, and then only slightly. In fact, considering the circumstances, I'm doing wonderfully well. I have a continuous appetite, as I have never known in my life before.

It was a great privilege that on May 17th, I could attend Holy Mass, and that on Pentecost Sunday and Monday, I also have been able to receive Holy Communion, after more than four months.

The suit you sent by express mail to Scheveningen, I fortunately received on May 16 on my departure from there. I already despaired of receiving it. Many thanks for everything. It contained everything I had asked for, but in case you sent more, or sent a letter with it, I haven't received these. I was looking forward to it, and would be happy to hear something.

Here I was allowed to keep Breviary, Missal and rosary. How will it be in Dachau? I hear though that there is Holy Mass on Sundays. I hope eventually to meet colleague Regout, Galena the Pastor and various other priests.

Please pay a personal visit to Professor Hoogveld, von Genechten, Bellon and Sassen to thank them for taking my place. Extend my condolences to the former on the death of Scintilla. The family will be comforted to know that after such deep preparation in such a sublime frame of mind and with an expression of such great affection for her family members she went to face death. It's good that she joined the Third Order. Many greetings to all. It's better so. You should remain the Director. The other changes are also very good. Greetings and thanks to Mrs. Span. Tell Hubert that in my solitude I've decided first of all to finish the edition of St. Teresa. Today is Teresa's birthday. I am spiritually at Jongemastate. On leaving Amersfoort, Father Hettema arrived. He thought they would free me. He is in good spirits and I heard he feels well.

Kindest regards to all. Pray for me.

In Christ, your Titus, Carmelite.

18

(Original text in German)

Dachau, July 12, 1942

From
Brandsma Anno
Dachau No 30492

Dear Brother-in-law and Sister,

If until now I wrote to the Prior of Nijmegen, now it is better to write to you. You forward the letter to the Prior. He will take care for further expedition and also for the answer in your name.

The answer must be written in German. No abbreviations that are not easily understandable. If not, the letter is not passed on. I have been allowed to read the letter the Prior sent to Kleve but not to keep it, as it was in Dutch.

Many thanks for all the kind words, from yourselves, the Prior and all the others. I am all right. One has to adapt oneself once more to new circumstances and with the help of God, I'll succeed here also. Our dear Lord will also continue helping. I may write once a month only. This is now for me the first occasion. Best greetings to all. I was pleased to receive information about the number of new novices, the new priests, the results of Oss and Oldenzaal, the health of Hubert, Cyprian, Vitalis and the other patients. Best wishes for a good recovery of Fr. Subprior.

If one wishes, one can send me each month 40 Marks. The Prior will gladly look after that.

As Henry wrote, Kaeter the pastor has been transferred to Eibergen. Congratulate him for me. Have any other pastors whom I know been transferred? I'm still waiting for news from Akke Kramer regarding his brother John.

Many greetings to the parish priest and curates at Bolsward, to Father Provincial and all the Confreres. Let us remain united, under the protection of Jesus, Mary and Joseph. Not too much worrying about me.

In Christ yours
Anno

GRAB TAUSENDER
UNBEKANNTER
GRAVE OF THOUSANDS
UNKNOWN

CHRONOLOGY OF THE ESSAYS

SCUOLA TIPOGRAFICA S. PIO X – VIA ETRUSCHI, 7 – ROMA